The Suffering Body

"The Suffering Body is a comprehensive account of the history of persecution of Christians in different contexts, corroborated by scholarly research and careful thought from the perspective of the Charismatic stream of Christian practice. With suffering and persecution as points of reference, these essays provoke one to discover afresh the meaning of the cost of discipleship in the light of the demands of Christian faith in different contexts. This book is an important contribution to the ongoing endeavours of the ecumenical movement in its relentless search for prophetic forms of witness in an increasingly broken world."

Samuel Kobia, General Secretary of the World Council of Churches

"An important and timely publication, the more so because it is edited by leading Pentecostal academics from the USA, where the role of suffering in Christian experience is often ignored and sometimes denied. A comprehensive theological, historical, and socio-political analysis of the role of suffering internationally, this is an important corrective to 'health and wealth' gospels and ideologies of power."

Allan Anderson, Professor of Global Pentecostal Studies, University of Birmingham

"The Church of Jesus Christ was born in suffering and our contemporary experience in India and indeed in Asia shows the church is purified and its witness strengthened as it passes through the fires of suffering. It is sheer joy to suffer for the sake of the Lord of truth and love. *The Suffering Body* leads the reader on the Calvary Road. A must-read for Christians engaged in witnessing to a world hostile towards God and wrapped in materialism."

Richard Howell, General Secretary Evangelical Fellowship of India, Vice-Chairman World Evangelical Alliance International Council

"This book is very timely and much needed. I belong to the Russian Orthodox Church, which is a Church of martyrs. For seven decades it was persecuted by an atheistic regime, persecutions that began immediately after the revolution of 1917. In the course of the 1920s and 1930s most bishops and priests, many monks and lay people were executed or imprisoned, all monasteries and theological schools were closed, many churches were destroyed or refashioned to suit other needs. A task was undertaken to eradicate 'religious prejudices' and to transform the Soviet Union into an atheist state, in which 'the last remaining priest' would be 'exhibited in a museum'. But 'God is not mocked' (Gal. 6:7), and the atheists' plans were never to be fully realized. In spite of decades of the most cruel acts, faith did not die in the people. And as soon as the grip of militant atheism started to weaken, people began returning to the faith of their forefathers. In the 1990s, this return took place on a mass scale. Nowadays the Russian Orthodox Church is one of the fastest growing Churches in the world. As Tertullian said, 'The martyrs' blood is the seed of Christianity.' The truth of this saying has been proven by the entire experience of the Church over the centuries. This painful but sanctifying experience of martyrdom is necessary for the Church, and we are eternally grateful to thousands and millions of martyrs who died in order that we may live in Christ."

+Bishop Hilarion of Vienna and Austria, Representative of the Russian Orthodox Church to the European Institutions

The Suffering Body

Responding to the Persecution of Christians

Edited by
HAROLD D. HUNTER
and
CECIL M. ROBECK, JR.

Paternoster:
thinking faith

Copyright © 2006 Harold D. Hunter and Cecil M. Robeck, Jr.

First published in 2006 by Paternoster Press

12 11 10 09 08 07 06   7 6 5 4 3 2 1

Paternoster Press is an imprint of Authentic Media,
9 Holdom Avenue, Bletchley, Milton Keynes MK1 1QR, UK
and
129 Mobilization Drive, Waynesboro, GA 30830 4575, USA
www.authenticmedia.co.uk

Authentic Media is a division of Send The Light Ltd,
a company limited by guarantee (registered charity no. 270162).

British Library Cataloguing in Publication Data
A catalogue record for this book is available from the British Library

ISBN 1-84227-378-7

Cover Design by James Kessell for Scratch the Sky Ltd (www.scratchthesky.com)
Typeset by Waverley Typesetters, Fakenham, Norfolk
Print Management by Adare Carwin
Printed and bound in Great Britain by J. H. Haynes & Co., Sparkford

Dedicated to
Suffering Christians Everywhere

Contents

Section III
The Middle East

Section IV
Central and Eastern Europe

Section V
Asia

List of Contributors

Dr. Dariusz Mikolaj Cupial is the chair of the Fundacja Cyryla I Metodego (Foundation of St. Cyril and St. Methodius) in Poland, which has a ministry to fathers. He is also the author of *Na Drodze Ewangelizacji I Ekumenii* (Katolickiego Univwersytetu Lubelskiego, 1996).

Dr. Thomas Finger was Professor of Systematic Theology at Northern Baptist Seminary in Lombard, IL (1976–86) and Professor of Systematic and Spirit Theology at Eastern Mennonite Seminary in Harrisonburg, VA (1989–2000). He is an ordained pastor in the Mennonite Church, USA and is one of its very few representatives to official ecumenical organizations. Dr. Finger is presently writing, traveling and teaching short-term in various places.

Bob (Xiqiu) Fu was born and reared in mainland China. A house church pastor in Beijing and English lecturer in Beijing Administrative College and Beijing Party School of the Chinese Communist Party, he was arrested along with his wife as an "illegal evangelist" in 1996. After the Fus were released, they escaped to Hong Kong, then came to the United States in 1997 before the handover of Hong Kong to Communist China. Bob is presently a Ph.D. candidate at Westminster Theological Seminary in Philadelphia and the China Analyst for The Voice of the Martyrs (USA). He has been appointed Visiting Professor in Religion and Philosophy at Oklahoma Wesleyan University for the 2003–2005 academic year.

Dr. Chin Khau Khai is the pastor of Myanmar Full Life Mission Church, Alhambra, California, USA. In 1999, he graduated with a Ph.D. in Intercultural Studies from Fuller Theological Seminary. He is the author of *The Cross Among Pagodas: A History of the Assemblies of God in Myanmar* (APTS Press, 2003).

Monsignor Felix A. Machado was born in Karadi (near Mumbai), India. Currently he is Undersecretary (appointed directly by Pope John Paul II in 1999) of the Pontifical Council for Interreligious Dialogue in the Vatican. As Undersecretary he is editor of *Pro Dialogo*, a trimestrial review of the Pontifical Council for Interreligious Dialogue. He also looks after the Catholic Church's dialogue with Hinduism and Buddhism. He has a doctorate in Catholic theology from Fordham University, New York (1984). He has taught theology in the Major Seminary in Bombay and is a Visiting Professor of theology at several Pontifical Universities in Rome.

Archbishop John Onaiyekan is the Roman Catholic Archbishop of Abuja, Nigeria. He currently serves as president of the Association of the Episcopal Conferences of Anglophone West Africa, the Nigerian Catholic Bishop's Conference, and the Nigerian Episcopal Conference, where he plays a mediating role in Christian-Muslim relations. He has also served as a representative of the Catholic Church on the Standing Commission on Faith and Order of the World Council of Churches.

Dr. Despina D. Prassas is an Assistant Professor of Theology at Providence College in Providence, RI, where she teaches Early Christianity and Early Byzantine theology. She represents the Ecumenical Patriarchate of Constantinople on the Central Committee of the World Council of Churches and takes part in the World Council of Churches – Pentecostal Joint Consultative Group sponsored by the World Council of Churches. She is a representative of the Greek Orthodox Archdiocese of America to the General Assembly of the National Council of Churches of Christ, USA, as well as a member of the Faith and Order Commission of the NCCCUSA.

Dr. Helen Rhee holds a Ph.D. in Church History from Fuller Theological Seminary, Pasadena, CA, USA. She joined the faculty of Westmont College in September, 2004, where she is Assistant Professor of World Christianity. She is also pastor of young adult ministry and adult education at Hana Church, California and she is associated with the Silkroad Mission. She is the author of *Early Christian Literature: Christ and Culture in the Second and Third Centuries* (Routledge, 2005).

Dr. Patrick Sookhdeo holds a Ph.D. from the School of Oriental and African Studies, London University and was awarded a Doctor of Divinity by Western Seminary, Portland, Oregon for his work on pluralism. He serves as the international director of the Barnabas Fund which supports suffering Christian minorities by reporting on their situations, facilitating prayer on their behalf, and funding projects run by national Christians in the affected countries. He also directs the Institute for the Study of Islam and Christianity, the educational arm of the Barnabas Fund. The institute conducts ongoing research on the status of the church in the Muslim world. He has written and lectures widely in the field of other faiths.

Rev. Dr. Valdis Teraudkalns is Docent in Philosophy in Rezekne Higher Education Institution and Lecturer in Sociology of Religion at the Faculty of Theology, University of Latvia, Riga. He is also General Secretary of the Latvian Bible Society. He has served as a board member for the Latvian Publishers Association. He is a minister with the Latvian Baptist Church.

Rev. Dr. Ioan Tipei received his Master of Divinity degree from the Church of God Theological Seminary in Cleveland, TN, USA (1987) and a Ph.D. degree in Biblical Studies from the University of Sheffield, UK. He is now the Rector of the Pentecostal Theological Institute of Bucharest, Romania, and the Assistant Pastor of the Philadelphia Pentecostal Church of Bucharest. He is editor of *Plērōoma: Studii Şi Cercetări Teologice* and the author of four books.

Rev. Dr. Keith Warrington is Lecturer in New Testament Studies and Director of Postgraduate Studies at Regents Theological College in the UK. Before that he was a minister and church planter in the Elim Pentecostal Church. He has a doctorate from King's College, London University. He is founder/Chair of the Pentecostal and Charismatic Research Fellowship and is a past editor of the *Journal of the European Pentecostal Theological Association.*

Biographical Information on the Editors

Rev. Dr. Harold D. Hunter is ordained by the International Pentecostal Holiness Church and has served in denominational executive positions and seminary teaching positions for over thirty years. Currently Director of the IPHC Archives & Research Center, he has lectured in seminaries spread across five continents. Hunter co-edited with Peter Hocken *All Together In One Place* (Sheffield Academic Press, 1991) and released *Spirit Baptism: A Pentecostal Alternative* (University Press of America) in 1983. His articles have appeared in international journals of varying disciplines in addition to entries for dictionaries.

On the ecumenical front, he continues to participate in various projects involving the World Council of Churches, the World Alliance of Reformed Churches – Pentecostal Dialogue, the NCCCUSA Faith and Order Commission and various grassroots organizations like the North American Renewal Service Committee (NARSC) and the International Charismatic Consultation (ICC). He is past president of the Society for Pentecostal Studies (1984).

Rev. Dr. Cecil M. Robeck, Jr. is an ordained minister with the Assemblies of God. He serves as Professor of Church History and Ecumenics and as Director of the David DuPlessis Center for Christian Spirituality at Fuller Theological Seminary in Pasadena, CA. He edited *Charismatic Experiences in History* (Hendrickson, 1985) and is the author of *Prophecy in Carthage: Perpetua, Tertullian, and Cyprian* (Pilgrim Press, 1992), and *The Azusa Street Mission and Revival: The Birth of the Global Pentecostal Movement* (Thomas Nelson, 2006). For nine years he was editor of *Pneuma: The Journal* *of the Society for Pentecostal Studies*. His many articles (over 200) have been published in a range of historical, theological, and ecumenical journals.

For over two decades, he has served as an apologist for and an interpreter of Pentecostalism in international ecumenical circles such as the International Roman Catholic-Pentecostal Dialogue, the World Council of Churches, the World Alliance of Reformed Churches-Pentecostal Dialogue, the Lutheran World Federation, and the Secretaries of Christian World Communions. He is a past President of the North American Academy of Ecumenists (1998 and 1999), and of the Society for Pentecostal Studies (1983).

Introduction

HAROLD D. HUNTER and CECIL M. ROBECK, JR.

From January 20–24, 2004, the triennial meeting of the International Charismatic Consultation convened around the theme of "The Suffering Church" in Salina Beach, Salina, Malta. We were invited to assemble a small academic consultation that would run alongside the larger gathering of several hundred people. Approximately fifty scholars from several continents gathered to discuss "The Suffering Church" around the world. The papers from this consultation form the core of this book.

Suffering, persecution, and martyrdom have been part of the Christian vocabulary since the beginning of the church in the first century AD. Jesus predicted that his followers would suffer, that they would be persecuted, and that some would die because of their faith. And so it has been.

Both of us have been reared and become ministers and scholars within the classical Pentecostal tradition. In North America, at least, where both of us make our homes, classical Pentecostalism as well as much of the later charismatic renewal has struggled with the place of suffering in the church. The minority voices that have pondered the divine mysteries have frequently been drowned out by those who have thundered from their pulpits that miracles remove the sting of pain.

We are convinced that just as there is a role for miracles, however, there is a continuing role for suffering in the church. C. S. Lewis postulated many years ago in *The Problem of Pain* that there is undoubtedly a grand design that will ultimately become evident in which suffering will be put into its proper perspective. Until that time, it often remains a mystery. Not all pain, not all suffering can be explained at the present time. After reflecting on this idea for a number of years, however, Lewis came to wonder whether all pain could ever be understood, or whether it did fit a grand design. Yet, there are those among us who attempt to explain suffering, either by offering it back to God as a mystery that only he can interpret, or by attempting to make sense of it within the limited boundaries of our understanding, or in more radical ways, by lifting up the role of miracle as the potential cure for all suffering.

The title we have chosen for this volume is *The Suffering Body*. To those who have eyes to see, it is a double entendre. Readers will see a reference to the human body and the suffering that results from pain, illness, and even death. On another level, the reference to the "body" is an equally clear reference to the church, which in the Pauline writings (1 Cor. 12:12–27; Rom. 12:1–8; Eph. 4:11–16), is frequently portrayed as the "body of Christ." While we do not wish to ignore the significance of suffering in the human body, it is on the latter subject, the suffering of the church that we have chosen to focus in this book. The church has been a "suffering body" for centuries, and many events in the twentieth and twenty-first centuries make it abundantly clear that in many places around the world, there are Christians who continue to suffer, endure persecution, and, in some cases, face martyrdom.

The first section of this volume begins with a series of historical and theological chapters that set the stage for the later case studies. Helen Rhee begins by pointing out that suffering has played a powerful role in Christianity since its inception. It has helped to provide Christians with an identity, that is, as those who trust in God through Jesus Christ, to the extent that they are willing to pay the ultimate price of suffering and death over against the offerings and demands of the present world. Keith Warrington moves the argument forward by locating the subject of suffering in pneumatology. Pentecostals and charismatics, he argues, often miss the fact that the Spirit is present "with us" when we suffer. Undoubtedly, this oversight comes with the emphasis upon power and miracle that these Christians tend to highlight, but in a day when the health and wealth gospel seems to be making inroads at some of the more unexpected places around the world, this idea that suffering is a normal part of the Christian life, and that the Spirit makes Christ present in the life of suffering believers is a well-timed corrective.

The discussion continues with a contribution by Thomas Finger, who represents a tradition that was born in suffering at the time of the Reformation. Mennonites in southern Germany, Switzerland, Austria, and the Netherlands were often pursued and murdered because their understanding of the gospel was perceived to be too radical. An extended period of persecution, as many of Menno Simon's followers can attest, can breed a psychological response that is not always helpful – a persecution complex. Such a complex brings with it potential dangers once that period of suffering and persecution is over. Cecil M. Robeck, Jr. understands this danger. He draws from his studies as a church historian and his experience as a Pentecostal ecumenist, when he asks all Christians to consider once again, the teaching of Jesus with respect to those who persecute or in other ways contribute to the suffering and martyrdom that many Christians around the world continue to face. Paul reminds us, "Bless those who persecute you; bless and do not curse" (Rom. 12:14). Robeck concludes with a series of prayerful actions that Christians can take that will make a difference, not only in the lives of those who suffer persecution, but also of those who pray for them.

A series of case studies originating from countries around the world transforms this discussion by providing the stories of places and people who are wrestling with the subject on a daily basis. Many of us do not live in contexts where suffering, persecution, and martyrdom are common fare. In North America, for instance, it is rare to hear of cases in which Christians are made to suffer for their faith. It is the case that at the beginning of the twentieth-century Pentecostals were often publicly ridiculed, arrested, and placed on trial because of some of their actions. At a more sinister level, some were tarred and feathered, had rocks or Molotov cocktails thrown at them, were sprayed with acid, were shot at, suffered church invasions, had their tents and churches destroyed, and bore the indignities of other forms of suffering and persecution. It was because they suffered such indignities that they often claimed that God stood with them.

Today, with the enormous growth of the Pentecostal and charismatic movements around the world, many in North America look triumphantly and claim that their success is the sign that God stands with them. Such sentiment has, at times, spilled over, even where one might not anticipate it. Archbishop John Onaiyekan makes it clear that there are many Pentecostals and charismatics in Nigeria who embrace a form of the gospel that ignores their suffering by concentrating on miracles.

Religious conflict, especially as it is seen in nations where there are sizeable numbers of Muslims and Christians living together such as Nigeria, or nations in which there is a Muslim majority or an Islamic government such as are found in varying degrees throughout the Middle East, has produced apocalyptic predictions of the future such as *The Clash of Civilizations*.[1] Patrick Sookhdeo provides a candid evaluation of the types of persecution that is taking place throughout the Muslim world, especially in regions of the Middle East and in southern Asia. Although he did not deliver a paper at the conference in Malta, Patrick's work with the Lausanne Continuation Committee has contributed substantially to this article.

In the contemporary world, it is difficult to remember that much of the Middle East and northern Africa was Christian long before Islam made its presence known. Among the oldest Christian groups in the region are the many Orthodox churches that call that part of the world home. Often misunderstood in the West, and frequently the subject of varying degrees of persecution in the region from at least the eighth century, the Orthodox churches of the Middle East have borne consistent witness to the Christian faith. Despina Prassas discusses the current status of Orthodox or, in this case, Coptic responses to persecution as they have been taking place in recent years, particularly in Egypt.

Clashes between religions are not, of course, the only or even necessarily the primary source of the suffering, persecution, and martyrdom of Christians. Often it comes as the result of conflicting ideologies. None of them was clearer throughout most of the twentieth century than was the conflict that came through the implementation of a form of communism that was atheistic. As teenagers we prayed for Christians, regardless of denominational affiliation, in this region of the world. Such prayers were part of the Christian response to the Cold War that existed between East and West following the Second World War and especially the repression of Christianity that came at the pleasure of the Soviet premiers, Josef Stalin and Nikita Kruschev.

Three scholars – Ioan Tipei from Romania, Valdis Teraudkalns from Latvia, and Dariusz Cupial from Poland – take a penetrating look at some of the events that occurred in Central and Eastern Europe from the time of the Bolshevik Revolution to the end of the Soviet regime and the emergence of glasnost and perestroika at the end of the 1980s. The stories that they tell, and the lessons to which they draw our attention are worthy of renewed consideration as we face the future. Ioan Tipei reflects both historically and theologically on the plight of Christians in Romania during the communist era. Valdis Teraudkalns reminds us that every story has two sides. Christians in the East sometimes differ in the retelling of the same story told by Christians in the West. He helps us see that perceptions are reality for many, and that misperceptions sometimes play a role in continuing the conflict even between Christians. What is needed is for the church to face these same histories together, to deal with the results, and to pray for a healing of memories. Dariusz Cupial provides a brief overview of Polish history, including its "Christian" history of over 1,000 years, the repression that it faced throughout the latter half of the twentieth century, and the role that hope and solidarity played in the renewal of the nation.

We conclude this volume with a section describing something of the situation of the church in Asia. With the changes that are presently taking place in China, new attention is being paid to the situation of the Christian community. Many people in the West operate under the false impression that Christianity first came to China through English and later American missionaries during the nineteenth century. The truth is that Nestorian Christianity was present in China from at least the seventh century, and Roman Catholic Christians were present from at least the fourteenth century through the eighteenth century. Throughout these 1,000 years, Christians were accepted and rejected a number of times. Christianity was, in a sense, re-introduced to China in the nineteenth century, largely with the aid of colonial power. Unequal treaties gave Christian missionaries freedoms that most Chinese citizens did not enjoy, and paved the way for the gospel message. With this history in mind, it may be easier to understand the common Chinese idea that the presence of Christianity represents a foreign, colonial imposition.

In spite of this history, the church in China has exploded in recent years. Like the situation that was common throughout the former Soviet bloc, there are "registered" Christians and there are "unregistered" or "underground" Christians in the area. Perspectives differ over how many of each kind of Christians exist within China, and on who can speak for the Christian faith. One thing is clear, however: the church in China is still subject to considerable suffering and persecution, and martyrdom is not out of the question. Bob (Xiqiu) Fu, who has been a house church leader in China, gives us insight on the current situation that governs church-state relations within communist China. Although this paper was not presented at Malta, its obvious relevance made its inclusion a necessity.

Elsewhere in southern Asia, limitations, suffering, persecution, and martyrdom are everyday realities in a number of countries. Vietnam, Indonesia, Sri Lanka, India, and Myanmar come immediately to mind. Chin Khua Khai discusses the status of human rights, and with them, the rights of Christians to practice their faith under the military government currently in place in Myanmar. The situation is complex and calls for prayer and political pressure to be brought to bear on behalf of such people.

The final contribution is one by Monsignor Felix Machado. In Pentecostal and charismatic circles specifically, and in evangelical circles generally, "interreligious dialogue" is often viewed as a code word for "compromise." Unfortunately, sometimes it is also confused with the idea of "ecumenism." At the present time, the term "ecumenism" which is derived from the Greek term οἶκος meaning "house" or "household," generally refers quite literally to the "household of faith," the church. Those who are engaged in ecumenism are engaged in discussions that hold implications for the "household of faith." On the other hand, interreligious dialogue speaks about discussions between members of two or more faith traditions. It may legitimately speak about a discussion in which members of the "household of faith," the Christian church, can take part in a broader discussion between Christianity and one or more other religions. One of the subjects appearing with increasing frequency on various ecumenical agendas is precisely this one.

For many Pentecostal, charismatic, and evangelical Christians this is viewed as threatening. How can we guarantee that Jesus' command to "make disciples" (Matt. 28:19) is not compromised or violated when we are engaged in interreligious dialogue? If we think about it for a moment, however, we might see that from the ministry of Jesus to the ministry of the Apostles, interreligious dialogue was present. For example, in Sychar, at Jacob's well, Jesus openly addresses the theological concerns of the Samaritan woman (cf. John 4:7–30). We can follow the dialogue with Jesus and the woman raising their respective questions and responding with their respective answers. In a sense, one could argue that Jesus' exchange with the Syrophoenecian woman (cf. Matt. 15:21–28) or his interaction with the Roman centurion might also be viewed in this way (cf. Matt. 8:5–13). Similarly, the apostle Paul was engaged many times in interreligious dialogue, Jewish-Christian, Epicurean-Christian, Stoic-Christian dialogue, following his conversion to faith in Christ (cf. Acts 17:16–21). When he spoke to the citizens in Athens, a city known for its pantheon of gods as well as its idols, Paul interacted at a significant level, acknowledging their tradition, but showing them how it pointed toward the Christian tradition as the truth (cf. Acts 17:22–32).

Monsignor Machado demonstrates that the call to engage in inter-religious dialogue is deeply rooted in the Christian faith. Furthermore, the Holy Spirit is both at work in the world (cf. John 16:8–11) and in the church. As a result, we can expect the Holy Spirit to be with us when we, who are rooted in faith in the Lord Jesus Christ and empowered by the Holy Spirit, speak of that faith in a dialogical way with people of other faiths. In this way, dialogue can be a useful tool in lowering the hostilities between people of different faith groups. This makes sense whether we approach people of a different faith who live next to us or in some far-off country somewhere around the world.

At present, there are many parts of the body that suffer. The type of suffering they bear varies from place to place. Why so many suffer is a mystery. As a result, we offer the doxology of Paul in Romans 11:33–36, as you, our readers, think anew about the place of suffering, persecution, and even martyrdom for those of the household of faith:

> Oh, the depth of the riches of the wisdom and knowledge of
> God!
> How unsearchable his judgments,
> and his paths beyond tracing out!
> "Who has known the mind of the Lord?
> Or who has been his counselor?"
> "Who has ever given to God,
> that God should repay him?"
> For from him and through him and to him are all things.
> To him be the glory forever! Amen.

Endnotes

[1] Samuel P. Huntington, *The Clash of Civilizations: Remaking of World Order* (New York: Touchstone, 1996).

Section I

THEOLOGICAL FOUNDATIONS

Persecution, Martyrdom, and Christian Self-Definition in the Early Church

HELEN RHEE

1. Introduction

Christian self-identities in the first three centuries AD developed as a result of various internal and external factors. One has to do with the Christians' relation with Judaism; another has to do with its in-house affairs and controversies with "heterodox" groups, such as the Gnostics and the Marcionites. Externally, Christian self-definition and identity was inevitably molded amidst Christians' interactions with the dominant Greco-Roman society. In response to the rapid growth of Christianity, the majority of pagans who came in contact with the movement reacted with fear, contempt, and hostility. The "new" religion with universal claims appeared as superstitious, irrational, and dangerous to the well-being of the empire. In the late second and early third centuries, public prejudices against Christians occasionally resulted in local violence against them, and learned aristocrats began to take Christianity seriously enough to launch major intellectual attacks on Christians and their doctrines. The last half of the third century witnessed violence against Christians from the top – the emperors themselves. The pagan perception of and periodic opposition to Christians formed "a negative starting point." This provided the situation to which Christians reacted and the categories that shaped their own self-understanding.[1]

This chapter deals with this Christian self-definition in relation to the persecution and martyrdom reflected in the Christian Martyr Acts. The first part briefly surveys the history of persecution as a context for the Martyr Acts; the second part treats the Christian self-identity presented in that literature in three aspects – religious self-definition, social self-definition, and political self-definition.

2. Christian Interaction with Greco-Roman Society

2.1 Persecutions up to the mid-third century

In the early second century, as evidenced in the famous letter of Pliny to Emperor Trajan, Christians were denounced and punished for their confession of the *nomen christianorum* in association with alleged crimes accompanied by the name Christian. In the course of his investigation, Pliny ordered a "sacrifice-test" as proof of their innocence; only those who recanted, conformed to the worship of the gods and the emperor, and cursed Christ, were pardoned. Although Pliny found no specific crime of Christians, he declared Christianity a "depraved and excessive superstition" (*superstitio prava, immodica*; *Ep.* 10.96). Describing the fire in Rome under Nero, Pliny's contemporary Tacitus attached to Christians the charge of "hatred of the human race" (*odio humani generis*) and the stigma of a "pernicious superstition" (*superstitio exitiabilis*; *Annals* 15.44). Suetonius, also writing about Nero, regarded Christians as "a class of men given to a new and mischievous superstition" (*genus hominum superstitionis novae ac maleficae*; *Nero* 16.2). These distinguished men of the senatorial rank perceived Christianity as a "superstition" in association with the Christians' guilt and punishment.[2] Superstition, a term in general usage that designated the irrational and fanatical religious groups or practices alien to Rome, rendered itself contrary to the high religious and ethical ideals of Rome. In essence, it meant irreligion and impiety, leading to a denial of the gods, i.e. atheism, as opposed to true piety, whose fruit was "to worship God according to the tradition of one's fathers."[3]

In the Greco-Roman world, where there was a fundamental unity in religion, society, and politics, the established idea of *pax deorum* provided its ideological basis.[4] *Pax deorum*, a sacred contractual relationship between gods and people, preserved the essential unity between religion and politics and governed the basic rules of life in the empire. The order, success, and prosperity of the empire would be maintained so long as the worship of the Roman gods continued by means of appropriate cults. *Pax deorum* was the bedrock and goal of the Roman way of life (*Romanitas*), and this *Romanitas* stood in continuity with the past and stood for the past, i.e. its ancestral tradition (*mos maiorum*). *Mos maiorum* was "the bond and foundation of society, a common fund of wisdom amassed in the course of centuries" that controlled the way the Greeks and Romans thought.[5] The ancient customs, especially in religion, guaranteed personal, familial, and political security and protection; they functioned as the firm stronghold in the midst of and against the infiltration of the countless new and dubious religious and social practices. Thus, piety embraced both the sense of loyalty to the traditional customs of Rome and the public devotion to the gods in the established cultic acts.[6]

Given this cultural mold, it is not surprising that the Christians in the second and third centuries attracted intense hostility and criticisms from their pagan neighbors. All the vices of superstition were ascribed to the ominous name of Christianity. In the mid-second century, as the church expanded her mission into urban culture, the Christians' neglect of the traditional gods became increasingly noticeable and turned into the frequent blame for the local disasters. A rescript of Emperor Antoninus Pius to the Council of Asia indicates the Christians having been denounced as "atheists" and a cause of evil in the society; it mentions the provincials' anger against them following the severe earthquake in Asian provinces (ca. AD 152).[7] In the reign of Marcus Aurelius (ca. AD 165), the great plague, which eventually devastated the entire eastern and central parts of the empire, was followed by local persecutions of the Christians. Tertullian's sarcastic sneer, though not without exaggeration, still reflected the pungent reality at the end of the century: "If the Tiber rises to the city walls, if the Nile does not cover the flood-plains, if the heavens don't move or if the earth does, if there is a famine or a plague, the roar is at once: 'The Christians to the lion!' Really! All of them to one lion?" (*Apol.* 40.2).

This charge of atheism (Christians' refusal to worship the traditional gods), which had been a familiar accusation against the Jews, was now turned against Christians and lay at the core of enmity toward them.[8] Among the pagans, it generated intense anxiety and fear of the gods' wrath and identified Christians as a direct enemy of the *pax deorum* and *mos maiorum*; enemies of the gods were the enemies of the people and of the empire. Hence, Justin in his apologies (ca. AD 150–55) singled out "atheism" as the most serious anti-Christian slander.[9] At the martyrdom of Polycarp (ca. AD 155–60), bishop of Smyrna,[10] the confession of his Christian identity aroused such "uncontrollable wrath" of Jews and pagans that they condemned him as "the destroyer of our gods, who teaches many neither to offer sacrifice nor to worship."[11]

Other charges soon accompanied the essentially religious charge of atheism. The accusations of Cornelius Fronto, Marcus Aurelius' tutor, preserved by Minucius Felix, were undoubtedly scandalous: worship of a donkey's head, ritual murder of an infant and cannibalism, and incestuous and promiscuous unions on feast days (*Oct.* 9.6; 31.1–2). The practice of black magic, a prominent feature of superstition, constituted another serious social charge; to the pagan eyes, certain Christian rituals and practices such as exorcism and praying "in the name of Jesus," speaking in tongues, and the sign of the cross could have been hardly distinguishable from magical rites.[12] Furthermore, the Christians' secret assembly, nonparticipation in the imperial cult, and radical apocalypticism created public suspicion of the subversiveness of Christianity as a political threat to the empire.

Within this hostile environment, another kind of opposition developed – more systematic and rational indictments on Christianity by the pagan intellectuals. They first appeared in the late second century with the work of the Platonist Celsus and continued in the third century with the Neo-Platonist Porphyry and in the fourth with the Emperor Julian the Apostate. These anti-Christian writings served a twofold purpose. First, they attempted to undermine the Christian doctrines and make-up against the Greco-Roman philosophy and values; second, they attempted to demonstrate the superiority of the traditional polytheism and the Greek *paideia* (education, training) upon which the whole Greco-Roman culture was founded.[13]

Celsus' work *True Doctrine* (*alethes logos*) serves as an example. It was written between AD 177–80, when the Christian apologetic activity was at its peak, possibly as an intelligent pagan retort to the earlier apologies of Justin Martyr.[14] Celsus' philosophical and theological criticisms of Christian doctrines were fundamentally based on the Platonic notion of divine transcendence and immutability; they targeted the Christian claim of exclusive monotheism, especially in relation to the worship of Jesus and the doctrines of incarnation and resurrection. His rational monotheism combined a belief in the incorporeal and impassible Supreme God with an affirmation of traditional gods as the intermediaries, including the Demiurge who created the physical world (henotheism). The Supreme God cannot be in touch with the physical world, and God's nature is not such that he can undergo change or alteration from perfection to corruption (4.14). In this sense, the idea of incarnation, God or Son of God descending to earth in a mortal body, is not only irrational but also unnecessary. Faith in bodily resurrection as opposed to immortality of the soul is equally detestable and theologically impossible; it is a misunderstanding of reincarnation (7.32). These doctrines not only reveal Christians' deficiency of reason but also expose their faint distortion and falsification of the classical Greek tradition and philosophy.

From the outset, he declares Christians the open enemy of the Greco-Roman society – a secret, illegal, and revolutionary sect, bound by oaths, with intent to subvert the established order (1.1). Having no tradition of their own, Christians apostatized from Judaism with its worst features, namely, radical monotheism and sectarian exclusivism, and abandoned the ancestral custom (*mos maiorum*) and worship of the gods of the society. As like attracts like, their appeal to the social outcasts and abominable sinners disclose their own moral bankruptcy (3.50–59, 64, 76); they attract only the uneducated and wretched women with simple fideism (1.27; 3.18); and they destroy families and disrupt social structure by putting children against their parents (3.55). Celsus calls Christians to obey the emperor, to return to the ancestral customs, and to participate in the civic life and public responsibility for the common good of the society (8.63–75).

Under the reign of Marcus Aurelius (AD 161–80), all these accusations and polemics found a vent in local persecutions and pogroms, especially in connection with the eruption of the piling misfortunes of the constant wars and natural disasters in the eastern provinces. "At this time," wrote Eusebius, "there were the greatest persecutions excited in Asia" (*Hist. eccl.* 4.15.1). In Rome, after a trial by the city prefect Urbicus, the Apologist Justin was put to death with other Christians (AD 163–67) (*Acts Just.*; cf. *Hist. eccl.* 4.16). The most vivid account of the local persecution under Marcus Aurelius came from Lyons and Vienne in Gaul (France) (*Hist. eccl.* 5.1; *Mart. Lyons*). In the summer of AD 177, during the festival of the imperial cult, sudden mob rage unleashed itself on the Christians who were accused of atheism, incest, and cannibalism. After suffering from robbery, imprisonment, torture, stoning, and a series of social sanctions, the Christians were driven by the mob to the governor's tribunal. They were suspected of treason, and their alleged crimes were confirmed by the false confessions of their slaves under torture. Then, the governor, by the emperor's directive, followed the precedent set by Trajan: the apostates were to be freed but those who persisted were to be condemned to death by beasts or beheading. The account singles out the heroism of the slave girl Blandina and the youth Ponticus, and it reports some forty-eight martyrs, including those who perished in prison. Even after the Christians' deaths, the crowd exposed, burned, and scattered the bodies in the Rhone River with scorn for the doctrine of resurrection.

Between AD 195 and 212, there were sporadic persecutions of various intensities in major parts of the empire.[15] In AD 203 Septimus Severus issued a general edict prohibiting conversion to Judaism or Christianity. Although this edict had a rather short duration, its impact was considerably felt among the upper-class converts, and it provided a precedent for future official actions. In Alexandria, Clement, who fled the city, reported "roastings, impalings, and beheadings" of Christians (*Strom.* 2.20.125); victims included Origen's father Leonides and a number of students of the Catechetical School, where Clement taught (*Hist. eccl.* 6.1, 4–5). In Carthage, Tertullian reported tortures, rackings, burnings, and condemnations of Christians (*Apol.* 40.12–13); the famous martyrdom of the noble woman Perpetua and the slave Felicitas, together with four other catechumens, took place in the amphitheater in March, AD 203 (see *Mart. Perp.*). The account of their martyrdom clearly depicts the total disruption of family life brought about by a conversion to Christianity and the vehement hostility of the crowd toward Christians. In Rome, Hippolytus described brutality of angry mobs turning on the Christians.[16] This precarious state of Christians under the threat of popular accusations and subsequent sporadic condemnation by the authorities and their perceptions of persecutions defined and redefined their mode of self-representation and attitude toward the dominant Greco-Roman society and culture.

2.2 Imperial crises and persecutions in the mid-third and early fourth century

From the mid-third century onward, persecutions were not confined to popular pogroms but initiated by the emperors with a "universal" impact. In the mid-third century, the empire was in deep crisis. In AD 249, Gothic tribes crossed the Danube and invaded the Balkan provinces of the empire. In January of AD 250, the Emperor Decius sought to regain the lost *pax deorum* by ordering a sacrifice to the gods of the empire throughout the empire.[17] The commissioners were appointed to supervise the sacrifice and the certificates (*libelli*) were issued to those who had performed it.[18] The edict was not specifically aimed against the Christians but rather at ensuring the favor of the Roman gods (*pax deorum*) and restoring the traditional cult in a time of national crisis. Decius' general edict had an initial success – until his death in AD 251. Bishops of Rome, Antioch, and Jerusalem were executed. In Caesarea, Origen was tortured and died in prison (*Hist. eccl.* 6.39.5); in Carthage, Cyprian went into hiding (*Hist. eccl.* 6.39.4). Many Christians likewise suffered from imprisonment, torture, exile, and death, but a vast majority of Christians lapsed by offering sacrifices and denying their religious identity.

After the interim period of peace, the Emperor Valerian (AD 253–60) renewed a systematic persecution on Christianity (AD 257) now as a church, as a hierarchically organized institution.[19] The first edict in AD 257 required bishops, presbyters, and deacons to offer sacrifice to the gods, prohibited Christian assemblies in public, and confiscated church property. The second edict in AD 258 ordered bishops, presbyters, and deacons to be arrested and executed. Christians in senatorial and equestrian classes would lose their dignities and property (Cyprian, *Ep.* 80). Valerian specifically targeted the church leadership and the Christians in the high ranks; Christians were not merely obliged to conform and compromise, but their worship and corporate life were threatened with extinction. At this time, Cyprian in Carthage was tried and martyred,[20] as were many other bishops and deacons in Rome, Spain, and North Africa.[21] The number of martyrs far exceeded that of the persecutions of Decius, but with much less apostasy. In AD 260, Valerian was captured by Shapur I, King of Persia; his son Gallienus restored the church's places of worship and properties and allowed freedom of existence as a corporate entity.[22] Under Gallienus and his successors up until AD 303 there were no general persecutions of Christians, and the church prospered during the forty years of relative peace.

When Diocletian took the imperial throne in AD 284, he found the empire in a dire situation as in the time of Decius: its frontiers constantly threatened by the Germanic tribes and Persians, the army rebellious, and the economy in depression. In order to revive the empire, he attempted to unite all the forces of the empire for the work of imperial reform and restoration on the foundation of the traditional Roman religion. In order to expedite the reform, in AD 293, he divided the empire into four regions and established the Tetrarchy, a rule of four emperors. Diocletian and Galerius ruled the East, and Maximian and Constantius Chlorus ruled the West. The Great Persecution (AD 303–12)[23] can be seen as the culmination of the measures of Diocletian and his fellow rulers (tetrarchs), aimed at imposing on the empire a strictly uniform administration inspired by the cult of the Roman gods and the practice of the traditional virtues of Rome.

For the first twenty years, Diocletian was tolerant of the church. In fact, his wife and daughter and many court officials were Christians. From the year AD 298 on, however, pressure against Christians gradually built up. Measures were undertaken to expel Christians from the army, and the oracle of Apollo in AD 302 confirmed Christian disruption at the sacrifice.[24] Diocletian issued the first of a series of edicts on February 23, AD 303; on the same day the church near the imperial palace at Nicomedia was destroyed. The edict ordered the following: churches were to be destroyed, assemblies forbidden, property confiscated, scriptures handed over to the authorities for burning. Christians of rank were to lose all privileges; imperial servants were to be reduced to slavery. It recalled the edicts of Valerian, without the death penalty. Diocletian had forbidden bloodshed; there were to be no martyrs.[25] A few months later, a second edict was issued, ordering the arrest of the higher clergy.[26] In the fall of AD 303, on his way to Rome, Diocletian issued a third edict that the arrested clergy should make sacrifice and be freed. On his return from Rome, however, Diocletian became ill and Galerius took advantage of the situation. In the spring of 304, Galerius issued the fourth edict, commanding all subjects of the empire to sacrifice to the gods on pain of death or hard labor in the mines; it renewed the demand made by Decius half-a-century earlier. While persecution in the West ended in AD 305, this edict was the beginning of the real horror in the East and lasted until AD 312.

3. The Martyr Acts

3.1 *The Martyr Acts and Christian self-definition*

The Martyr Acts describe and celebrate, sometimes with gruesome detail and arresting images, the undaunted faith, noble endurance, and incredible valor of Christians imprisoned and brutally executed by the Roman authorities. The martyrs are the heroes of the church whose deaths witness to their unshakable allegiance to Christ. They are noble athletes[27] who are engaged in a supernatural combat (*agon*) against the devil beyond the earthly struggle opposed to the crowd or the governors. They are the partakers of Christ's sufferings and the imitators of his death; Christ was the protomartyr or the first martyr of Christianity in his self-giving death on the cross.

All of these themes are explicit in the earliest account of a Christian martyrdom, *The Martyrdom of Polycarp*, a congregational letter from Smyrna to the church in Philomelium in response to the latter's request for a detailed account of the aged bishop Polycarp's martyrdom, which took place between AD 155 and 160.[28] Recognized as an "authentic" contemporary account, it became the model for what would soon become a popular genre of literature, Martyr Acts; it set forth "a martyrdom in accord with the gospel" (1.1) through Polycarp's example and bore the earliest testimony to the cult of the martyrs in the church (17.1 – 18.3). Here the words *martyr (martys)* and *martyrdom (martyrion)* in the definite sense of witnessing to Christ by death at the hands of hostile secular authority first appear.[29] Only those who die in accordance with God's will are the true martyrs: the imitators of the Lord (1.2; 19.1) and partakers of Christ (6.2) in his death. The twin theme of *imitatores Christi* and athletic heroism governs not only this piece but also all the subsequent Martyr Acts.

Martyrdom was a public spectacle charged with powerful emotions and rich symbolism. It took place in the middle of the urban surroundings and religious rituals as part of athletic contest or sacrifice. In these spectacles, martyrs made "an ultimate statement of commitment to the group and what the group represented."[30] The *acta martyria* deal with two primary concerns: a demand to sacrifice/swear allegiance to the gods and the emperors, and the question, "Are you a Christian?"[31] These two concerns are closely related in such a way that the answer to the question of Christian identity involves a refusal to partake in pagan ritual and to give allegiance to the pagan gods/emperors. The climax in the Martyr Acts then is the final confession of the martyr made in public: "I am a Christian."[32] As Ekkehart Mühlenberg observes in those texts, "while death is part of the confession, death or manner of dying has no value of its own apart from the confession."[33] It is this final confession that unites the martyr with "all the sojourners of the holy and catholic church everywhere"[34] and serves to draw the Christian "group identity and self-definition."[35] The Christian Martyr Acts present martyrdom as the supreme religious value for the group and tell the "collective stories" of dying for God in and with all of their collective cultural traditions: Socrates,

Maccabees, the Roman generals' *devotio*, Greek tragedies and their heroes, gladiators, games and athletes, philosophers, and Jesus on the cross.[36] In this way, the Martyr Acts culturally legitimize the martyrs' deaths and define the Christian identity and ethos represented by their words and deeds.

The public executions of Christians needed an explicatory context for outsiders and insiders alike.[37] The fact that martyrdom was used as a positive "demonstration of religious truth" is beyond doubt,[38] and the Martyr Acts shared some common literary elements in describing martyrs' heroism[39] with the theological thrust of witnessing to God over against pagan gods. Thus, martyrology carried strong missionary messages to the outsiders, and martyrs constituted "strong 'apologies' for the faith to pagan audiences"[40] resulting in conversions.[41] In a world where people were seized by "a sort of fascination with death … surrounding voluntary death in legend and life, a desire for theatrical prominence, the very widespread idea of the body as a prison for the soul, and pessimism,"[42] and where different religious and philosophical schools contended over the merit of their respective "martyrdoms,"[43] the Christian Martyr Acts placed an exclusive claim on theirs as the only "authentic" martyrdom to the one true God over against any other causes or beings. As such, they imparted an indelible impression and power to the pagan minds. In the *Martyrdom of Perpetua and Felicitas*, the jailor Puden became a Christian by the martyrs' display of extraordinary virtues and strength (9.1; 16.4). Moreover, the soldier Basilides, who led the heroine Potamiaena to her death, professed his Christian faith in public after her noble death and even joined her in martyrdom (*Mart. Potam.* 5–7). The Apologist Justin, who himself would be martyred for his faith, was profoundly impressed as a pagan by the scene of Christian martyrdom (2 *Apol.* 12). To the insiders, Martyr Acts certainly provided the teachings on the true nature of martyrdom and an inspiration and heroic model to follow or at least to commemorate. Other Christians became martyrs as did Agathonices, who threw herself into the flame when inspired by the vision of Christ at the martyrdom of Carpus (*Mart. Carp.* 42–44 [Greek]). Likewise, Lucius and an unknown man shared the fate of Ptolemaeus, protesting on his behalf in the trial (*Mart. Ptol.* 15,

20). Tertullian's famous statement, "the blood of the martyrs is seed" (*Semen est sanguis Christianorum*), was not mere rhetorical hype (*Apol.* 50.13).

The martyrs transformed the stigma of deviance into a badge of honor.[44] The martyrs struggle against the persecutors who personify the demonic powers but overcome them not with the sword but with blood. They loom larger than life as the exemplar of faith and the embodiment of Christian ideals; they represent a kind of spiritual perfectionist along with the ascetics. Their desire and contempt for death and defiance to the Roman authorities set themselves against the established culture and society and deny the socio-political paradigm of power. The Martyr Acts, so deeply embedded in the life and spectacles of the Greco-Roman world, put forth the Christian resistance to the life this world offers for the glory in the next.

3.2 Religious self-definition: Christianity as true sacrifice and piety

In the form of both athletic contest and sacrificial rite, martyrdom was a public ritual and dramatic "liturgical sacrifice in which the word of Jesus and his kingdom was confessed and acted out, and an offering made that repeated his own."[45] The martyrs, "the athletes of piety," proclaimed loud and clear that Christianity was the true piety over against the pagan piety by virtue of their public confession and self-offering: the supreme sacrifice in imitation of Jesus Christ. If one recalls that the purpose of the sacrifice is to restore *pax deorum* and harmony to the community, the Martyr Acts' portrayal of martyrdom and thus of Christianity as true sacrifice indeed turns the table on the pagan piety and disrupts the entire structure of the Greco-Roman religion and society. The Christians' daring refusal to participate in the pagan sacrifice is juxtaposed with their joyous offering of their prayers, praises, and finally their own lives to the one true God of creation. When Perpetua and her fellow martyrs entered the arena for their combat, she firmly resisted the authorities' attempt to dress them as the priests of Saturn (for men) and the priestesses of Ceres (for women).[46] Not only was the authorities' attempt a deliberate insult to the Christian monotheism, but it also might have meant using them as both ministers and sacrifice to those gods.[47] These martyrs instead insisted on their "free will" and "freedom" to die as Christians (*Mart. Perp.* 5) – as the pure and noble sacrifice to the true God.

The martyrs publicly testify that the so-called traditional gods to whom pagans offer sacrifice are only dead idols and in fact evil demons; therefore, the pagan sacrifice is false and ineffective and a mere semblance of the true sacrifice. However, since the Christian God is the only true God, the Christian sacrifice, most remarkably in the form of dying for God, is the true sacrifice. Hence, the Christian worship is the only authentic worship. One has only to remember that a major function of martyrdom as a cosmic contest and efficacious sacrifice to God was conquering the Devil, the chief of the pagan gods. Thus, Justin Martyr replies to the prefect's urge to sacrifice: "What person of sound mind … would choose to turn from piety (*eusebeia*) to impiety (*asebeia*), from light to darkness, and from the living God to soul-destroying demons?" (*Acts Just.* C.4.4).

The presentation of Christianity as the true sacrifice to the true God, thus as the true piety, centers on the Christian confession, "I am a Christian." It is significant and inevitable that this confession of Christian identity immediately follows the martyrs' rejection to partake in pagan sacrifice and their affirmation of Christian monotheism.[48] This confession also answers the question, "Are you a Christian?" which usually precedes the demand to offer sacrifice, and thus provides a valid reason for the Roman officials to persecute and execute Christians.[49] Therefore, this confession is a crucial part of martyrs' training[50] and constitutes the most resounding declaration of the Christian self-definition.

3.3 Social self-definition: Christian rejection and redefinition of traditional family relations

The Martyr Acts also portray the martyrs as renouncing their natural family ties in favor of their commitment to martyrdom and the new Christian identity and kinship. For instance, Sanctus, one of the martyrs of Lyons, when asked by the governor about his identity, refused to recognize any other identity but his Christian one: "instead of giving his name, birthplace, nationality, or anything else," he kept on repeating, "I am a Christian!" (*Mart. Lyons* 1.20). Similarly, one of Justin Martyr's companions, Hierax, when asked about his parents, answers, "'Christ is my true father,' … and our faith in him is our mother. My earthly parents have passed away" (*Acts Just.* B.4.8). The martyrs deny any earthly or natural ties and acknowledge only their spiritual identity and kinship. In light of the newfound eternal family, the transient and earthly family identity and loyalty are meaningless and discarded.

As the martyrs reject physical family ties and experience separation from them, they join the new Christian kinship relations. When the "mother-martyrs" withdrew from their maternal responsibilities for martyrdom, their children were placed in the Christian parental care. Agathonice was confident that God the heavenly Father would take care of her children. Though Perpetua's son remained at the hands of her earthly father, Felicitas's newborn girl was taken up by a Christian woman who brought up the baby as her own daughter. Moreover, as Perpetua rejects her earthly father, she gains her heavenly Father. There is an inverted parallel between her physical father and the old shepherd in her first vision. In her fourth vision, after Perpetua defeats the devil in the form of an Egyptian, the *lanista* (president of the game[51]) of marvelous stature rewards her with golden apples and a kiss, saying, "Peace be with you, my daughter (*Filia, pax tecum*)!" (*Mart. Perp.* 10.13). In contrast to the disturbing appearances of her pagan father in real life, "it is a serene father-figure – not tormented and tormenting, but solacing – who appears to Perpetua in her first and last visions."[52] Thus, her heavenly Father replaces her natural father whom she has rejected and honors her with paternal welcome and recognition of her commitment to Christ.

In fact, God is the only Father explicitly identified in the Martyr Acts.[53] While the prominent women martyrs are mothers and/ or take maternal roles for fellow Christians, no male martyr is identified as father or takes the paternal role.[54] The genuine father figure and paternal role are reserved only for God; Perpetua's father (the only human father identified) is portrayed as an evil menace to Christians' loyalty to their heavenly Father. This may have been a literal interpretation of Jesus' command to "call no man Father" in Matthew 23:9.[55]

As the new Christian kinship defies natural blood relations and is redefined by the relation to God the Father as siblings and mothers, it also crosses social barriers and embraces people from radically different socio-economic statuses. Martyrdom is a great social equalizer: slaves, mistresses, noble matron, senator, physician, aged bishop, and youth all belong to the same family of God as brothers and sisters and share the same honor of martyrdom. In particular, the portrayals of the heroism of the weak and the lowly (e.g. women and slaves) strongly indicate the social reversal: "Christ proved that the things that men think cheap, ugly, and contemptuous are deemed worthy of glory before God," because of their love for him (*Mart. Lyons* 1.17). Indeed, according to Everett Ferguson, persecutions provided an "equal opportunity" of martyrdom for both men and women,[56] and for women martyrs, martyrdom meant "gaining of personhood" and authority.[57] Along with the ascetic call to virginity and continence, the call to martyrdom offered women empowerment and "liberation" from the traditional female sex and gender roles.[58] The women martyrs experienced transformation of their gender stereotypes and empowerment on the way to martyrdom. This kind of alternative relationship and perspective counteracted the established social boundaries.

3.4 *Political self-definition: Christ versus Caesar*

As previously mentioned, in the Martyr Acts, the Roman magistrates consistently demand the Christians to offer sacrifices to the gods and/or the emperors or to take an oath by the gods and/or the emperors' genius. With the traditional cults, the imperial cult provides the litmus test for Christian loyalty to the empire. The Christian confession of the one true God precludes not only the worship of the traditional gods but also the cult of the emperors; thus, the martyr's confession is a political act as well as a religious one. The Christian "atheism" resulted in the Christian subversiveness to the Roman Empire.

Since "Caesar and Christ are … the archetypical heroes of two antithetical cosmologies,"[59] the contest of power between the Lord Christ and the Lord Caesar becomes significant in several Acts.[60] In the earliest Acts, the *Martyrdom of Polycarp*, the two confrontations of Polycarp with the government focus on this issue. First, the police captain Herod tries to persuade Polycarp, saying, "Now what harm is there for you to say 'Caesar is lord,' to perform the sacrifices and so forth, and thus your life?" (8.2).

Then, at the trial, the governor demands that Polycarp "swear by the Genius of the emperor," "recant" (9.2), and "curse Christ" (9.3). Both the captain and governor represent the deeply ingrained Roman imperial ideology that religiously legitimated the (supposedly) absolute power of the emperor. Thus, in the *Acts of the Scillitan Martyrs*, the proconsul Saturninus defines the *mos Romanorum* in that manner: "our religion is a simple one: we swear by the genius of our lord the emperor and we offer prayers for his health" (3). He then commands the Christians to take oaths by the genius of the emperor (5). In the *Martyrdom of Apollonius*, after Apollonius's confession of his Christian identity, the proconsul Perennis urges Apollonius the same command: "swear by the Genius of our lord the emperor Commodus" (3). Later, he repeats, "do what I tell you: offer sacrifice to the gods and to the image of the emperor Commodus" (7). The underlying command comes from the emperor,[61] which requires a religious enactment of their political loyalty and the acknowledgment of the "imperial salvation."

To this pressure, the martyrs distinguish the worship of the emperor from the proper honor and obedience due to the emperor. Polycarp does recognize the Christian teaching "to pay respect to the authorities and power that God has assigned [Christians]" (*Mart. Pol.* 10.2), but he rejects the command: "I do not intend to do what you advise" (*Mart. Pol.* 8.2). Speratus, one of the Scillitan martyrs, stresses Christian civil obedience, "I have not stolen; and on any purchase I pay the tax," but articulates who his Lord is: "I serve that God whom no man has seen, nor can see, with these eyes" (*Acts Scill.* 6). According to Apollonius, Christians "obey any law passed by the emperor" and "respect him" but "worship the immortal God alone" (*Mart. Apol.* 37).

Apollonius would swear to pay honor to the emperor and pray for his authority only by "the one, true God, the One existing before all the ages" (ibid.).

The martyrs' distinction of religious and political loyalty and persistent refusal to conform to the authorities' orders amount to blaspheming the "sacred emperors"[62] and instantly make them outlaws, traitors, and threats to the empire; for they desacralize and destabilize the imperial myths and ideology, which claim absolute power. Polycarp's famous retort comes in response to the governor's demand: "For eighty-six years I have been his servant and he has done me no wrong. How can I blaspheme against my king and saviour?" (*Mart. Pol.* 9.3). It is impossible for a Christian to take the imperial cult for granted and to render to the emperor what he demands, especially because "Jesus Christ [is] reigning eternally" (*Mart. Pol.* 21). Speratus replies to the proconsul, "I do not recognize the empire of this world. Rather ... I acknowledge my lord who is the emperor of kings and of all nations" (*Acts Scill.* 6). Christians do not live by the Roman imperial ideology but unmask its hollow reality in light of God's heavenly kingdom.

The depiction of Christ or God as "king" and "emperor of kings" carries an apocalyptic imagery set above and against the emperor and his earthly empire. The portrayal of God / Christ as the heavenly monarch who is the final Judge accentuates the contrast between God's eternal and universal kingship and the temporal reign and limited authority of Caesar. Therefore, the extent of the Christians' loyalty to the emperor or the empire is determined not by what Caesar requires but by what their God requires.

Hence, Apollonius declares that sacrifices and oaths – the typical signs of loyalty – belong only to the "almighty God, the lord of heaven and earth and of all that breathes" (*Mart. Apol.* 8). After all, "a divine decree cannot be quelled by a decree of man" (*Mart. Apol.* 24).

4. Conclusion

This chapter presented the ways in which the Christian Martyr Acts defined Christian self-identity with respect to the volatile relation of Christians with the Greco-Roman society. The Martyr Acts define the "fundamentals" of Christianity with the negotiable and the nonnegotiable. These "fundamentals" project the ideals as well as the realities; the assertion of what Christians believe and practice delineates in turn what they should believe and practice. Furthermore, the essentials of "what it means to be a Christian" answer the question "What difference does and should Christianity make?" The Christian ideals are unabashedly universal in claim and scope, but it is the very universal ideals that disclose a deliberate selectivity in drawing the boundaries. Here, Christian monotheism set up the clearest boundary against the Greco-Roman polytheism. The worship of the God Almighty who created and rules the universe and of his Son Jesus Christ demarcates the true worshipers from the false. The Christians' belief in the one true God determined their moral, social, and political outlook and practice against the traditional social norms and values. Ultimately, Christians were willing to pay the price for their faith; the victims of violence became the victors of the spiritual battle in their martyrdom.

Endnotes

[1] R. L. Wilken, "The Christians as the Romans (and Greeks) Saw It," in B. F. Meyer and E. P. Sanders (eds.), *Jewish and Christian Self-Definition* Vol. 1 (3 vols.; Philadelphia, PA: Fortress Press, 1980), 124.

[2] On the topic of superstition in the Greco-Roman world in general and its relationship with the persecution of the Christians, see further L. F. Janssen, "'Superstitio' and the Persecution of the Christians," *Vigiliae Christianae* 33 (1979), 131–59.

[3] Wilken, "The Christians as the Romans (and Greeks) Saw It," 105–106.

[4] On the idea of *pax deorum*, see F. W. Fowler, *The Religious Experience of the Roman People* (London: MacMillan, 1911), especially 184–86.

[5] M. Simon, "Early Christianity and Pagan Thought: Confluences and Conflicts," *Religious Studies* 9 (1973), 387.

[6] R. L. Wilken, *The Christians as the Romans Saw Them* (New Haven, CT: Yale University Press, 1984), 53, 56.

[7] Eusebius, *Hist. eccl.* 4.13; cf. W. H. C. Frend, *Martyrdom and Persecution in the Early Church* (Oxford: Blackwell, 1965), 239–40.

[8] J. J. Walsh, "On Christian Atheism," *Vigiliae Christianae* 45 (1991), 255–77, attributes the significance of this charge to the second half of the second

century and the third century, especially from the reign of Marcus Aurelius onwards.

[9]   *1 Apol.* 6; *2 Apol.* 3; contra Walsh, "On Christian Atheism," 262.

[10]   For the account of Polycarp's martyrdom and the circumstance that led to it, see *Hist. eccl.* 4.15 and *Mart. Pol.* in H. Musurillo (ed.), *The Acts of the Christian Martyrs* (Oxford: Clarendon, 1972; repr. 2000), 2–21. Subsequent references to the individual Martyr Acts come from the Musurillo's edition.

[11]   *Hist. eccl.* 4.15.26; *Mart. Pol.* 12.2.

[12]   C. S. de Vos, "Popular Greco-Roman Responses to Christianity," in P. F. Esler (ed.), *The Early Christian World* Vol. 2 (2 vols.; London & New York: Routledge, 2000), 878; cf. S. Benko, *Pagan Rome and the Early Christians* (Bloomington, IN: Indiana University Press, 1984), 103–31.

[13]   M. B. Simmons, "Graeco-Roman Philosophical Opposition," in Esler (ed.), *Early Christian World* Vol. 2, 841.

[14]   See C. Andresen, *Logos under Nomos: Die Polemik des Kelsos wider des Christentum*, Arbeiten zur Kirchengeschichte 30 (Berlin: Walter de Gruyter, 1955), 312–44.

[15]   On this issue, see W. H. C. Frend, "Open Questions concerning Christians and the Roman Empire in the Age of the Severi," *Journal of Theological Studies* 25 (1974), 334–43.

[16]   *Commentary on Daniel* 4.51, cited by Frend, *Martyrdom and Persecution*, 323.

[17]   On Decius's religious policy, see H. A. Pohlsander, "The Religious Policy of Decius," *ANRW* 2.16.3 (1981), 1826–42.

[18]   On Decian *libelli*, see J. R. Knipfing, "The *Libelli* of the Decian Persecution," *Harvard Theological Review* 16 (1923), 359–61.

[19]   Cf. M. Sordi, *The Christians and the Roman Empire* (trans. A. Bedini; Norman & London: University of Oklahoma Press, 1986), 108–21.

[20]   See *Mart. Cypr.*

[21]   Eusebius, *Hist. eccl.* 7.11.12–14.

[22]   Eusebius, *Hist. eccl.* 7.11.13.

[23]   On the events preceding the Great Persecution and its aftermath, especially in the East, see Eusebius, *Hist. eccl.* 8 and 9; *Mart. Pal.*

[24]   See Frend, *Martyrdom and Persecution*, 489–90.

[25]   Lactantius, *Mort.* 11.8.

[26]   Cf. Eusebius, *Hist. eccl.* 8.6.9.

[27]   On the prominence of the athletic image in the Martyr Acts and its historical development, see V. C. Pfitzner, "Martyr and Hero: The Origin and Development of a Tradition in the Early Christian Martyr-Acts," *Lutheran Theological Journal* 15 (1981), 9–17; K. L. Brodin, "Athletic Exemplars in the New Testament and Early Christian Martyrological Literature" (Ph.D. diss., Fuller Theological Seminary, 2000), 138–71.

[28]   There has been a great deal of scholarly debate on the date of Polycarp's death. There is a conflict between the date given by Eusebius, who places it in the (early) reign of Marcus Aurelius (AD 160–80) and the date of proconsul

Quadratus mentioned in 21 who was *consul ordinaries* in AD 142. T. Barnes, "Pre-Decian Acta Martyrum," 511–12, based on the average length of office, suggests three possibilities: 155/6 (possible), 156/7 (most probable), 157/8 or 158/9 (possible). This is followed by Musurillo, *The Acts of the Christian Martyrs*, xiii; Grant, *Greek Apologists*, 53–54; and Bisbee, *Pre-Decian Acts*, 120–21. The Eusebian date (AD 165–68) is followed by Frend, *Martyrdom and Persecution*, 240; and H. F. von Campenhausen, "Bearbeitungen und Iterpolationen des Polykarpmartyriums," *Sitzungsber der Heidelberger Akad., Phil.-hist. Kl.* (Abhand. 3; 1957); repr., in *Aus der Frühzeit des Christentums* (1963), 253.

[29] G. W. Bowersock, *Martyrdom and Rome* (Cambridge: Cambridge University Press, 1995), 13.

[30] J. Lieu, *Image and Reality: The Jews in the World of the Christians in the Second Century* (Edinburgh: T&T Clark, 1996), 82.

[31] Cf. G. A. Bisbee, *Pre-Decian Acts of Martyrs and Commentarii* (Harvard Dissertations in Religion 22; Philadelphia, PA: Fortress Press, 1988), 103–104.

[32] See, for example, *Mart. Pol.* 10.1; 12.1; *Mart. Carp.* 23, 34 (Greek); 3.5 (Latin); *Mart. Lyons* 1.19, 50; *Acts Scill.* 9, 13; *Mart. Apol.* 2; *Mart. Perp.* 3.2; 6.4; cf. *Mart. Pion.* 15.7; 16.2. On this topic, see further J. Bremmer, "'Christianus Sum': The Early Christian Martyrs and Christ," in G. J. M. Bartelink, A. Hilhorst and C. H. Kneepkens (eds.), *Eulogia* (Instrumenta Patristica 24; The Hague: Nijhoff International, 1991), 12–18, where he states, "the only occasion where the followers of Jesus publicly used the self-designation 'Christian' was the confrontation with the Roman magistrate" (18).

[33] E. Mühlenberg, "The Martyr's Death and Its Literary Presentation," *Studia Patristica* 29 (1997), 90.

[34] *Mart. Pol.* 1.1.

[35] Lieu, *Image and Reality*, 82.

[36] Cf. D. Boyarin, *Dying for God: Martyrdom and the Making of Judaism and Christianity* (Stanford, CA: Stanford University Press, 1999), 116–17.

[37] Mühlenberg, "The Martyr's Death," 87.

[38] Boyarin, *Dying for God*, 101; cf. idem, "Martyrdom and the Making of Christianity and Judaism," *Journal of Early Christian Studies* 6/4 (1998), 595.

[39] For a list of these literary features, see K. Hopkins, *A World Full of Gods: The Strange Triumph of Christianity* (New York: A Plume Book, 2001), 113–14.

[40] E. Clark, "Response," in E. Castelli (ed.), *Visions and Voyeurism: Holy Women and the Politics of Sight in Early Christianity* (vol. 2 of Protocol of the Colloquy of the Center for Hermeneutical Studies, New Series; Berkeley, CA: Center for Hermeneutical Studies, 1995), 28, also quoted by Boyarin, *Dying for God*, 101.

[41] See for example, *Mart. Perp.* 9.1; 16.4; *Mart. Potam.*

[42] A. D. Nock, *Conversion: The Old and the New in Religion from Alexander the Great to Augustine of Hippo* (Oxford: Oxford University Press, 1933), 198.

43 Boyarin, *Dying for God*, 101; cf. idem, "Martyrdom and the Making," 595.

44 E. Weiner and A. Weiner, *The Martyr's Conviction: A Sociological Analysis* (Brown Judaic Studies 203; Atlanta: Scholars Press, 1990), 57.

45 R. D. Young, *In Procession before the World: Martyrdom as Public Liturgy in Early Christianity* (Milwaukee, WI: Marquette University Press, 2001), 12.

46 *Mart. Perp.* 18.4–5; cf. Tertullian, *Apol.* 15.4–5.

47 K. M. Coleman, "Fatal Charades: Roman Executions Staged as Mythological Enactments," *Journal of Roman Studies* 80 (1990), 66.

48 *Mart. Pol.* 10.1; *Mart. Carp.* 5, 23, 34 (Greek); 6.1 (Latin); *Mart. Lyons* 1.19, 20, 26, 50; *Acts Scill.* 9, 10, 13; *Mart. Apol.* 2; *Mart. Potam.* 5.; cf. *Mart. Perp.* 3.2.

49 *Mart. Ptol.* 10–12, 15, 18; *Acts Just.* A.3.4; 4 passim; *Mart. Lyons* 1.10; *Mart. Apol.* 1–2; *Mart. Perp.* 6.4.

50 Cf. *Mart. Lyons* 1.19f., 33, 50.

51 For the translation of *lanista* as a "president of games" equivalent to ἀγνωθετηε, see J. den Boeft and J. Bremmer, "Notiunculae Martyrologicae II," *Vigiliae Christianae* 36 (1982), 391; Bowersock, *Martyrdom and Rome*, 51; cf. L. Robert, "Une vision de Perpétue martyre à Carthage en 203," *Comptes rendus de l'Acad. Des Inscr. Et Belles-Lettres* (1982), 228–76.

52 P. Dronke, *Women Writers of the Middle Ages: A Critical Study of Texts from Perpetua to Marguerite Porete* (Cambridge: Cambridge University Press, 1984), 5.

53 Cf. Christ in *Acts Just.* B.4.8.

54 As M. H. Griffin, "Martyrdom as Second Baptism: Issues and Expectations for the Early Christian Martyrs" (Ph.D. diss., University of California, Los Angeles, 2002), 87, notes, although Papylus claimed spiritual children, he did not call himself father or was called father, *Mart. Carp.* A.32 (Greek); B.3.2 (Latin).

55 Cf. Griffin, "Martyrdom as Second Baptism," 85.

56 E. Ferguson, "Women in the Post-Apostolic Church," in C. D. Osburn (ed.); *Essays on Women in Earliest Christianity* Vol. 1 (Joplin: College Press, 1993), 497.

57 Young, *In Procession before the World*, 13.

58 See D. M. Scholer, "And I Was a Man: The Power and Problem of Perpetua," *Daughters of Sarah* 15.5 (September/October 1989), 10–14.

59 C. A. Barton, "Savage Miracles: The Redemption of Lost Honor in Roman Society and the Sacrament of the Gladiator and the Martyr," *Representations* 45 (1994), 59.

60 Cf. *Mart. Pion.* 19–20; *Mart. Iren.* 2.4.

61 Cf. *Acts Cypr.* 3.4; *Mart. Carp.* 4 (Greek); *Acts Just.* B.2.1.

62 Cf. *Mart. Carp.* 21.

2

A Spirit Theology of Suffering

KEITH WARRINGTON

1. Introduction[1]

The concept of suffering has largely been a neglected subject by Pentecostals and charismatics alike. This neglect has largely resulted from two issues. Historically, it has been due to a tendency by Pentecostals to concentrate on defending fundamental characteristics of Classical Pentecostalism (especially the baptism of the Spirit) and to use references to the Spirit in the New Testament as evidence for their interpretation of the phenomenon. Secondly, it has been due to an emphasis on certain core elements of the role of the Spirit to the exclusion of this one. Thus, the association of the Spirit with prophecy, empowering for mission, or for the purpose of sanctification has tended to obscure the awareness that a core role of the Spirit relates to the issue of suffering.

It may also be adduced that for Western Christianity, the experience of suffering is an infrequent one and that may have influenced our limited observation of suffering in relation to the Spirit-led lifestyle of the believer. If it does not happen to us, then it may not be a central characteristic of the work of the Spirit. However, the New Testament paints a different picture.

Robert Garland wrote, "Life in the ancient world was nasty, brutish and short."[2] It has been a quest for centuries to try to discover a rationale for it. However, the New Testament while not providing a comprehensive explanation of suffering, does portray the Spirit as having a central role in the life of the believer who suffers. My aim is not to explain possible reasons for suffering, but to identify the role of the Spirit in the lives of believers who are suffering. There are many good books exploring the former topic,[3] but less exploration has been undertaken with regard to the role of the Spirit in association with suffering.

2. Suffering and the Spirit in Judaism

The Jews identified a number of reasons for suffering. It resulted from chastisement due to sin, persecution, a desire by God to evaluate and improve his people, as well as satanic/demonic activity, though this was always under the sovereign rule of God.

Suffering was explained largely as being beneficial (in that it demonstrated their love for God and helped them in their fight against sin), proof of their being God's people (thus, they were persecuted by people and demons), and evidence of God's affection for them (thus, he disciplines them when they sin and uses suffering in his refining of their characters, thus enhancing their potential).

The Jews also identified a number of characteristics that enable appropriate responses to suffering. They believed that they were living in the end times, a period that was associated with suffering; it was therefore understandable that they should suffer. At the same time, they were fortified by the assurance that God would vindicate the righteous and eventually deliver them from their suffering. Thus, it was appropriate to persist and be patient. The fact that the Messiah was to come was viewed as evidence that the cries of the poor had been heard. Suffering was thus always to be viewed in the context of a future hope.

Furthermore, God used suffering for his purposes. Thus, the deaths of the martyrs were understood to have brought about the religio-political changes in the history of Israel. Indeed, they believed that suffering also had vicarious value. The idea that suffering could atone for the sins of others is located in the writings of the Maccabees in the context of exploring reasons for martyrdom.

Of benefit also was the recognition that suffering provided opportunities to demonstrate care for those suffering, while some suffering was recognized as being senseless, occurring for no specific reason, but because one was a member of humanity where suffering is often indiscriminate.

The Jews also recognized the important role of the Spirit in times of suffering. In the Old Testament, the Spirit empowered people to undertake extraordinary responsibilities that would result in the people being sustained in or redeemed from severe circumstances (Judg. 6:34; 11:29). On other occasions, he is described as being present in times of suffering (Ps. 51:11; 139:7), strengthening people in times of suffering (Isa. 11:1–4; 1 Enoch), identifying some suffering as being caused by sin (Isa. 48:16; Zech. 7:12) and offering hope after the suffering (Isa. 43:19; Ezek. 37:11–14). In particular, the Messiah was expected to be the Spirit-endowed person who would support those suffering (Isa. 42:1–5; 61:1–3).

Thus, the Old Testament prepares the readers of the New Testament with information that locates the Spirit centrally as the one who empowers people who are in situations of personal weakness that, if not resolved, may inhibit their fulfilment of the destiny God had set for them. On other occasions, the Spirit functions supportively in the lives of those who are suffering. Although the suffering may sometimes be removed, on the many occasions when it is not, the Spirit provides himself as the sustainer for God's people. The New Testament will more clearly identify the comprehensive role undertaken by the Spirit for believers in this regard.

3. Suffering and the Spirit in the Synoptics

The New Testament offers an innovative and distinct contribution to a better appreciation of the work of the Spirit in relationship to suffering. It is in the writings of Luke and Paul that the Spirit becomes a central element in this regard, though he is also introduced in the Synoptics with regard to suffering.

For example, in situations where his readers may have felt isolated, Matthew (10:20/Mark 13:11/Luke 12:12) informs them that the Spirit is with them, inspiring them and empowering them. Their position of potential helplessness in the face of opposition forces is to be re-categorized as one of supreme sufficiency because of the presence of the Spirit. Although their families may betray them, the Spirit will buttress them.

The readers of each Synoptic Gospel would have benefited from the encouraging words of the writers as they affirmed the role of the Spirit to guide them in their responses to their accusers. Matthew's Jewish audience knew what it was like to be accused of betraying the ancient faith and to be marginalized by their religious constituencies. Mark's audience, probably in Rome, faced different pressures. To believe that Jesus was God was viewed as an act of folly, given that he died and on a cross as a criminal. It was at Rome that the first significant persecutions were to take place, and these would be of a different ferocity than those experienced elsewhere in the empire up until that time. If ever there were believers who needed the comfort of a supernatural being who would give them the words to say and the authority with which to present them, it was the readers of Mark's Gospel.

Luke's audience, including sophisticated Gentiles, would face yet another form of interrogation from those in their communities who would find the message of Jesus unacceptable when compared with the philosophies of the day. Christianity was intellectually unsatisfying and simplistic. Thus, he offers the promise that the Spirit will be with them, not just to provide words of support and defence for their beliefs, but also to enable them to hold on to the truth and not to reject it in the face of opposition.

4. Suffering and the Spirit in Luke–Acts

Although Luke describes the Spirit-inspiring prophecy (1:41, 42, 67–69; 2:25–32) and preaching (1:15; 4:15, 18), he also records an association with suffering. Thus, Simeon (2:25–35), who is described in association with the Spirit three times in three verses, prophesies of suffering for Mary and opposition for Jesus. The first recorded reference to Jesus after his being baptized is at Nazareth (4:14–29), where he preaches from Isaiah 61:1–2. Luke informs the readers that Jesus is "in the power of the Spirit" (4:14), but the response of the people is not favorable for they question him (4:22) and attempt to kill him (4:28–29). This opposition will continue through the life of Jesus despite the fact that he ministers in association with the Spirit.[4] In his second volume, Luke traces the same consequence of Spirit-inspired ministry receiving acceptance and also opposition in the lives of the apostles.[5] Mittelstadt appropriately concluded, "As Jesus, the Spirit-anointed one, drew hatred and was finally killed, so also the Spirit-anointed messianic community will become the objects of hate and persecution."[6]

Stephen functions as an example of a believer who was led by the Spirit (Acts 6:5, 10; 7:55). However, although there is a passing reference to the fact that he achieved signs and wonders (6:8), the immediate aftermath to the reference to Stephen's appointment as one of the Seven is that he experienced opposition followed by his sermon and martyrdom. Although the Spirit is associated with his appointment, his miracles, and his sermon, Luke concentrates on the opposition and suffering of the Spirit-inspired Stephen (6:9–7:60).

What is more remarkable is that Luke presents Stephen in parallel to Jesus. As Jesus was led by the Spirit and died a martyr's death, so also does Stephen. The message to the readers is clear. To be led by the Spirit assumes the possibility, indeed probability, of suffering. Although the message of Acts is that the gospel triumphs, it is in association with the fact that it does so through suffering. More particularly, the Spirit who sets the agenda for the development of the church and assures that it will succeed does so on a route catalogued by opposition and suffering.

5. Suffering and the Spirit in Paul

Paul, in particular, redeems the concept of suffering from the assumption that it is associated with the displeasure of God. Instead, he associates suffering with positive benefits. Thus, whereas the Galatians assumed that weakness in a representative of a god indicated an insignificant deity, Paul presents his suffering as the divinely ordained plan of God as a result of which the Galatians heard the good news of Jesus (4:14). Similarly, the thorn in the flesh (2 Cor. 12:7–10) is presented as of benefit to Paul in that its objective was to remind Paul of his own weakness and inability to succeed without the support of God.[7]

5.1 *The Spirit is associated with and works through suffering*

The consequence of being a child of God is that one will suffer (Rom. 8:17). However, in that suffering, the power of God is made manifest. The undefined weakness of the believer referred to in Romans 8:26 results in the unilateral involvement of the Spirit to support the believer in his/her time of powerlessness. His role is to empower believers, especially those who are suffering.

The Spirit is not only related to miracles, signs, and wonders, but also suffering and weakness. It is not the case that life lived in the shadow of the cross and life lived in the power of the Spirit are mutually exclusive. There is no contrasting theology between a theology of the cross and a theology of the Spirit. The former does not signify suffering and the latter glory. Both are complementary, involving suffering and glory – indeed, glory through suffering. Thus, when in 2 Corinthians 2:14–16 Paul describes the life of suffering associated with his ministry which resulted in their hearing the gospel, he concludes that the Spirit of God has been part of the enterprise (3:3). He associates suffering with being led by the Spirit (Acts 14:22). Luke writes with a similar agenda, identifying Paul's journey to Jerusalem to suffer as not only being prophesied by the Spirit (21:11) but also resulting from the leading of the Spirit (Acts 20:22).

5.2 *The Spirit provides adoption for believers (Rom. 8:14–17)*

Paul wrote his letter to Rome against a background of social, financial, verbal, and physical suffering. The context of the readers may be easily overlaid in our contemporary world in which Christians are suffering. The world is as alien a home for many contemporary believers as it was in the early years of the church.

The issue of suffering as a believer in Romans 8 is located in the context of adoption. Paul has been declaring the difference made by the presence of the Spirit in the lives of believers

(8:1–13). Now he declares the activity of the Spirit that results in sonship while the world in which they live abandons them to suffering. This relationship as adopted children of God is certain because the Spirit who is part of their lives is none other than the Spirit of adoption who, coming into their presence, places them in God's presence. The reference to the cry, "Abba! Father," may relate to a joyful consideration of their relationship with God or their cry in time of need. Whatever the occasion the Spirit acts as a reliable friend who affirms that such a relationship is valid and not presumptuous.

Paul is not declaring that believers must suffer in order to receive their adoption. Rather, he is reflecting on the fact that the readers may well suffer for their faith (the persecution of Christians by Nero (AD 64) is only a few years off) but they do so following in the footsteps of their Saviour. This is only the preface to a life characterized by glory. Present sufferings do not undermine their right to be called children of God, such a position being determined by God, assured by the Spirit, to be enjoyed eternally.

5.3 *The Spirit seals the believer*

The introductory verses of 2 Corinthians catalogue Paul's sufferings (1:5) on their behalf (1:6) and identify their partnership in suffering (1:7). He graphically describes the intensity of his past afflictions (1:8–9) and informs them of his reliance on their prayers for him (1:10). In a context of suffering, he reminds them of the role of the Spirit to seal believers (1:22). Although not specifically mentioned, the reference to sealing is probably a description of that which takes place at salvation.

The concept of "sealing with the Spirit" provides Paul with an opportunity to explore the radical nature of the supportive role of the Spirit to them in their sufferings. The practice of sealing letters, objects, and even people was common in the ancient world. The seal represented a number of features, each of which help explicate the comprehensive nature of the Spirit's involvement in the life of a believer.

Fundamentally, the seal signified ownership; that which was sealed was owned by someone. The fact that believers are sealed with the Spirit indicates that the one who arranged for the sealing to occur, namely Christ, owns them. In a society that was quickly becoming inhospitable to Christians, it was of considerable encouragement to them to realize that someone had chosen to own them and had affirmed this by the presence of none other than the Spirit in them.

Secondly, the seal signified security. In the commercial center of Corinth, buyers would seal goods that they intended to purchase by stamping them with a seal. It indicated that the goods were spoken for; they were no longer for sale. The Spirit is described as functioning as security for believers. Not only does someone own them; he also happens to be the one who owns all authority. To seek to harm a believer would thus be equivalent to attempting to harm God.

Finally, the seal signifies that the object sealed is valuable. To a group of Christians who will soon experience persecution when they will be treated as worthless objects, Paul reminds them that they are valuable to God. Although marginalized by society, the Spirit has sealed them.

5.4 *The Spirit acts as a guarantee*

In Ephesians 1:14, Paul uses the word ἀρραβών (2 Cor. 1:21, 22; 5:5); each occurrence of the word has reference to the Spirit. It is a technical term for a first installment or guarantee. The Spirit is God's down payment in the believer's life, and as such he acts as a guarantee and a taste of the future. Two facts in particular are guaranteed: (1) believers will possess the inheritance graciously promised by God to them; (2) God will possess the inheritance chosen by himself, the church, for himself. The cumulative effect is to provide the readers with a sense of well-being and security; they are secure beyond their understanding and the Spirit is their guarantee.

There was a great deal of uncertainty in the ancient world. In Ephesus, a fire was kept burning to act as a guarantee that the city would not be destroyed. On a broader level, security was an important feature of Ephesian life, represented by a six-mile-long wall around the city. Life for the people of the time was fragile.

Issues of health were frequently on their minds, though for the vast majority, it was not an area over which they had much control. Not only were the social conditions of many inadequate, resulting in malnutrition and diseases that come with a poor diet, but the health professions were insubstantial, often restricted to the wealthy, and of uncertain quality. Postnatal infant mortality rates were very high, perhaps up to 25 percent in the first year of life. At the same time, life expectancy was not anticipated far beyond thirty years of age. If health issues dominated much of the thoughts of people, however, life after death was much more uncertain for Jews and Gentiles alike. Paul, however, is convinced of his eternal destiny and encourages his readers to be as confident about theirs, concluding with the fact that the presence of the Spirit in their lives acts as a constant reminder of their eternal security despite their present struggles.

5.5 The Spirit inspires boldness

Acts 4:31 describes the boldness of the believers as the result of their being filled with the Spirit. This boldness, coupled with wisdom, was, for example, to be the experience of Stephen who was opposed by the Jews (6:10). Similarly, Paul encourages his readers to use what the Spirit supplies (Eph. 6:17–18), in particular, his provision of "the sword of the Spirit" for inspired speech at a given point in time, especially in times of confrontation.

5.6 The Spirit inspires hope

Paul ascribes a significant role to the Spirit with regards to the concept of hope (Rom. 5:3–5). When the pressure of one's situation results in despair edging ever closer, Paul describes the presence of the Spirit as enabling believers to retain the belief that their suffering is the prelude to something better. His promise to them is that this suffering is to be considered in the light of the fact that as the children of God they will be glorified with him hereafter (8:17). The Spirit enables the suffering believer to abound in hope (15:13), the word *abound* meaning abundance, to the point of excess.

Paul is thus able to encourage his readers to believe that their suffering does not result from the superior power of the enemies of God. On the contrary, God is supreme and the Spirit affirms this fact (8:28). The future glory will wipe out the contradictions of the present.

5.7 *The Spirit inspires love*

The first time love is mentioned in Romans (5:5) is in the context of suffering (5:3–4) and the Spirit. The Spirit has an important part to play in channeling the love of God to believers with lavish generosity.[8] Paul expresses the notion of the love of God in a way that anticipates an experiential more than an intellectual way. The reference to love being located in the believers' hearts further expresses the emotional nature of this reception of God's love. Paul expects God's love for the believer to be felt. The tense of the verb "has been poured" is perfect; in Greek, this has the meaning of an act in the past that has ongoing significance. The experience of the love of God is thus intended to be an ongoing reality for the believer, having commenced at salvation, but especially present in times of suffering.

5.8 *The Spirit helps believers*

The Spirit is being described as doing something *for* believers. In the context of the weakness of believers, the Spirit is presented as operating on their behalf (Rom. 8:26).

Paul uses a verb for "help" that occurs nowhere else in the Bible and prefaces it with another word (ὑπέρ) that emphasizes the intensity of the help offered. Not only does the Spirit help, but also he helps significantly those who are weak.

5.9 *The Spirit prays for believers*

Paul refers to the fact that the Spirit prays for believers (Rom. 8:26–27) in their weakness. Paul's reference to the Spirit praying is a metaphor which must be carefully unwrapped. He is declaring a truth that is precious and therefore to be appropriated but also a mystery and therefore not necessarily to be completely understood, though there is a welcome to explore it intellectually and experientially. The picture is of the Spirit, who is God, so intimately relating to believers that for a moment, it is as if his closeness to them is greater than it is to God, enabling him to pray for them.[9]

This concept of the Spirit demonstrating empathy with believers is remarkable. The believer is not praying; the Spirit is praying for us. This does not mean that Christians are inactive. For the believers, the fact that they do not know how to pray is part of their weakness. They are encouraged to recognize that the Spirit who affirms them (Rom. 8:16–17), himself prays for them (8:26) in accordance with God's will (8:27) and purpose (8:28).

5.10 The Spirit groans with believers

Paul refers to the fact that the Spirit identifies with believers with groans that are too deep for words (Rom. 8:26). The term translated "too deep for words" is of significance. It may be translated "without words" or "unable to be expressed." Paul may therefore be not seeking to identify the occurrence of the Spirit's intercession on the behalf of the believer but to simply specify that he is doing so and that the believer may depend on the fact that such intercession is full of sincerity and meaning, even though one may not hear it. It may be silent, but it taps at the very heart of the fact that the Spirit is committed to suffering believers and expresses the most complete advocacy on behalf of the believer. The significance of the Spirit being involved on the part of the believer is that he will ensure that God's will be enacted. This is a foregone conclusion since he is God.

5.11 The Spirit offers a new perspective on suffering

Thus, believers are informed that the suffering they experience is part of a wider context. Believers are not exempt from the suffering experienced by the world; in reality, they participate in its pain (Rom. 8:18–23), but so does the Spirit. The suffering experienced by both is not the fault of the sufferers; rather, it is sin that is at fault, and both the created order and the church suffer as a result. However, both will be redeemed from this situation when God resolves the issue of sin, while the expectation of Paul is that the Spirit-empowered church will positively impact the suffering world also whilst being individually and corporately supported by the Spirit.

6. Conclusions

In a world that is often dominated by suffering, the New Testament writers identify the role of the Spirit in contexts of weakness and suffering. Although suffering is inextricably linked to life on earth and Christians are not immune to it, it is to be remembered that it is an earthbound condition and the Spirit's involvement in the suffering of the believer is certain, motivated by his inexhaustible love.

Endnotes

[1] I am indebted to my student Marijke Hoek, whose doctoral dissertation "An Examination of the Concepts of Suffering and Weakness in Relation to the Spirit in Romans 8," has provided much stimulating thought on this issue especially as it relates to Paul. Insofar as this was originally presented in the context of a conference, footnotes had been kept to a minimum.

[2] R. Garland, *The Eye of the Beholder: Deformity and Disability in the Graeco-Roman World* (Duckworth: London, 1995), 11.

[3] P. Brand and P. Yancey, *Pain: The Gift Nobody Wants* (New York: HarperCollins, 1993); D. A. Carson, *How Long, O Lord* (Leicester: InterVarsity Press, 1990); I. M. Dau, *Suffering and God*, Nairobi: Paulines, 2002); R. Dunn, *When Heaven Is Silent* (Milton Keynes: Authentic Media, 2004); E. Elliot, *A Path through Suffering* (Carlisle: OM Publishing, 1997); E. Farley, *Divine Empathy: A Theology of God* (Minneapolis, MN: Fortress Press, 1996); P. Fiddes, *The Creative Suffering of God* (Oxford: Clarendon, 1988); D. J. Hall, *God and Human Suffering: An Exercise in the Theology of the Cross* (Minneapolis: Augsburg, 1986); S. Hauerwas, *Naming the Silences: God, Medicine and the Problem of Suffering* (Grand Rapids: Eerdmans, 1990); R. Hays, *The Vision of the New Testament* (New York: Harper Collins, 1996); H. S. Kushner, *When Bad Things Happen to Good People* (New York: Avon, 1981); A. E. McGrath, *Suffering and God* (Grand Rapids, MI: Zondervan, 1995); K. D. Richmond, *Preaching to*

Sufferers: God and the Problem of Pain (Nashville, TN: Abingdon, 1988); G. Walters, *Why Do Christians Find It So Hard to Grieve?* (Carlisle: Paternoster, 1997); P. Yancey, *Where Is God When It Hurts?* (London: Pickering & Inglis, 1998).

4 Luke 6:1–11; 11:14–54; 19:39–47; 20:19.

5 Acts 4:16–18; 5:17–18, 27, 33, 40; 8:1–3; 9:1–2; 12:1–4; 13:44–45, 49–51; 16:19–24; 17:5–9, 13; 18:6, 12, 17; 19:9, 23–24; 21:27–36.

6 M. W. Mittelstadt, "The Spirit and Suffering in Luke – Acts: Implications for a Pentecostal Pneumatology" (Ph.D. diss., Marquette University, 2001), 108.

7 For Paul, weakness was understood as a prerequisite element in his life necessary to identify the power of Christ (See particularly S. J. Hafemann, *Suffering and Ministry in the Spirit* [Carlisle: Paternoster, 1990]). Savage writes, Paul's "weakness in some sense actually serves as the grounds for divine power" (T. B. Savage, *Power through Weakness: Paul's Understanding of the Christian Ministry* [Cambridge: Cambridge University Press, 1996], 166). It is the vehicle through which the gospel is revealed in the life of Paul as it was in the life of Christ. For Paul, suffering has potential value. Although it is not to be assumed that suffering *per se* is good, it is to be maintained that on occasions it may be harnessed by God for the benefit of the believer and the development of the kingdom.

8 Cf. Joel 2:28; Mal. 3:10, where God pours out his blessings/Spirit on his people.

9 Some have stated that he is describing the opportunity for believers to engage in glossolalia. Thus, the believer presents his/her prayer while speaking in tongues, the assumption being that the desire of the individual is being articulated in the process of speaking in tongues (1 Cor. 14:14, 15). The problem with this view is that it assumes that all believers have received the gift of tongues, which is not reflected elsewhere in Paul's writings (1 Cor. 12:30). There is also no evidence in the New Testament that the Spirit operates via the gift of tongues though tongues are viewed as a prayer/praise language (1 Cor. 14:2, 14). It would also indicate that the Spirit only acts on behalf of the believer when he or she is speaking in tongues. This limits the advocacy of the Spirit in a way not reflected in the text.

3

An Anabaptist–Mennonite Theology
of Suffering

Some Features

THOMAS FINGER

Today's Mennonite churches trace their origins to the Anabaptist movement, which arose during the Protestant Reformation. Probably no group which called itself Christian has ever suffered so much at the hands of others who called themselves Christians as the original Anabaptists did. Between 1527 and 1575, around 4,000 Anabaptists were cruelly drowned, burned, beheaded, and broken on racks or wheels. Countless others suffered torture, imprisonment, confiscation of property, and banishment. As members of an outlawed group, Anabaptists were denied civil rights, education, and most forms of employment. For at least two centuries thereafter, their heirs frequently migrated from place to place on society's margins, officially regarded as illegal and subject to sporadic persecution. Who were these Anabaptists, and what beliefs and practices occasioned this massive suffering?

Sixteenth-century Anabaptism arose from several relatively distinct origins. Like most scholars today, I distinguish three main geographical sources: Switzerland, South Germany / Austria, and the Netherlands.[1] Nearly all Anabaptist leaders were killed off within a short span of years. The movement developed no single institutional structure, body of writings, or theology. Much surviving information on Anabaptism was penned by its enemies, including records of many trials. Given both the relative scarcity and the unevenness of historical sources, it is not surprising that several different interpretations of historic Anabaptism exist. By *historic Anabaptism* I mean the movement from 1525 to 1575. By the end of that period, most Dutch Anabaptists were called

Mennonites, after their leader Menno Simons (1496[?]–1561). This name eventually spread to the majority of Anabaptists in other countries.

During the Reformation, and then by church leaders and historians until the early twentieth century, Anabaptists were usually regarded as heretics, as idealistic religious fanatics (*Schwaermerei*), as at least potential revolutionaries and/or divisive sectarians. Since the 1930s, the recovery, discovery, and study of original documents have been altering this portrait. Nonetheless, it still appears surprisingly often in church and secular histories.

One more recent interpretation, which approaches Anabaptism largely from a theological standpoint, regards it as "consistent evangelical Protestantism."[2] Anabaptism, on this reading, arose mainly among people who emphasized Scripture, following the early Reformers' lead, and accepted many of their interpretations, but took the implications of some ideas further. For example, the claim that salvation comes through faith entailed, for Anabaptists, that baptism, the rite by which people enter the church, was only for those who made conscious faith commitments to Christ. The great majority of Europeans, though, had been baptized as infants. They regarded such a later rite as rebaptism. (This is why the label *Anabaptist*, which meant re-baptizer and was intended as derisive, came to identify its proponents.) Anabaptists, further, insisted that all teachings of Jesus, including renunciation of violence, applied to all Christians. Since Protestant leaders did not affirm this, here again Anabaptists can be interpreted as applying a Protestant theological teaching, *sola Scriptura*, more consistently, and taking its implications further than these Protestants.

Such theological teachings, however, carried enormous social implications. For well over a millennium, only one official religion, to which nearly all citizens belonged, had existed in each European political territory. Yet if only citizens who made conscious faith commitments were to join a church, many would likely remain unchurched. Eventually, different churches might even arise. For many centuries, though, it had been assumed that any such distinctions between the body politic and the church body would divide, and likely destroy, the former. Moreover, nearly all Anabaptists refused to participate in armies or police forces. This seemed to endanger the state's security further. Anabaptists, in fact, were most often prosecuted for treason, not heresy.

Anabaptist understandings of faith, baptism, and church, then, challenged the hierarchical unity of late medieval civilization. These beliefs, moreover, ascribed greater value to human choice. Consequently, Anabaptism has also been interpreted, mainly from a socio-cultural standpoint, as a forerunner of the Enlightenment, or modernity. According to this second interpretation, Anabaptists prioritized inner, spiritual experience over outward church ceremonies, and conscience over the authority of tradition. Anabaptists become not consistent evangelical Protestants, but incipient liberal Protestants, heralds of Western progress and civilization.[3]

A third, largely socio-economic, interpretation emphasizes that most historic Anabaptists were peasants or artisans. Anabaptists stressed medieval, peasant, communal values like social equality and economic sharing. These had been promoted, on similar biblical grounds, in the failed Peasant Wars that convulsed Germanic lands from 1524 to 1526. Anabaptism, indeed, arose in their wake, which helps explain why governments often feared them as divisive revolutionaries. In that apocalyptically charged era, moreover, most Anabaptists expected Jesus to return soon and punish the godless, especially their rulers. Some among the earliest Anabaptists also supposed that, at this final moment, they could assist Jesus by taking up arms.[4] For most, however, Anabaptism offered a peaceful route to ideals which the violence of the Peasant Wars had failed so drastically to attain.

In any case, during the Peasants Wars most Protestant and Catholic leaders sided with the merciless noble conquerors, or otherwise identified with prosperous classes.[5] For most peasant-artisans, however, the defeated socio-economic ideals comprised much of the Reformation's meaning.[6] Since the Reformers had failed to champion these, Anabaptism often spread rapidly among the lower classes, until it was suppressed even more severely. Stressing this connection with prior peasant-artisan aspirations, Friedrich Engels lauded Anabaptists as forerunners not of Western liberalism, but its socialist opposition.[7] This, of course, strengthened the prevailing estimate of them as fanatical revolutionaries.

While the three foregoing interpretations construe Anabaptists as heralds of future movements, a fourth turns towards their medieval past. Anabaptist ideals did not appear *de novo* at the Reformation. The sharp critique of current church practices, the striving for holiness by following Jesus, the formation of distinct religious communities to embody God's kingdom – these had appeared, most clearly in monastic movements, as far back as Basil the Great.[8] By the fifteenth century these impulses were spreading widely among religious communities that included married people who remained in secular vocations.[9] Moreover, a Rhineland spirituality, stretching back to Meister Eckhart and the Beguines, which had often attracted lay people, clearly impacted South German/Austrian and Dutch Anabaptists. Anabaptism, in this fourth reading, was a further expression of such time-honored aspirations, and owed about as much to Catholicism as to Protestant Reformers.

While all these interpretations contain some truth, I incline towards this last one. Accordingly, I will seek to explain the theme of suffering by showing, first, how historic Anabaptists developed some medieval Catholic themes, and then indicating some surprising similarities with Orthodox and Pentecostal emphases. Next, I will describe how some of these notions were deformed in later Anabaptist–Mennonite experience. Finally, I will indicate how Anabaptists are re-forming these deformations today, and how a contemporary Anabaptist theology of suffering might contribute to mission and ecumenical interaction among all churches.

1. Historic Anabaptist Emphases

1.1 Catholic influences

Beginning with, and perhaps before, Meister Eckhart (1260?–1328?), the "Rhineland Spirituality" associated estrangement from God with the human tendency to value "creatures" – finite realities such as possessions, social reputations, spouses, children, ethnic or national identity – more highly than the creator. Humans become inordinately attached to these creaturely goods, which in turn, so to speak, send down roots into their bodies and souls, entangling and cluttering them, and obscuring the souls' deepest Ground, God. Return to God involves painful detachment from these creatures – an *Abgescheidenheit* or *Gelassenheit* – ripping up, or allowing God to rip up, the roots we let them plant within us.

Human souls, for Eckhart, originally came forth from God, as the Son came forth from the Father. Indeed, the Son's birth from the Father, and his return to Father through the Spirit, actually continues, in a spiritual manner, in the soul's Ground. But we, who have been diverted by creaturely attachments, can become conscious of and blessed by this deep inner reality only if we make our way back to the Father painfully through the process of detachment from this world, as did the Son though his life, death, and resurrection. Eckhart could call this journey a path on which we follow Jesus, or the way of the cross. This, however, was largely symbolic language for the soul's inward return to God. Eckhart, moreover, often portrayed the soul, in its depths, as already divine.[10] Union with God was ontological, or a union of being.

These emphases shifted somewhat as the Rhineland current rolled on through Eckhart's younger contemporary, Johannes Tauler (1300[?]–1361) and the anonymous *German Theology* (ca. 1430). Spirituality's goal became less a union of being and more a union of wills, through grace, where God and the soul remained distinct. As this spirituality was practiced by many lay people, Jesus' earthly journey not only symbolized the inward process, but provided the pattern for participating in it outwardly, in daily life. Tauler urged his hearers to accept "the cross, from whichever direction it comes, *from outside or from within* … follow your crucified God with a humble spirit, in true abnegation of yourself, *both inner and outer* … and unite yourself with him."[11] Eventually, this inner/outer crucifixion led to resurrection.

As the Rhineland stream poured into South German/Austrian Anabaptism, it branched in two further directions. First, while inner, spiritual participation in Jesus' "conception, birth, death, and resurrection in us"[12] remained central, it was even more closely linked with outer sufferings. Anabaptists, through their mission and consequent persecution, came to believe that they were experiencing "none other than Christ experienced."[13] They conformed their public behavior ever more precisely to his, including his nonviolent response to evil. Second, Anabaptists identified creaturely attachments – possessive grasping after finite goods and values – as the source of not only individual, but also social, sin. That desire to own and control more and more – lands, persons, wealth, large territories, and much else – bred conflict and war, through which some people accumulated vastly more possessions and power than others, and kept on subjugating the latter.[14] The *Gelassenheit* process, then, not only purified people "inwardly from greed and lust," but also outwardly and socially "from injustice in our way of living and our misuse of the creatures."[15] For some Anabaptists, like the Hutterites, this meant that salvation involved the surrender of everything that had been wrongly appropriated – including all private property.[16] For Hutterites, salvation also involved participation in a religious community of production and consumption, where creaturely goods were harvested, manufactured, and shared in common.

In sum, from medieval, Catholic, Rhineland spirituality, South German/Austrian Anabaptists (and later some Dutch Anabaptists) drew the notion that creaturely attachments become deeply entangled in human souls and bodies through sin, and that *salvation necessarily involves the suffering, which accompanies their uprooting.* Like Rhineland mystics, Anabaptists experienced this process inwardly as spiritual participation in Jesus' life, death, and resurrection. As for Rhineland spirituality's many lay practitioners, this process occurred mainly in everyday life, where Jesus provided the model for outward behavior. Intense persecution prompted Anabaptists to conform even more closely to Jesus' pattern, including nonviolence. They also recognized the social consequences of creaturely attachments, and that authentic community life and social justice could not be attained unless the attachments were uprooted.

1.2 Similarities with Orthodoxy

Significant contact between historic Anabaptists and Eastern Orthodoxy has never been discovered. Most of what follows could perhaps be traced to Catholic influences. Nonetheless, certain similarities with Orthodoxy are striking. Dutch Anabaptists, for instance, normally affirmed that the Holy Spirit proceeds from the Father.[17] Anabaptists most commonly portrayed atonement in *Christus Victor* fashion, which was much more prominent in the East than the West.[18] Anabaptist soteriology, however, with its strong ethical concern, is usually considered in light of Protestant and Catholic alternatives. Historians often find it more like the Catholic – as did the Reformers, who construed it as "works righteousness." This ethical emphasis, however, was more likely an expression of a deeper, transformative apprehension of salvation as *divinization*. Divinization, to be sure, was a Rhineland theme. Yet Anabaptist soteriology usually sounded quite foreign to Catholics, and, in many respects, more like that of the East.[19] Like the Orthodox, South German / Austrian and Dutch Anabaptists frequently spoke of sharing the "divine nature" (cf. 2 Pet. 1:4) and yet denied, sometimes explicitly, that humans become God.[20] Orthodoxy had developed a technical distinction to express this: we participate in God's *energies*, but never God's *essence*. Dutch Anabaptists also coined a formal terminology: humans were born "out of (*uit*)" the Father through Christ and the Spirit, but not, like the eternal Word, "from (*van*)" the Father.

Talk of divinization, of course, can imply that people do become God, as it may have for Eckhart. It can arouse unrealistic expectations about salvation, and sometimes did on Anabaptism's fringes. Melchior Hoffman, Anabaptism's first Dutch evangelist, taught that his "apostolic messengers" could not be physically harmed.[21] So did Jan Matthijs, who engineered the take-over of the city of Muenster, with disastrous results.[22] For most Dutch and South German / Austrians, however, divinization was clearly *Christomorphic*. It was attained not by leaping over the human sphere,[23] but by following Jesus through the very concrete struggles of witness and daily life, all the way to the cross.[24] *When Anabaptist salvation is understood as divinization*, inward and outward suffering, which their Catholic forerunners stressed, again appear intrinsic to it, but *participation in Jesus' resurrection becomes more central and rich.*

1.3 Similarities with Pentecostals

As previously mentioned, apocalyptic expectation pervaded
the Reformation era, and early Anabaptism even more so. Its
first evangelists were clearly influenced by a tripartite historical
scheme devised by Joachim of Fiore (d. 1202). Joachim divided
history into three (somewhat overlapping) eras: the Age of the
Father, ruled by the law; the Age of the Son, governed by the
gospel; and the age of the Spirit, when God would teach people
directly, eventually transcending written Scripture. This final age
would be spearheaded by an elite spiritual community (monks
for Joachim) and a returned Elijah. God's Spirit, though, would
also speak through simple people.

This last theme strongly appealed to Anabaptism's peasant-
artisan, mostly illiterate, audiences. In their eyes, not only had
Lutheran, Reformed, and Catholic leaders sided with the upper
classes. Their educated scholars had also controlled, and perverted,
the interpretation of Scripture. Anabaptists, in contrast, assured the
masses that God's Spirit could reveal the Bible's meaning, hidden
from the scholars, directly to repentant, humble people. Illiteracy
was no obstacle. The Spirit would speak as they memorized large
portions of Scripture, or gathered to hear a rare literate person
read it – and perhaps, as we will see, even apart from the biblical
text.

Pentecostalism emerged among people who also expected the
End's imminent arrival, preceded by the Spirit's final outpouring.
Pentecostals interpreted the charismatic phenomena which
erupted as evidence of that penultimate event.[25] Pentecostalism
also appealed strongly to lower classes. Aided by the Spirit, they
could understand the Bible better than apostate scholars of the
liberal Protestant establishment. As among Anabaptists and many
other movements in church history, God's Spirit was the great
equalizer. This same Spirit was directly available to women and
men, poor and rich, uneducated and educated – and was received
more often by the first than the second members of these pairs.

Pentecostalism first spread, and still spreads, among social
classes much acquainted with suffering. Unlike the liberals
of their day, but like historic Anabaptists, early Pentecostals

organized no grand schemes of social transformation. Yet, as among Anabaptists, their intense sharing of life in the Spirit led to sharing what resources they had. The new joy and purpose given by God's Spirit enabled, and still enables, many Pentecostals to find ways out of poverty and suffering to more stable lives. Similarly, when Anabaptists and Mennonites found opportunity to work, their social situations almost always improved, and sometimes astonishingly.

For Pentecostals, as for early Anabaptists, God's Spirit provides strength and direction amid dire circumstances, and consolation and joy even when earthly suffering waxes too great to be overcome. When we recognize that divinization and participation in Jesus' resurrection, for early Anabaptists, were bestowed by the Spirit in this way, we perceive that *personal suffering, intrinsic as it was to salvation, and social suffering, inescapable as it was, was not the last word. Early Anabaptism, at least, was highly pneumatic.* Indeed, could Anabaptists possibly have risked and endured such barbaric suffering apart from joyous experience of God's Spirit and joyous expectation of Jesus' imminent return?

2. Anabaptist Emphases Deformed

I have described the foregoing Anabaptist emphases in a positive, fairly idealistic way. Even from the beginning, however, these emphases were affected by, or intermingled with, contrary tendencies. As time passed, some of the latter emphases became common enough to characterize Anabaptism as a whole. The following deformations, which first surfaced quite early, have strongly impacted the Anabaptist–Mennonite tradition ever since. Numerous exceptions to these trends, of course, also appeared. But due to space limitations, I must generalize very broadly.

2.1 Cross overshadows resurrection

Anabaptists experienced the martyr's cross almost from the outset. They were able to endure it, and traverse the path to it, through the fellowship of, or inward participation in, Jesus' own sufferings. The Rhineland mysticism on which they drew, however, also stressed the power of, or participation in, Jesus' resurrection (cf. Phil. 3:10). When we realize that most Anabaptists vividly experienced this overall process as divinization, empowered by God's Spirit, we recognize that their sufferings, hideous as they were, were suffused by awareness of Jesus' risen presence and hope for their own resurrection. Resurrection and divinization's positive side were celebrated by the later South German / Austrian leaders, Pilgram Marpeck and Peter Riedemann.[26] And though divinization was rather etherialized among early Dutch Anabaptists, their successors retained it in somewhat more sober form.[27]

Nevertheless, intense suffering and martyrdom were so widespread that Anabaptist spirituality's painful, purgative, ascetic side often predominated. Suffering, indeed, frequently became *the* mark of a true Christian, something routinely expected. The reverse could easily be assumed: if you do not suffer, you are not a Christian.

Eventually, persecution's severity diminished slowly, even if it did so unevenly. But this occurred partly because many Anabaptists had withdrawn, for the sake of survival, from the social arena and mission, into somewhat separated communities. Over the next centuries, Anabaptist–Mennonites experienced much less outer, public suffering, generally speaking. Yet internalized memories and expectations of suffering often lived on. The world at large, for many Mennonites, was evil and dangerous, filled with people who hated them. Life was hard, weighted down with toil. The future was uncertain, and heaven a distant, albeit real, hope. Resurrection's present, participatory reality faded. Earthly life, for many, was marked far more by the cross.

2.2 *Letter overshadows Spirit*

The Holy Spirit, in historic Anabaptism, was exceptionally active in a highly charged apocalyptic atmosphere. To Anabaptism's mostly illiterate audiences and mostly literate evangelists, God's Spirit revealed the meaning of biblical texts. Eschatological texts, of course, were among the most crucial, and the Spirit provided keys to their interpretation. These interpretations, however, sometimes involved details – identities of persons, places, dates – not found in those texts. These details often led to predictions, some of which disastrously failed. Hans Hut, South Germany / Austria's leading evangelist, predicted Jesus' return for Pentecost 1528. When Hut was martyred before that date and Jesus failed to appear, many a follower defected or fled. In the Netherlands, Melchior Hoffman identified himself as Elijah and Strasbourg as the place of Jesus' advent – and was imprisoned there for life. Not to be outdone, Jan Matthijs identified himself as Enoch and Muenster as the city. Thousands followed his call to Muenster, to establish and defend God's kingdom there – militarily. Catholics and Protestants, alarmed enough to combine armies, eventually slaughtered them. No episode has been cited nearly as often as proof of Anabaptism's fanatical, revolutionary intentions.

Among early Anabaptists, God's Spirit was sometimes invoked to justify not only faulty predictions, but also scandalous behavior. Like nearly all pneumatic movements, historic Anabaptism found it necessary to critique and sometimes exclude its more radical leftward fringe to avoid disintegration.[28] Most Anabaptists communities sought to curb spiritual excesses and unrealistic expectations of divinization by strong disciplinary procedures.[29] Further, since Scripture was often invoked to justify erroneous predictions and behavior, Anabaptist exegesis became more rigorous and literalistic. Since the Holy Spirit, moreover, was the alleged source of dubious extra-biblical revelations, many Anabaptists became suspicious of any insight or leading not directly substantiated by the biblical letter.

Such intra-Anabaptist controversy and outward persecution posed enormous challenges. Consider, for instance, what Menno Simons faced in rebuilding a credible Dutch church after the wild prophesyings and behaviors at Muenster. The necessity of some church discipline and careful exegesis becomes obvious. Yet while Menno continued to extol divinization and its transformative potential, his biblical exposition became increasingly repetitive, wooden, and intolerant of anyone who differed. Over the next centuries, the Bible became an ethical and doctrinal codebook for many who were named after Menno. The significance of more figurative, doxological, and expressive passages faded. The sober, disciplined life under the cross was often ordered by a black-and-white literalism.

2.3 Flesh overshadows Spirit

Nearly every brand of historic Anabaptism, I propose, can be understood as an effort to incarnate divine Spirit in creaturely matter: to express inner, spiritual reality in the outer, material world.[30] Different Anabaptist groups attempted this in various ways, with varying success. Still, they shared a common aim – that every task and feature of daily and church life be transformed by living as Jesus did, empowered by his transforming Spirit. This, I submit, presupposed a profound, even if unarticulated, *sacramental* apprehension of reality: an implicit conviction that the visible, material, creaturely world was a fit vehicle for expressing invisible, spiritual, divine grace.[31] (Many Mennonites today, however, are hesitant to use *sacramental*, for it still carries crude, magical connotations for them.)

This necessary presupposition of Anabaptist practice, however, was contradicted by several conceptual, though seldom examined, assumptions. Most historic Anabaptists assumed that an *ontological barrier* distanced Spirit from matter. Matter, that is, could never really embody Spirit, but at most point towards it, indirectly.[32] In practice, however, Anabaptists insisted on water baptism at the risk of their lives, and on the Lord's Supper, rightly celebrated, as essential to any true church. Most Anabaptists, indeed, experienced Christ vividly present in these rites. Nevertheless, the realistic sacramentalism of their day (Catholic and Lutheran) seemed crudely physical to them, and they lacked any alternative concept for what they experienced, save "spiritual."

Perhaps most significantly, Anabaptists tended to equate the human body with "the flesh" in the negative biblical sense and consider it incorrigible in this life.[33] This last assumption produced tremendous intrapersonal tensions. On one hand, lofty, Christ-like impulses flowed (or were supposed to flow) from their souls and/or spirits, since these were taking on the divine nature. On the other hand, their bodies, the channels for expressing these impulses, inevitably opposed the latter. Taken literally, this theory implied that the body could obey only when the soul/spirit overrode, or suppressed, its irreversible carnal orientation.

Further, since this theory assigned Christ-like acts to the soul/spirit, and contrary behavior, dualistically, to the body, Anabaptists often supposed that when their brethren faltered, there was a simple explanation: they had deliberately turned from the Spirit's guidance to the flesh. The obvious solution, it seemed, was strict disciplinary measures, including threat of the ban, or excommunication, to turn them back from the body to the Spirit. If such brethren truly turned back, Anabaptists often assumed, their behavior would quickly improve; if it did not, such people must still be following their irredeemable bodies, and probably should be banned.

Alone among historic Anabaptists, Pilgram Marpeck clearly differentiated the body from the sinful "flesh," and conceived the latter more as an energy. While he acknowledged that "the flesh" often operated *through* the body, Marpeck insisted that the body was being transformed by God's Spirit. Undesirable behavior, then, would not always signify that someone had clearly turned towards the flesh. It might signify, instead, a salvific kind of suffering: an ongoing effort by God's Spirit to free people – bodies included – from "the flesh" and divinize them. Such people would be better helped by patient encouragement than by swift discipline.[34]

Frequently, however, Anabaptism's negative estimate of the body combined with its prioritizing of the cross and the biblical letter to foster a legalistic lifestyle, preoccupied with outward behavior. Christ-like living often became more a task of human effort than a fruit of divinizing renewal. As centuries passed, this task continued to involve inner suffering, sometimes in the face of outer, public opposition. It produced highly ethical, stable, and sometimes admired communities. But the Spirit's spontaneity and joy, with their missionary thrust, were often lacking.

3. Re-forming the Deformations

By the late nineteenth century, Mennonites became involved in world mission. Today, the Mennonite World Conference lists churches in sixty-six countries, with about 1.3 million baptized members – a number that should perhaps be tripled if unbaptized children are included. Next to the United States (323,000 baptized members), the Congo has the most Mennonites (194,000), with India and Canada about tied for third (128,000), and Ethiopia fifth (98,000; Europe as a whole has shrunk to 53,000). The Mennonite Central Committee is well known for its relief work in fifty-seven lands. True to their history, Mennonite missions often concentrate on marginalized, suffering populations. Brothers and sisters from Colombia, who face threats from right- and left-wing death squads, or Ethiopia, who flourished underground during the Marxist years, could inform you far more concretely about suffering than I can.

For over half a century, Mennonites have also become increasingly involved in mainstream North American society. They often recognize that themes like the cross, the letter, and the flesh were disproportionately stressed in their past. Various ways of redressing this balance are sought. Some Mennonites, sadly, plunge rather uncritically into the quest for status, pleasure, and wealth. However, the resurrection, the Spirit, and the body are reappearing in Mennonite thought and practice in constructive ways that may benefit the wider church as well. These insights, I believe, are biblical. They belong to all of us. Still, Anabaptist–Mennonite experience has shed important light on them. From this angle, these insights might be considered our particular gifts to the broader church. Still, we have seen how these insights were often deformed in Mennonite experience. Elements needed to re-form them have been better appropriated by other churches. To better understand and practice these insights, then, Mennonites must learn from others. Let me now propose four themes for a re-formed Anabaptist–Mennonite theology of suffering, enhanced by Catholic, Orthodox, and Pentecostal contributions.

3.1 Suffering is intrinsic to Christian transformation

Society today, at least in wealthier nations, is geared towards avoiding suffering. Enticing images of ever improved, more efficient, pleasure-enhancing products, and of healthy, attractive people enjoying them, continually assault the senses through the mass media. The media, of course, also convey images of want, tragedy, and violent conflict – but often simply as vivid impressions, without analysis of causes or possible solutions, and therefore as surds, as frightening, threatening specters to be avoided. Suffering close to home – poverty, unemployment, serious illness, death in our own neighborhoods – is kept off the streets. This massive flight from suffering, nonetheless, betrays a profound subliminal awareness and fear of it. When suffering leaks through the usual defenses, people often fall back on churches for protection.

These bodies of the crucified Lord can accompany people who pass through suffering in profound ways. Yet even many who suffer want not to pass through it, but to avoid it as much as possible. In response, churches that compete with countless other institutions, causes, and products for peoples' attention, are tempted to market themselves as even better routes to enjoyment, status, security, and prosperity. In Anabaptist perspective, however, suffering actually arises from inordinate desires to possess such things and to cling to them, and from the inequality and oppression that arise among people driven by conflicting desires of this sort. These desires and conflicts plant roots in individuals, groups, and institutions too deep for suffering to be avoidable – even if some people manage to drown awareness of it in a deluge of activities, possessions, or glittering images thereof.

Suffering, moreover, is unavoidable in the Christian life. For these roots clutter, corrupt, and darken those deep levels within people, and those deep channels which interconnect people, which God's Spirit wants to touch and transform by divine energy – that is, where God wants to dwell. These roots simply must be extirpated. However this occurs, it will cause pain. Suffering, then, is overcome only by facing that pain and dealing with the inordinate desires which bind one. These desires, moreover, are often energized by deeper fears of poverty, loss, rejection, and ultimately of abandonment, even by God. To people who face these fears and this deeper, threatening emptiness, churches can offer the crucified but now risen Jesus. He will bear these sufferings with them, and never forsake them, no matter how deep the terror or pain.

The churches' message, in Anabaptist perspective, is not that suffering, or the cravings and powers that cause it, are unreal, or have been *destroyed* (though someday they will be). Instead, these forces, though they seem to govern so much of reality, have been *defeated*; they no longer need have *dominion* over us, for nothing in all creation can separate us from God's love in Christ Jesus. This message may not be very marketable among people who want to avoid suffering, especially in societies that suppress awareness of it. But this news will sound very good to people who learn, in way or another, that suffering cannot be avoided, and hear that there is indeed a path through it, along which God can bring everlasting health and joy.

3.2 Churches address suffering by providing spiritual nurture

If churches are to form the context for this journey through Jesus' life and death to his resurrection, they must provide the sensitivity, patience, nurture, and wisdom needed to face life's deepest sufferings and questions.

Mennonite churches have usually provided ethical guidelines for following Jesus and also a communal atmosphere for living this out. Given their late Medieval, peasant-artisan, continental origins, Mennonites have usually resisted the individualism of many American-born churches and renewal movements. In fact, sharing of not only experiences but also material goods marked all historic Anabaptist communities, and many others later on.[35] Like Catholics and Orthodox Christians, Mennonites cannot separate being a Christian from belonging to a church.

Nonetheless, as experience of the Spirit and resurrection faded, and as Mennonites became more ethnically ingrown, community often existed on a more social or "horizontal" level, with less spiritual height or depth. Though Pietistic influences sometimes impacted them, Mennonites, like most Protestants, were reluctant to articulate or adopt specific spiritual practices. Piety was something which some Mennonites somehow "caught" – but many did not. Over the centuries, a fairly steady stream of Mennonites trickled into movements more spiritually vital, from early Quakers to Pentecostals.

Today, many Mennonite congregations seek to provide spiritual nurture for suffering people – and realize that to do so, they need to be more deeply grounded, spiritually, themselves. To this end, Mennonites are borrowing from Catholic sources and beginning to discover the Orthodox. Unfortunately, though, most Mennonites seem to assume that their tradition contains no such spiritual resources. They do not realize that drawing from Catholic streams, at least, and intermingling them with their own currents, is consistent with their own origins.

Spiritual resources to meet suffering can also be provided by a deeper sacramental and aesthetic life than Mennonites have usually practiced. Though historic Anabaptists experienced God's presence vividly in their worship and sacraments, they usually called this simply "spiritual," as previously mentioned. Over time, the Swiss Anabaptist emphasis, which extended Zwingli's demotion of symbols and rituals further than he did, came to characterize most Mennonite worship. Catholics and Orthodox can help Mennonites recover that original sensitivity which, I have argued, was really more sacramental.

3.3 Churches address suffering by being celebrative

Though suffering is intrinsic to divinization, it is not the last word. The final goal, which sustains churches through suffering, is resurrection, and ultimately a whole new creation. In Anabaptist perspective, suffering must be viewed within an eschatological horizon. Historic Anabaptists called people to live as Jesus did, not simply because he taught it, but also because God's kingdom was already present, and with it God's divinizing Spirit, who alone made that lifestyle possible. Suffering's intensity corresponded to the Spirit's fuller, final outpouring, which aroused God's enemies to greater fury because their reign was nearly over. Some imprisoned Anabaptists even invited people to attend their martyrdoms – and bring their friends! For these would be their final conquest of satan, their entry into glory, their supreme witness to God's kingdom. Indeed, these gruesome spectacles often were just that. Many governments initially made executions public to deter people from the Anabaptists. Later, governments held them secretly, because these witnesses had swelled Anabaptist ranks.

To deal with suffering today, churches must have ways, even in the midst of suffering, of expressing celebrative joy. Here Pentecostals are contributing much to other communions, Mennonites included. I am often struck by similarities between Mennonite and Pentecostal understandings of suffering – particularly among African American and Hispanic Pentecostals. Yet the staid, sober, regulated pace of much Mennonite worship and life contrasts sharply with Pentecostalism's expressive, happy, spontaneous alternatives.

To be sure, expressive worship can provide escape from suffering, and even awareness of it, especially in societies saturated with enticements to novel, ever more pleasurable experiences. The Anabaptist reminder that true spiritual experience produces discipleship with its fruits can check these tendencies. Otherwise, if pleasurable experiences are only superficial, they likely will arouse desires for more intense ones. And these experiences, when they inevitably fail to satisfy, will give rise to still stronger longings, which will clutter and bind people's hearts.

Freedom from these attachments, however, requires not only that they be uprooted, but also that true joy, brought by divine life, fills the void that they leave behind. Churches, in a re-formed Anabaptist perspective, provide not only companionship through suffering and crucifixion of attachments, but also channels for experiencing and expressing resurrection joy.

In Anabaptist–Mennonite perspective, moreover, only *inordinate* attachments require crucifixion. Many creaturely desires – for sustenance, friends, children, spouses, and others – are good in themselves. To be sure, these often become inordinate, and therewith idolatrous, by usurping or obscuring the allegiance due to God alone, and to fully following God's call. Creaturely reality itself, however, is not the obstacle, as Meister Eckhart sometimes implied. It is the arena, the theater, for sacramental expression of God's glory. Mennonites seek not only to experience Jesus' life, death, and resurrection inwardly, but also to manifest them outwardly, as God's Spirit transforms matter. In this way also, it becomes apparent that the life of God's new creation, which is really, though only partially, present, is the last word, the goal of their faith – even though the sufferings of the old creation and of release from it are unavoidable, and intrinsic to the journey.

3.4 Church mission opposes social suffering and communicates alternative visions

In light of God's goal, suffering cannot be good or desirable *in itself*. Suffering has value only as a necessary means for avoiding greater suffering, or, otherwise said, for attaining greater good (as when someone suffers hunger pangs to overcome obesity). God, indeed, can utilize suffering in unexpected ways to attain greater goods, as is most evident in the outcome of the greatest suffering ever: Jesus' death. Yet this never provides churches a warrant for sanctioning suffering; or even for putting up with suffering, except when it is absolutely unavoidable or it is indispensable for acquiring greater good. To witness to the coming and present reality of God's new creation, churches must oppose all forms of social suffering and their causes.

My Anabaptist perspective on how inner and outer reality are intertwined, and how inordinate attachments operate in both dimensions, leads to a sober appraisal of social sin, but also suggests a particular way of combating it.[36] If personal sin arises when inordinate desires for creaturely goods take root in the heart, then social sin arises from conflicts among people to attain these desired goods.[37] Inordinate individual desires give rise to self-centered grasping after their objects, to efforts to possess and control them. Social sin emerges when some people band together in order to possess and control certain goods, and forcibly prevent others from acquiring them. Inevitably, some groups gain control of more goods than others. They then ally with other successful groups to control even more goods and dispossess still other groups. In most societies, this leads to relatively few people controlling the sources of wealth, enjoying their products, and, through superior force (whether exercised or only threatened) greatly limiting the access of the rest to wealth and power. This analysis, I believe, can be corroborated and enriched by Scripture.

For now, I simply note that the apostle James well described the initial stages.[38]

This understanding means, first, that unjust social structures originate in violent conflict, whose developed form is war, and are maintained largely by threats of violence and war. From this perspective, war is not simply one among multiple sources of injustice. War and violence are at, or at least very near, the root of all social injustice and unjust suffering. Consequently, an alternative, peaceful, nonviolent way of dealing with differing human desires and aims must be central to God's coming and already-present new creation. Jesus' peaceful comportment was not simply one, perhaps dispensable, feature of his life, death, and resurrection. It was central to that saving process in which *all humans* must participate, inwardly *and outwardly*, to attain divinization.

Second, if social and personal evil are so deeply intertwined, the former cannot be greatly ameliorated simply by altering broad social structures or processes. If the roots of social injustice are not affected, it will find ways to operate through any social form. This does not mean that churches should never deal with social, economic, and political structures. Obviously, some are better than others. Neither does it mean that mission should concentrate wholly on the personal realm, for it and the social realm are profoundly connected.

Instead, this general outlook leads mission to focus on the local level and on initiating personal transformation *and* alternative forms of community life there. Among Mennonites, this most often happens when congregations or the church, in some other visible, corporate form, share in the life of a neighborhood or region, including its sufferings. Since life patterned after Jesus takes distinct, perceptible forms, this presence will not only communicate with local people on personal levels, but suggest different ways of dealing with the social issues affecting everyone. For instance, if Christians share not only personal and emotional burdens, but also material goods, and resolve differences in peaceful, creative ways – these can suggest alternative forms of social interaction that might well, in time, take root in the neighborhood or region, and then spread beyond. Food cooperatives and conflict mediation centers are examples.

To be sure, this mission focus may seem much narrower than those which concentrate on broad structural changes. Yet if social sin's roots sink as deeply into people as I propose, structural changes, while important, may mostly affect life's surface. Perhaps local projects, where God's Spirit begins disentangling sin's personal roots, will plant something significantly different, and finally more effective. Moreover, if Jesus' way, the pattern for all authentic human life, is as different as Mennonites suppose from those of our world, pervaded by greed, violence and suffering – perhaps what society needs most is visible evidence that real alternatives are possible. If these alternatives are closely linked to churches that invite people to participate in the new creation's divinizing energy, perhaps these will make greater and ultimately even broader impact.

In any case, this has been the main mission focus in the Anabaptist–Mennonite tradition, which has sought to actualize God's new creation both inwardly and outwardly, both spiritually and materially, both personally and socially, in a world where suffering is unavoidable, but by no means the last word.

Endnotes

[1] The classic statement of this perspective is James Stayer, Werner Packull, and Klaus Deppermann, "From Monogenesis to Polygenesis: the historical discussion of Anabaptist Origins," *Mennonite Quarterly Review* 46.2 (April 1975), 83–121. For some qualifications, see Arnold Snyder, "Beyond Polygenesis: Recovering the Unity and Diversity of Anabaptist Theology," in H. Wayne Pipkin (ed.), *Essays in Anabaptist Theology* (Elkhart, IN: Institute of Mennonite Studies, 1994), 1–33.

[2] Harold Bender, *The Anabaptist Vision* (Scottdale, PA: Herald, 1944), 13. Bender helped this approach become highly influential among Mennonites, who were gaining acceptance by evangelical Protestants by mid-century. Bender traced it as far back as Max Goebel's *Geschichte des christlichen lebens in der Rheinisch-Westfaelischen Kirche* (Coblentz, 1848).

[3] See Ernst Troeltsch, *Protestantism and Progress* (Philadelphia, PA: Fortress Press, 1986 [1912]), esp. 37–38, 68.

[4] E.g. the early South German/Austrian evangelist, Hans Hut. For the Muenster episode, see Section I.C below.

[5] Martin Luther sided rather dramatically with the nobles (see Roland Bainton, *Here I Stand* [New York: New American Library, 1950], 205–22. To introduce

the Reformation, Ulrich Zwingli relied on the Zurich town council, which often opposed peasant interests (see Ulrich Gaebler, *Huldrych Zwingli: His Life and Work* [Philadelphia, PA: Fortress Press, 1986]).

6 James Stayer, *The German Peasants' War and the Anabaptist Community of Goods* (Montreal: McGill-Queen's University, 1991), 45–60.

7 Friedrich Engles, *The Peasant War in Germany* [1850], in *The German Revolutions* (Chicago: University of Chicago, 1967).

8 Kenneth Davis, *Anabaptism and Asceticism* (Scottdale, PA: Herald, 1974), 39–54.

9 Especially the Fransiscan Tertiaries and the Brethren of the common life (see Davis, *Anabaptism*). Much earlier, Albrecht Ritschl considered Anabaptists the successors of mystical and ascetic groups, particularly the Tertiaries and monasticism (*Geschichte des Pietismus* I [Bonn: Adolph Marcus], 1880).

10 "God is present in the soul in the whole of his divinity" (quoted in Oliver Davies, *God Within* [New York: Paulist, 1988], 48). When critiqued by the Inquisition for calling the human soul divine, Eckhart replied that only a faculty or power within it was divine. The rest was "touched by createdness" and was therefore "itself created" (49). See *Meister Eckhart: The Essential Sermons, Commentaries, Treatises and Defense* (trans. Edmund Colledge and Bernard McGinn; New York: Paulist, 1981), esp. 42–44, 80.

11 Johannes Tauler, Sermon 51, quoted in Davies, *God Within*, 89 (italics mine). According to Maria Shrady, "the decisive difference between Tauler and Eckhart … is the imitation of Christ, placing an emphasis on his humanity never to be abrogated" (trans. Shrady, *Johannes Tauler: Sermons* [New York: Paulist, 1985], xv). For *The German Theology* on following Jesus, see *The Theologia Germanica of Martin Luther* (trans. Bengt Hoffman; New York: Paulist, 1980), esp. 67–68, 97.

12 Leonhard Schiemer, "Three Kinds of Grace," in Daniel Liechty (ed.), *Early Anabaptist Spirituality* (New York: Paulist, 1994), 90.

13 Leonhard Schiemer, "The Apostles' Creed: An Interpretation," in C. J. Dyck (ed.), *Spiritual Life in Anabaptism* (Scottdale, PA: Herald, 1995), 33.

14 These Anabaptists were applying Rhineland themes literally and socially. *The German Theology* (trans. Hoffman), for instance, had taught that sin arises "when the creature assumes for itself some good thing … as though the Good *belongs* to the creature" or assumes that it is one's "own property." (62).

15 Hans Hut, "The Mystery of Baptism," in Liechty (ed.), *Early Anabaptist Spirituality*, 70.

16 *Peter Riedemann's Hutterite Confession of Faith* (trans. John Friesen; Scottdale, PA: Herald, 1999), 94, 120.

17 More precisely, this was from the Father through the Son. See Cornelius Dyck, William Keeney, and Alvin Beachy (eds.), *The Writings of Dirk Philips* (Scottdale, PA: Herald, 1992), 259, 362, 381; J. C. Wenger (ed.), *The Complete Works of Menno Simons* (Scottdale, PA: Herald, 1956), 496, 810. Since these writers seldom used formal terminology, this usage, though relatively

infrequent, and the absence of the Western *filioque* (though perhaps echoed in *Dirk Philips*, 65) is significant. Dirk (62–63, cf. 361, 413, 500) and Menno (496, cf. 860) may also have considered the Father the source of the Son's and Spirit's being, as in the East.

[18] See my "Pilgram Marpeck and the Christus Victor Motif," *Mennonite Quarterly Review* 78.1 (Jan. 2004), 1–25; and Thomas Finger, *A Contemporary Anabaptist Theology: Biblical, Historical, Constructive* (Downers Grove, IL: InterVarsity Press, 2004), 333–52.

[19] Alvin Beachy seeks to show how most major historic Anabaptist themes are best understood on the assumption that salvation was viewed as divinization (*The Concept of Grace in the Radical Reformation* [Nieuwkoop, Netherlands: B. De Graf, 1977]). After comparing sixteenth-century Anabaptist soteriology with Protestant and Catholic understandings, I argue that it was closer to divinization (*Contemporary Anabaptist Theology*, 115–35).

[20] Dyck, Keeney and Beachy (eds.), *Dirk Philips*, 145; William Klassen and Walter Klaassen (eds.), *The Writings of Pilgram Marpeck* (Scottdale, PA: Herald, 1978), 530–31.

[21] Klaus Deppermann, *Melchior Hoffman* (Edinburgh: T&T Clark, 1987), 257.

[22] See Obbe Phillips' gruesome account in George Williams and Angel Mergal (eds.), *Spiritual and Anabaptist Writers* (Philadelphia, PA: Westminster, 1957), 216–19.

[23] Marpeck critiqued this notion strongly, much as Irenaeus once critiqued the Gnostics (Klassen and Klaassen [eds.], *Pilgram Marpeck*, 52, 57, 80, 83, 84, 86, 103). While several statements by early South German/Austrians might seem to imply this exaggerated notion, I seek to show how they really do not (Finger, *A Contemporary Anabaptist Theology*, 123).

[24] Many Swiss and South German/Austrian Anabaptists considered Christian life a three-phased baptismal process, where a *baptism of the Spirit* was followed by *baptism of water* and finally *baptism of blood*. The last always included mortification, or inward participation in Jesus' cross, and too often outward, literal martyrdom.

[25] See Donald Dayton, *Theological Roots of Pentecostalism* (Metuchen, NJ: Scarecrow Press, 1987).

[26] E.g. *Peter Riedemann* (trans. Friesen), 61, 84, 85, 97, 116–117, 178–179, 196–197; Klassen and Klaassen (eds.), *Pilgram Marpeck*, 92; cf. 91, 94, 100, 101, 122, 134, 137, 233, 453. These emphases entered the Anabaptist stream again in the early eighteenth century when the German Baptist Brethren joined it with Radical Pietism (their North American successors are known mainly as The Brethren Church and The Church of the Brethren). The Swiss Anabaptist understanding of salvation should not be called divinization, but (following Beachy, *Concept of Grace*) was a less thorough sort of ontological transformation (meaning transformation *by* a different, divine kind of being, *not into* it).

27 For Dirk Phillips and Menno Simons, divinization involved participation in Jesus' risen flesh. However, they thought that if this flesh had originated *from* Mary, it would have derived ultimately from Adam's sinful flesh, which they considered irredeemable. Consequently, they taught that Jesus' flesh was created supernaturally *in* Mary, and merely born *through* her. Dirk and Menno insisted that this flesh, like Adam's before sin, was fully human. Yet they expected people divinized by such purity to live more righteously than most Mennonites did. As a result, many Mennonites became preoccupied more with crucifixion of their corrupted Adamic flesh than participation in Jesus' risen flesh (see 3.3 below).

28 By February 1527, slightly two years after their origins (January 21, 1525), Swiss Anabaptists affirmed the "Schleitheim Confession," in part to counter the "very great offence ... introduced by some false brothers among us ... thinking to practice and observe the freedom of the Spirit," though they have "given over to the lasciviousness and license of the flesh" (in Howard Loewen, *One Lord, One Church, One Hope and One God: Mennonite Confessions of Faith* [Elkhart, IN: Institute of Mennonite Studies, 1985], 79).

29 Cf. 2.3 below. Such measures were also necessary to form tight-knit communities that could avoid detection, and to help identify spies attempting to infiltrate them.

30 A major theme of Arnold Snyder, *Anabaptist History and Theology* (Kitchener, ON: Pandora, 1995).

31 Cf. my "Are Mennonites Sacramental?" *The Mennonite* 7.18 (Sept. 21, 2004), 9–11; also "How 'Sacramental' were the Original Anabaptists?" address at Conference on Ritual in Anabaptist Communities, Hillsdale College (MI), June 27, 2003.

32 John Rempel, *The Lord's Supper in Anabaptism* (Scottdale, PA: Herald, 1993), 29–30.

33 According to Balthasar Hubmaier, "the flesh has irretrievably lost its goodness ... and has become entirely and wholly worthless and hopeless unto death. It is not able or capable of anything other than sin, striving against God ..." (Wayne Pipkin and John H. Yoder [eds.], *Balthasar Hubmaier: Theologian of Anabaptism* [Scottdale, PA: Herald, 1989], 433, cf. 87, 147, 442, 446). According to Menno Simons, Those who are "born of flesh and blood ... are altogether deaf, blind, and ignorant of divine things." Any such person "has nothing in common with God, but is ... of a contrary nature ... unmerciful, unjust, unclean, quarrelsome, contrary, disobedient, without understanding, and irreverent" (Wenger [ed.], *Menno Simons*, 54, 55). Menno was referring to a "fleshly nature" that extended even further than the body (cf. note 27 above).

34 Klassen and Klaassen (eds.), *Pilgram Marpeck*, 309–68, cf. 108.

35 Snyder, *Anabaptist History*, 93, 237–52, 374. However, only a few groups, like the Hutterites, practiced total community of goods.

36 Frequent use of these South German/Austrian mystical concepts is still rare among Mennonites. However, I find them largely congruent with the

way most Mennonites view society. I find them very helpful for further articulating this social theology while connecting it with a spiritual theology. See my "An Historic Anabaptist Social Spirituality," *Conrad Grebel Review* 22.3 (Fall 2004), 93–104.

37 I am not attempting to describe sin comprehensively, but only a major feature of it.

38 "These conflicts and disputes among you, where do they come from? Do they not come from your cravings that are at war within you? You want something and do not have it, so you commit murder. You covet something and cannot obtain it; so you engage in disputes and conflicts" (Jas. 4:1–2, NRSV).

Christians and Persecution

Making an Appropriate Response

CECIL M. ROBECK, JR.

You have heard that it was said, "Love your neighbor and hate your enemy." But I tell you: Love your enemies and pray for those who persecute you, that you may be sons of your Father in heaven. He causes his sun to rise on the evil and the good, and sends rain on the righteous and the unrighteous. If you love those who love you, what reward will you get? Are not even the tax collectors doing that? And if you greet only your brothers, what are you doing more than others? Do not even pagans do that? Be perfect, therefore, as your heavenly Father is perfect. (Matt. 5:43–48, NIV)

The body is a unity, though it is made up of many parts; and though all its parts are many, they form one body … If one part suffers, every part suffers with it; if one part is honored, every part rejoices with it. (1 Cor. 12:12, 26, NIV)

1. Introduction

I do not consider myself to be an expert on the subject of suffering or of "persecuted churches," but my primary ministry as a seminary professor of church history and ecumenics frequently takes me to countries where religious tensions exist. While the persecution of Christians is common in many places around the world, the level of persecution that Christians must suffer and the reasons that Christians are persecuted vary from place to place. Jesus told us how we are to treat those who persecute the church.

We are to love them. The apostle Paul helps us understand how we are to view our persecuted sisters and brothers. They gain our support as we enter into their suffering with them. In this chapter, it is my desire to help us see more clearly what we can do to live up to both of these expectations. I will do this by asking four questions.

2. How has Persecution Looked Through the Centuries?

Persecution is nothing new to the church. It has been persecuted and it has done its share of persecuting through the centuries. When we read the New Testament, we quickly realize that persecution surrounded the earliest Christians at every turn. When they tried to share the gospel message, the earliest Christians were often arrested, run out of town, beaten, thrown into prison, or even executed.[1] Technically, it was against Roman law to be a Christian until AD 313, although the law was often unevenly enforced. The Roman government, which ruled the ancient western world, viewed Christianity as a threat to the stability of the empire.[2] The church proclaimed a different king and it anticipated a different kingdom. As a result, the government developed strategies for undermining the church or keeping it in check. Sometimes, it arrested every new convert it could find, hoping to scare people away from converting.[3] When that did not work, it jailed and executed church leaders, believing that without leaders, the church would collapse.[4] Neither tactic was ultimately successful.

In AD 313, that all changed. That year the co-emperors, Licinius and Constantine, issued an edict from Milan, which for the first time declared that it was legal for people to pursue their Christian faith.[5] It provided for the "toleration" of Christianity. Within a decade, however, Licinius had died, and Constantine embraced Christianity as the religion of the empire. A new era, the era of what came to be known as Christendom, came into being.

Constantine was a pragmatist. It was he who embraced Christianity as part of his imperial policy. Even before he had sole responsibility for the empire, his mother had become a Christian. At one point, he claimed that he had a dream that revealed the "chi-rho" symbol. When he asked his advisor for the meaning of his dream, he was told that if he supported the Christian God revealed through this symbol, he would conquer the world. Constantine did just that. Once he had sole control of the empire, Constantine included state grants to support members of the clergy. In AD 313 he exempted the clergy from certain public duties, in AD 319 he suppressed soothsayers, and in AD 321 he granted official recognition to Sunday as the day for Christian worship.[6]

During this period, Constantine also began to dabble in issues related to church discipline, from his judgment concerning Donatism in North Africa to his calling of the Ecumenical Council at Nicaea in AD 325. As a result, he recruited chaplains and distributed prayer books to his soldiers. He proceeded to invade much of what would become Europe, from England on the west, to Russia on the east. In a sense, his soldiers became his evangelists. When they entered a village or town, the people were given an ultimatum. They could convert or die; seldom did the people refuse baptism.[7]

When the church aligned itself with the state, the emperor's subjects became loyal, tax-paying Christians.[8] In return the emperor paid the clergy, and built and cared for their churches. As a result, the church grew and even prospered. But its growth and prosperity came at a great price. Constantine and his successors, especially Justinian with his theory of συμφωνία τις ἀγαθὴ / *symphonia tis agathe* determined that the emperor was responsible for day-to-day life, the earthly kingdom; the bishops were responsible for the life to come, the kingdom of God.[9] And so it was that the symbol of the empire became an eagle with two heads. The one head represented the authority of the emperor. The other head represented the authority of the church. In places like Cyprus and Greece, all Orthodox churches still fly a flag with a two-headed eagle in black, against a yellow background. This flag is the Ecumenical Patriarch's coat of arms and it dates back to the Byzantine Empire. In one of the eagle's claws is a sword, representing the power of the state. In the other claw is the cross, representing the power of the church.

Today it is difficult to find places where the church does not exist in one form or another. But in a few countries, especially in those noted for their ties with Islam, one will find few Christians. The Qur'an, of course, was allegedly revealed to a man who was concerned, in part, by the constant bickering among Christians over theological and, especially Christological issues. Mohammed, who lived in Arabia during the seventh century, desired to be a spiritual man. He regularly practiced both prayer and fasting. But he was annoyed at the way Christians from the West and Christians from the East argued about the nature of Jesus. He was also concerned with the way Christians talked about God. For him, Trinitarian language sounded as though Christians worshiped three gods, not one. He was committed to preserve the message of God as one. While it may be the case that he did not fully understand the theological discussions of his day, his "revelations" ultimately denied the sacrificial death and resurrection of Jesus, declaring him to be merely a prophet. They also rejected the doctrine of the Trinity.

The authoritarian methods by which Christianity spread following the Council of Nicaea, the ways in which the Nicene Creed came to be imposed upon dissident voices, and the subsequent and sometimes relentless pursuit of "heretics" following its adoption often carried a backlash. At this time it encouraged many to embrace the more "liberal" way of viewing life, the faith of Islam. As Mohammed's military power increased and his followers overran Christian centers throughout Arabia, then the Middle East, North Africa, and ultimately Central Europe, those they conquered were encouraged, sometimes also at the point of the sword, to convert to Islam. On the whole, however, Islam provided a limited toleration to Jews (people of the Law) and greater toleration to Christians (people of the Book). It accepted the Jewish prophets as divinely inspired and it included Jesus among the divinely inspired prophets.

While Mohammed tolerated both Jews and Christians because they shared some of the same Scriptures, he gave preferential treatment to those who converted to Islam. His followers forced those who did not convert to wear clothes that marked them as Christians or Jews.[10] They subjected Christians to extra and ever-increasing taxes.[11] They did not allow them to build new churches. And they limited their employment opportunities.

With the coming of the crusades during the eleventh through the thirteenth centuries, Christians, now aligned with the heirs to the Roman Empire, ran military campaigns to rid the world of Jews and Muslims. Sadly, Jews were often portrayed as "Christ killers," while, especially in Spain, Muslims were considered to be "infidels" and "blasphemers" because they did not accept Jesus as the Son of God. As a result, Jews and Muslims were either run out of countries such as Spain and Italy or completely massacred, all in the name of Christ. What resulted over the long-term were anti-Semitism and ultimately the Jewish Holocaust. Muslim–Christian relations were strained and have festered ever since.[12]

In those places where Muslims triumphed over Christians, Muslims converted church buildings into mosques and desecrated or destroyed many Christian symbols, especially crosses. Several years ago I visited Istanbul, Turkey, the former city of Constantinople, the capital of the Byzantine Empire. This is where Constantine's successors built the famous church Hagia Sophia. When the Muslims conquered that city and occupied Hagia Sophia, they turned it into a mosque. When I visited the former Hagia Sophia, I found that all crosses that had been carved in the stone throughout the building had been crudely broken off or removed. For Muslims, the cross stands as a sign of offense, a stumbling block because of what it symbolizes. In many Muslim lands, even in such "secular" countries as Turkey, Christians are not allowed to display or wear one.

Beginning with the fifteenth century, European colonialism enabled the church to make great missionary strides. But colonialism also imposed artificial divisions that created strife. Whole continents were carved up by various European governments and the pope, simply by drawing lines on a map. They divided up tribes and people groups and gave little regard to customs, histories, or language differences. And they sent their missionaries.

The 500th anniversary of Christopher Columbus's 1492 arrival in the western hemisphere was both highly celebrated and severely critiqued. The reasons were simple, and they included religious persecution in the form of forced conversions. Throughout Latin America, for instance, virtually every ship that came from Spain or Portugal came with soldiers and priests. The soldiers came to make it clear that all those they met were now subjects of the Spanish rulers. The priests came to guarantee that the people submitted to the Christ who had appointed these rulers and the pope, who led Christ's church. When the indigenous people did not accept these conditions for peace and did not rise voluntarily to the "opportunity" to submit to this demand outlined in the *Requerimiento*, their acceptance of Christianity was accomplished by force.[13]

Africa did not fare much better. The Portuguese claimed Angola, and today it is largely Catholic. The Germans claimed Tanzania, and today it is largely Lutheran and Catholic. The Dutch, followed by the English, claimed South Africa. Today it is heavily Reformed and Anglican. And so the division of the land and the Christian faith continued. With the end of colonialism in the 1960s, many predicted the persecution of Christians by governments and the demise of the church.[14] Instead, we have seen the reinvention of the church in Africa as new African denominations have been formed.[15]

In Asia, Christianity came early to India by ancient trade routes, but it expanded with the coming of the Portuguese who produced Catholic dominance around Goa, and later with the English, who introduced Anglican, Congregationalist, and Baptist versions of the church. A very successful Jesuit mission was established in Canton, China, in 1583. By 1692, the emperor, Kangxi issued an Edict of Toleration for Christians. When Dominican missionaries arrived in 1700, they found a church of some 300,000 people, but they accused the Jesuits of compromising the gospel. The resulting fight between Jesuits and Dominican missionaries became known as the "Rites Controversy," and the Chinese government was so disgusted that it expelled them all.[16]

Later, the British reintroduced Christianity to China, but it did not come by noble means. The British wanted the cotton and spices that India had to offer. The Indians wanted silver. But the English needed money, so they encouraged the Indians to grow cheap opium poppies. The English processed and sold the opium to the Chinese, who paid in silver so the English could buy what they wanted from India. Many Chinese became drug addicts. The Chinese government outlawed opium and fought the Opium Wars to end the drug trade, but because the English had bigger guns, the Chinese lost.

As the English negotiated the Treaty of Nanking and later treaties with the Chinese, churches in England pressured the English to require the Chinese to allow Protestant missionaries to evangelize in China. Such provisions made this treaty come to be known as an "unequal treaty." The negotiation of such "unequal treaties" became common, giving Christian missionaries freedoms that others did not enjoy, and leading to resentment against the church as complicit in the colonial expansionist policies of the British.[17] In 1899 the Chinese people rose up in what was called the Boxer Rebellion and killed thousands of Christians, both English and Chinese. A decade later the empire collapsed and a new Chinese government was created that was more tolerant of Christianity.

Following the Second World War, that government was forced into exile on Taiwan, and implementing a Communist agenda that was both nationalist and ideological, Mao Tsetung and his successors attempted to rid China of Christianity's unwelcome foreign influence, if not Christianity altogether.[18] Once again, the church was persecuted, and in spite of the veneer of recognition given to the Three-Self Patriotic Movement by the Chinese government, it continues, with strict rules and clear limitations. It has been especially difficult among the unregistered "house church" movement.[19]

What all of this adds up to is this: while there have been many fine missionaries that have selflessly spread the gospel throughout the world, the gospel has often been spread in the frailty of human sinfulness and human flesh. The persecution of Christians today needs to be understood, in part, as stemming from that sinful history. Division between churches, doctrinal disputes, the alignment of the church with various states and their policies, including those of the United States, and the use of force to guarantee submission to the cross are all part of the story of Christian persecution.

2. What is the State of Persecution Today?

What is identified as persecution today varies from place to place, from context to context. At its worst, the persecution of Christians involves the taking of lives. In most cases what is called persecution involves the placing of strict limitations upon the freedom of Christians to meet, to build churches, to evangelize, or to advertise themselves to those they seek to help. In fact, persecution can include everything from execution and martyrdom to the public ridicule of those who follow Jesus.

The earliest Pentecostals in the United States were widely persecuted through public ridicule. The sermons preached by pastors from churches in the historic mainline set the tone of many such attacks when Pentecostal worship was labeled as nothing more than "a disgusting amalgamation of African voodoo superstition and Caucasian insanity."[20] But such persecution originated even more forcefully in the public ridicule that they received from the press, where they were given names like "Holy Rollers," "Holy Jumpers," "Holy Kickers," and "Tangled Tonguers." They were even made the brunt of cartoons and poetry.[21]

Even I can remember when Pentecostal children had rocks thrown at them by others, simply because they were Pentecostals. But I want to concentrate on some of the kinds of persecutions that stem from government policies, cultural pressures, and religious protectionism.

2.1 *Some persecution is politically or ideologically motivated*

In October 2000, the USA government gave me permission to travel to Cuba. I had been invited to attend an ecumenical meeting there, to preach in three churches in Havana and Matanzas, and to meet with Fidel Castro. All of the churches in which I preached are subject to very strict laws. I had to receive permission from the Cuban government to preach in them. The congregations are not allowed to expand their church buildings or build new ones. One of the churches in which I preached was in an older woman's home that she has made available as a church for over twenty-five years. About seventy-five or

SUMMER SOLSTICE SEES STRENUOUS SECTS SASHAYING

"Religion stands on tiptoe," so an English poet puts it,
But here it goes a jumping when a pious brother foots it;
And sisters with the "gift of tongues"—is that a scoffer's jest?
Observe no more St. Paul's commands, but shout like all possessed.

This cartoon was published in Los Angeles, California, at the top center of page 1, just below the masthead of *The Evening News*, July 23, 1906. The title, "Summer Solstice Sees Strenuous Sects Sashaying" is clearly a tongue-twister intended to ridicule speaking in tongues. July 22 was the summer solstice, the longest day of the year. The characters demonstrate the derogatory names being hurled at the people of the Mission. The language of "tongues" surrounding the woman at the lower left, ranges from Oopsquee [Pig Latin] to *e pluribus unum* [Latin] with ditties and noises as well. The poem at the bottom of the cartoon criticizes the extensive role that women legitimately played in the Azusa Street meetings, based upon the Mission's understanding of Joel 2:28–29. The reference to Paul, on the other hand, is to 1 Corinthians 14:34a "Let your women keep silence in the church," the position of most traditional churches at that time. This cartoon not only ridiculed the Mission it acted as a form of free advertisement as well.

eighty of us met from 7–10 p.m. in 95-degree heat and very high humidity. The windows were open to the world. People stood in the tiny living room, on the sidewalks, and in the street. And we had church! There was singing and dancing and clapping and tambourines and guitars and shouting and testimonies and prayer. We made a lot of noise! Their neighbors had no choice but to listen, so they stood at their windows and in their doorways and joined in or listened.

Unfortunately, that week, the former prime minister of Canada, Pierre Trudeau, died. Because he had supported Castro against the USA, Fidel Castro flew to Canada for his funeral. But Castro sent Dr. Caridad Diego, Director of the Office of Religious Affairs for the Central Committee of the Communist Party of Cuba, to talk with us about religious freedom in Cuba. At the end of her speech, I asked her a question. "I am a Pentecostal," I began,

> Pentecostalism is a religion *of* the people, a grassroots movement that gets much of its vitality from lay participation. It often displays an exuberant liturgical life, with singing, guitars, tambourines, drums, dancing, shouting, speaking in other tongues, and other spiritual manifestations. It is worship that is hard to ignore, and is quite at home in a Latin context. I am sure that you have heard good things about it, but I am also quite sure that others complain about it at times. When the revolution came to Cuba, Pentecostal churches were already present. But at that time, none of us would have predicted the enormous popularity of the movement that we have seen throughout Latin America and the Caribbean.
>
> As I have preached to several congregations this week, they have told me that they are frustrated by the fact that they can't get literature and they are limited by the facilities in which they must worship. As many as 200 people are crowded into inadequate space in some 400–500 different "house churches." They don't have church buildings where they might worship freely and not disturb their neighbors. I would like to know what the Cuban government is prepared to do to bring about some change in the current situation that will meet their needs. They are, after all, good Cuban citizens who pray for their country's well-being, and I believe that the nation as a whole would benefit from seeing that their needs are met.

Dr. Diego was very clear in her response. In essence, she argued that Cuban churches are to be run by Cuban people without influence from outside Cuba. Cuban churches will not be allowed to compete with one another or with other churches for favors from the government. If neighbors do not like the noise, they can find some member of these noisy churches and trade housing with them. All churches are treated equally, so you cannot ask for special privileges for Pentecostals. Cuban churches will remain small, restricted churches. If they become too big, they will become too powerful.

Her message was clear. The Communist leadership does not want to be challenged. "Don't you want them to be biblical?" she quipped, explaining that New Testament churches were all house churches. I wanted desperately to respond, "Yes, and they were persecuted, too!" But I refrained.

2.2 Some persecution is culturally motivated

More recently, what are called anti-proselytism laws and anti-conversion laws are being enacted around the world. One such place is in the island nation of Trinidad and Tobago in the Caribbean, where Hindus now hold the political majority. These laws require the imprisonment of anyone who speaks negatively about any other religion. If a person is offended when listening to a Christian sermon in which Christians are made to look better than others, or Christ is proclaimed as the only means of salvation, the Hindu can file a complaint and the preacher will be arrested. In our politically correct climate, we may soon see attempts to pass such laws in the United States.

In North India, Hindu nationalists have passed similar legislation. They have argued that to be "an authentic Indian necessarily means being Hindu."[22] While the Indian constitution guarantees freedom of religion, Hindu nationalists, who are trying to preserve an ancient Hindu culture with a deeply entrenched caste system, are arguing that Christianity is their "cultural" enemy. In one extreme case in 1999, five of these Hindu nationalists poured kerosene on the vehicle of an Australian evangelical missionary and burned him and his two young sons to death as they slept.[23]

When missionary organizations began to focus their attention in the 1990s on the so-called 10–40 Window, these Hindu nationalists decided to exploit what they claimed were Christians targeting their culture. Here is a place in which the actions of well-meaning Christians in the West have had a negative effect upon the lives of Christians in another part of the world. As one Indian Pentecostal leader recently told me angrily, "I must now live with the consequences of decisions that American Pentecostals made about my country, and they didn't ask me what I thought!"

As a result of such decisions, Hindu nationalists have struck especially at evangelicals, Pentecostals, and Roman Catholics who have been leading the Dahlits to Christ. The Dahlits are the untouchable peoples in the ancient caste system of Hinduism. By bringing hope to the Dahlits, the Christian message is shaking the foundations of Hindu culture. With these new laws, in some areas it is now necessary for a person to apply to a local magistrate, often a Hindu, for permission to convert, or in some cases, it is required that a person register his or her conversion with the local magistrate. The result: increased pressure and discrimination against Christians.

2.3 Some persecution is religiously motivated

Persecution for religious reasons can be seen today in places like Nigeria, Sudan, Egypt, Syria, Iran, Saudi Arabia, Pakistan, and Indonesia. You may guess that these are mostly nations where Islam is dominant. But some Buddhists are now taking lessons in this regard in places like Sri Lanka. For the most part, Islam sees all of life as interconnected. It is not difficult to see the similarity that exists between the older, Byzantine understanding of the relationship between church and state, represented by the two-headed eagle, and the worldview that many Muslims hold in various Islamic states. In a sense, the state is merely the extension of the mosque. We can see this most clearly in Iran, where the imam, the religious leader, Ayatollah Ali Khomeini, is the acknowledged leader of the Islamic Republic of Iran.

The tradition of separation between church and state in the USA makes it very difficult for Americans to understand this. In any case, though by no means all sects of Islam would agree, there are many Muslims who would like to see the implementation of Islamic law as the law of the state. This is called Shari'a. The

Taliban of Afghanistan implemented this law, and it functions with variations in several Middle Eastern countries. Under this law, any conversion from Islam to Christianity comes with a death penalty. In places like Pakistan, this penalty has been sought within the recent years.

The state of Zamfara, in Nigeria, was the first of twelve northern states in Nigeria to introduce the Shari'a. Its introduction, in clear violation of the national constitution of Nigeria, set off riots in the city of Kaduna that claimed 2,000 lives in the year 2000, and again in December 2002, most of them Christian. The latest violence came after a Kaduna newspaper reported that the prophet Mohammed would have approved of the Miss World beauty pageant. Since this was spun as a "Christian" position, subsequent riots led to the burning of Christian churches and deaths of nearly 2000 Nigerian Christians.[24]

In countries like the Sudan, where the north is Muslim and the south is Christian, Shari'a has not yet been imposed, but the movement is in that direction. As the nation wages civil war, we have heard of the slave trade that has gone on in which Muslims kidnap Christian women and children and take them to the north. There they force the women to become their wives and adopt the children or use them as slaves.[25] Throughout Africa, Muslim men are being encouraged to marry Christian women in a form of Muslim evangelism. Muslim men are the undisputed head of the household. They often confine their women to veiled lives with no formal education, lives limited to doing menial tasks and child-bearing, with limited contacts with the outside world. Women who resist are frequently punished. The children are considered the property solely of the Muslim man, and Islamic courts inevitably rule in favor of the man.

Not all persecution that is religiously motivated is done by people of other faiths such as Islam. Some of it is also undertaken by other Christians, especially in places where proselytism has been alleged. Even Pentecostals have been guilty of persecuting other Christians when they believe that their proprietary "rights" have been challenged. In one case, Northern Irish Elim Pentecostal missionaries exported Northern Irish politics to northern Zimbabwe where they battled Southern Irish Carmelite missionaries with such ferocity that the regional government official labeled the entire affair as "quite un-Christian."[26]

On the other hand, there have been many cases where Pentecostals have been the victims. Between 1984 and 1986, Don Stephens and his coworkers in Youth with a Mission were charged with "proselytizing" a teenage boy in Greece. They were tried, found guilty, and ultimately sentenced to a three-and-a-half-year prison term. While the Orthodox Church argued strongly for their imprisonment, on appeal the court reversed the decision and they were freed. The Orthodox Church was trying to insure the homogeneous nature of Greek culture by preserving Orthodoxy as the only allowable religious expression of that culture.[27]

In Cyprus, there is only one recognized church. It is Orthodox. No other denomination can incorporate in Cyprus. If they attempt to do so, the state will close them down. The reason for this goes back to the message on that flag. To be Greek or a Greek Cypriot, even to be Russian, is to be culturally Orthodox. Similar things are said throughout the Americas about Latinos. It is assumed by many that to be a Latino is to be Catholic, that is, to be Latino is to participate in a Catholic culture. Thus, anyone who attempts to bring the gospel outside the structures of the Orthodox Church in Greece or Cyprus, or Russia, or outside of the Catholic Church in Mexico and elsewhere in Latin America, is viewed and sometimes treated as a sectarian who is undermining the religious as well as the cultural life of its citizens. The result often comes in the form of persecution.

3. What do the Scriptures Say about our Response to Persecution?

Scripture is very clear on the issue of our suffering and persecuted sisters and brothers. The apostle Paul summarizes it briefly when he notes, "The body is a unity made up of many parts … If one part suffers, every part suffers with it" (1 Cor. 12:12–26). As part of the larger Body of Christ, then, we are part of the body that suffers. We must stand in solidarity with our suffering sisters and brothers. We must remember them and pray for them and reach out to them in whatever ways we can. We must work to change the status quo, so that they might rejoice, for in their rejoicing, we are also participants, for if "one part is honored, every part rejoices with it" (1 Cor. 12:26).

Jesus also made some very important statements on this subject. In John 16:33, for instance, he tells us, "In this world you will have trouble. But take heart! I have overcome the world." Trouble! That is what persecution and suffering are. Trouble! It is important to understand that in this world there is trouble, and there is suffering, and there is persecution, because this world is not the kingdom of God. But we also have Jesus' claim that he has already overcome this world, and as a result, we can have hope, and as sisters and brothers to those who suffer from the effects of persecution, we must be prepared to offer them that hope.

But the text of Matthew's Gospel at the beginning of this chapter points us in yet another direction. Jesus has told those who follow him that it is not sufficient for them to be just like the crowd. It does not take much to love those who love you. Anyone can do that. What is much more difficult to do is to love those who are your enemies. Those who persecute Christians in any part of the world are enemies of the church. It does not matter whether they are governments interested in stamping out the Christian faith or crushing the influence of the church. It does not matter whether it is leaders in another religion or even in another church or misguided fanatics who wish to do Christians harm. It does not matter whether it is terrorists who, in the name of Allah, would destroy Christians as "children of Satan." It does not matter whether it is people from a culture that tries to keep the gospel from transforming that culture or who treat their Christian neighbors as less than the "children of God" that they are. It does not matter if it is an individual who speaks falsely against Christians when it comes to their faith and life, or the individual who seeks to undermine a Christian's testimony, or who criticizes Christians for the kind of witness they have. The response is to be the same: "Love your enemies and pray for those who persecute you, that you may be sons of your Father in heaven." Look once again at the text. The Lord causes the sun to rise and the rain to fall not only on us, but also upon those who are evil. We are called to be just like him.

4. How can we Respond to the Current Situation?

The persecution of Christians will continue into the foreseeable future. At times it may seem as though there is not very much that an ordinary Christian can do to bring it to an end or to intervene on behalf of those who suffer persecution. But there are a number of actions that can be taken that are consistent with the teachings of Jesus and of Paul and that will make a difference for "the suffering church."

1. Pray for the end of all religious persecution, but especially in cases where the loss of human life is a real possibility. No one wants persecution and no one deserves to suffer from persecution.

2. If persecution comes, however, realize that it often brings with it the growth of the church. The early church theologian, Tertullian, observed that "the blood of martyrs watered the churches and reared up many times as many champions of piety."[28] Similarly, persecution under the Soviet regime as well as under the Chinese government, particularly that persecution aimed at "unregistered" Christians, has contributed to the growth of the church in both places. Pray for the growth of the church wherever persecution flourishes, both in terms of the numbers of people who come to faith and in terms of the growth of spiritual vitality that often comes with persecution.

3. Pray that the leaders of our churches and the leaders of our nations will find ways to end religious persecution worldwide. While Jesus says that in this world we will have trouble, and that includes suffering and persecution, he does not say that it will always be present in every place. The more that our leaders can do to limit it, the better off will be the church.

4. Pray for the strength of our sisters and brothers undergoing persecution. We do not know about all the pressures they face. Pray that the Lord will remove their fear and provide them with the peace and assurance that only he can bring.

5. Pray that our sisters and brothers who are undergoing persecution do not take on a "persecution complex" that keeps them from becoming a positive influence when their circumstances change. This temptation is very difficult for them to overcome. At this moment the Chinese government in Beijing says it is looking for ways to foster collaboration with Chinese Christians who are not part of the official church in China. For decades, registered Christians have been controlled by the state and unregistered Chinese Christians have been persecuted by the state and subject to spies who have reported them to the state. It is difficult for them to trust *any claim* by the government that it is open to change, especially in the light of very recent closures of some 400 churches and temples of those who have chosen not to cooperate with the state. Pray that the Lord will provide our sisters and brothers with wisdom and relieve them of their fears.

6. Pray that the US government and all governments adopt foreign policies that are just and merciful – good for all parties concerned. But give hands to those prayers by speaking to, calling, or writing to your legislative representatives. Tell them what you think. Ask hard questions and vote for those who support policies that do not compromise the church or its message, policies that will break down barriers.

7. Pray that the Lord will give you a forgiving heart that will enable you to love your enemies. Our basic human instinct is to do unto others what they have done to us. But Jesus reverses this by telling us to do to them what we would like for them to do to us (Matt. 7:12; Luke 6:31). This cannot be done apart from the Spirit of God.

8. Evaluate your own life so that you do not become a persecutor. It is never "payback" time. To the extent that we are able, we are to resist using force on anyone and to ask for forgiveness any time we resort to force. In a country as powerful as ours, we live with the temptation to become the persecutors of the persecutors. But our job as Christians is to show the world a "more excellent way," and that is the way of love, most profoundly seen in Jesus (John 3:16).

9. Finally, pray that the Lord will save those who currently persecute our sisters and brothers. If we pray for those who currently engage in persecution and cause suffering to the church, the Holy Spirit will deal with them, and we may be surprised by the changes that will be made.

Endnotes

[1] See, for instance Acts 5:17–18; 6:8–8:3; 12:1–5; 16:16–40; 21:27–36, etc.

[2] Helen Rhee, *Early Christian Literature: Christ and Culture in the Second and Third Centuries; The Apologies, Apocryphal Acts and Martyr Acts* (London and New York: Routledge, 2005), 12.

[3] In Carthage, for instance, Christians were persecuted from AD 197–204. The persecution under Septimius Severus was aimed primarily at new converts, especially in AD 203–204. *The Passion of Perpetua and Felicitas*, which outlines the last days of several new converts, was written during this time.

[4] During the period when Cyprian served as Bishop in Carthage, AD 250–258, two waves of persecution swept over the church. One of them came during the reign of Decius, the other under Valerius. In both cases, Christian leaders seemed to be singled out. One can find evidence of this policy throughout many of Cyprian's epistles.

[5] Following their meeting in Milan, Constantine and Licinius announced in what became known as the "Edict of Milan" that "notwithstanding any provisions concerning the Christians in our former instructions, all who choose that religion are to be permitted to continue therein, without any let or hindrance, and are not to be in any way troubled or molested." Lactantius, *The Death of the Persecutors*, 48.

[6] Eusebius, *Ecclesiastical History* 10.vii; *Cod. Theod.* 9.16.1; *Corp. Jur. Civ.* 2:127; *Cod. Theod.* 2.7.1.

[7] Cf. Hans Lietzmann, *From Constantine to Julian: A History of the Early Church* Vol. 3 (trans. Bertram Lee Woolf; New York: Meridian Books, ca. 1949); and W. H. C. Frend, *The Rise of Christianity* (Philadelphia, PA: Fortress Press, 1984), 487.

[8] I do not wish to suggest that emperors only saw the church as a political tool. As Warren Treadgold, *A History of Byzantine State and Society* (Stanford, CA: Stanford University Press, 1997), 259, has reminded us, during this period, virtually every emperor was "devout often to the point of religious asceticism, and all showed deference to the churchmen they considered orthodox." Still, all politicians seem to recognize the power that religion and religious commitments engender in the masses, and most politicians either harness its power toward meeting their ends or they attempt to destroy it.

⁹ Justinian, *Novella*, preamble, "There are two great gifts, which God, in his love for humankind, has granted from on high: the priesthood (ἱερωσύνη / *hierosune*) and the imperial dignity (βασιλεία / *basileia*). The first serves divine things, while the latter directs and administers human affairs; both, however, proceed from the same origin and adorn the life of humankind. Hence, nothing should be such a source of care to the emperors as the dignity of the priests, since it is for their (the emperors') welfare that they (the priests) constantly implore God. For, if the priesthood is in every way free from blame and possesses access to God, and if the emperors administer equitably and judiciously the state entrusted to their care, general harmony (συμφωνία τις ἀγαθὴ / *symphonia tis agathe*) will result and whatever is beneficial will be bestowed upon the human race."

¹⁰ Aziz S. Atiya, *A History of Eastern Christianity* (Millwood, NY: Kraus, repr. 1967, 1968, 1980), 84, 89.

¹¹ Otto F. A. Meinardus, *Two Thousand Years of Coptic Christianity* (Cairo, Egypt: The American University in Cairo Press, 1999), 64–65, notes the occasional destruction of churches as well as the imposition of taxation of the Copts through the imposition of *cheirotonia*, a tax imposed for installing ecclesiastical leaders.

¹² On the origins of anti-Muslim sentiment and rhetoric in Spain see Steven Runciman, *A History of the Crusades*. Vol. 1 *The First Crusade and the Foundations of the Kingdom of Jerusalem* (3 vols.; Cambridge: Cambridge University Press 1951), 89–91.

¹³ Luis N. Rivera, *A Violent Evangelism: The Political and Religious Conquest of the Americas* (Louisville, KY: Westminster/John Knox, 1991), 33–34, quotes from such instructions given by the Spanish monarchs and to be read as follows: "I beg and require of you … to recognize the church as lady and superior of the universe and to acknowledge the Supreme Pontiff, called pope, in her name, and the king and queen … as lords and superiors … by virtue of said donation; and consent to have these religious fathers declare and preach these things to you. If you do so, you will be acting well … If you do not do it … then with the help of God I will undertake powerful action against you. I will make war on you everywhere and in every way that I can. I will subject you to the yoke and obedience of the church and of Their Highnesses."

¹⁴ Bengt Sundkler and Christopher Steed, *A History of the Church in Africa* (Cambridge: Cambridge University Press, 2000), 903.

¹⁵ Among the first to study these churches was David B. Barrett, *Schism and Renewal in Africa: An Analysis of Six Thousand Contemporary Religious Movements* (Oxford: Oxford University Press, 1968).

¹⁶ Robert E. Entenmann, "Catholics and Society in Eighteenth-Century Sichuan," in Daniel H. Bays (ed.), *Christianity in China: From the Eighteenth Century to the Present* (Stanford, CA: Stanford University Press, 1996), 8–23;

and Richard Madsen, *China's Catholics: Tragedy and Hope in an Emerging Civil Society* (Berkeley, CA: University of California Press, 1998), 29–31.

[17] Roger R. Thompson, "The Chinese Countryside and the Modernizing State," in Bays (ed.), *Christianity in China*, 54.

[18] See, for instance, "Document 9: Concerning Questions about Control of Religious Organizations and Affairs by Outside Forces," in Donald E. MacInnis, *Religion in China Today: Policy and Practice* (Maryknoll, NY: Orbis, 1989), 42. In a speech given to a National Catholic Representatives Meeting in Beijing in April 1983 by Qiao Liansheng, then Director of the Religious Affairs Bureau, he notes, "To maintain our nation's strength and power, and to undergird the independence and selfhood of all religious organizations in our nation, the restoration of foreign religious influence and power must be prevented ... Reflecting on the history of our nation since 1840, it is difficult for one to forget over 100 years of Catholic and Protestant propagation in China, coinciding with the aggressive incursions and oppression of imperialism against China ... The Catholic and Protestant churches of that period served as the vanguard and tool of imperialist aggression. No one can deny these historical facts."

[19] Luke Wesley, *The Church in China: Persecuted, Pentecostal, and Powerful* (Asian Journal of Pentecostal Studies Series 2; Baguio, Philippines: AHPS Books, 2004), 7–21.

[20] From a sermon by Dr. R. J. Burdette, preached at Temple Baptist Church, Sunday, September 23, 1906, and published in "New Religions Come, Then Go," *Los Angeles Herald* (September 24, 1906), 7. Cf. "Denounces New Denominations," *Los Angeles Express* (September 24, 1906), 5.

[21] "Summer Solstice Sees Strenuous Sect Sashaying," *The* [Los Angeles] *Evening News* (July 23, 1906), 1.

[22] Paul Marshall with Lela Gilbert, *Their Blood Cries Out: The Worldwide Tragedy of Modern Christians Who Are Dying for Their Faith* (Dallas, TX: Word, 1997), 99.

[23] James and Marti Hefley, *By Their Blood: Christian Martyrs from the Twentieth Century and Beyond* (3rd edn.; Grand Rapids, MI: Baker, 2004), 117–20.

[24] Obed Minchakpu, "Chronic Violence Claims 2000 Lives," *Christianity Today* 46:1 (Jan. 7, 2002), p. 23.

[25] "Swiss-Based Rights Group Helps Buy Freedom of 1,050 Slaves in Sudan," *Los Angeles Times* (January 29, 1999), A 14. See also, Allen D. Hertzke, *Freeing God's Children: The Unlikely Alliance for Global Human Rights* (Lanham, MD: Rowman & Littlefield, 2004), 237–300, especially 239–45 on Khartoum's policy of forced Islamization.

[26] David J. Maxwell, "The Spirit and the Scapular: Pentecostal and Catholic Interactions in Northern Nyanga District, Zimbabwe in the 1950s and early 1960s," *Journal of Southern African Studies* 23.2 (June 1997), 298.

[27] Don Stephens, *Trial by Trial* (Eugene, OR: Harvest House, 1985).

[28] Tertullian, *Apology* 50.

Section II

AFRICA

5

The Scandal and the Glory of the Cross

ARCHBISHOP JOHN ONAIYEKAN

1. Introduction

We live in a world where suffering is most unpopular. Nobody
wants to be on the receiving end of it. And yet, all around us we are
bombarded daily with news of all kinds of suffering and tragedy.
Natural disasters and man-made tragedies fill our news media.
All kinds of pains are inflicted on poor hapless victims, sometimes
unintended but very often by design through the wickedness of
fellow human beings. Injustice and oppression continue to cause
a lot of avoidable suffering among peoples and nations. The
modern mass media, which seems to have a predilection for bad
news, keeps these tragic events constantly before our minds and
attention.

The church of God is in the world even though she does not
belong to the world. If the world is full of suffering, the church
cannot be exempt from it. She is by the very nature of things part
of this phenomenon of suffering. It is therefore quite appropriate
that this International Charismatic Consultation should decide to
focus on the theme of the suffering church. I thank the organizers
for giving me the honor of being part of this consultation. I thank
especially those who have made my participation possible through
their sacrifice and generous contribution.

What I intend to share with you are simple reflections from
my perspective of faith and life. I do not intend to go into deep
theological or exegetical speculations. I am sure many of you
here have other and better opportunities to read such material
elsewhere. I believe it is more important that we have the feeling
for the theme and especially how it is relevant to the world of

our days and the church in our times. My point of departure is obviously where I come from. I am a Catholic Archbishop and I serve the Church in Nigeria as Archbishop of the Federal Capital Abuja. These two dimensions, Catholic and Nigerian, will obviously affect my approach to the topic.

I shall begin with some biblical foundation, with brief references to both the Old and the New Testament materials. Then I will move on to some simple theological reflections drawn from these biblical references. Finally, I will show how some of these biblical and theological insights have impacted the life of the church throughout Christian history, up to contemporary times. I hope to conclude on a positive note indicating how suffering in the church is an expression and part of the redemptive sacrifice of Christ.

2. Suffering in the Old Testament

For a biblical discussion of suffering, there is no better place to start than the beginning: the book of Genesis. "In the beginning, God made heaven and earth" by his free decision. He spoke and everything came to be. God looked at everything that he created, and it was all very good. But almost immediately after that, in the third chapter, our attention is drawn to the mysterious entrance of evil into a creation that God made "very good." The story of the serpent in the Garden of Eden is a parable of the mystery of evil in the world created good by a good God. Evil will always remain a mystery, especially for whoever believes in a God that is good and just. Ancient Hebrew faith clearly rejected the position of their neighbors which "explained" evil in terms of a rival divine Principle in an eternal combat with the Principle of Good. Rather, if there is any response at all to this dilemma of evil in a world created good, it is in the story of the Fall, which presents suffering in this world as punishment for the sins of our first parents. This was more or less the main thrust of the thinking of the Old Testament. If there is suffering in the world, it must be because there is sin. Sometimes, the suffering is believed to have been inherited from one generation to the other. This is expressed in the common saying, polemically quoted by the prophets:

The fathers have eaten unripe grapes,
And the children's teeth are set on edge.
(Ezek. 18:2; cf. Jer. 31:30)

Even the historical problems and tragedies of the nation of Israel were often explained in terms of infidelity to God. The basic concept of the covenant is that when the people are faithful, things go well with them, but if they refused to be faithful, God punishes them, either directly or through their enemies.

Although this explanation was generally accepted, the fact that innocent and just people sometimes suffer constantly posed not only a theological problem but a dramatic human difficulty. The book of Job takes up this issue head on. The just man at times suffers not because of his sins but because God has his own plans. The book of Job, at a deeper level, can be seen as a reflection of the history of Israel whose sufferings are part and parcel of God's plan for humanity.

3. *Ave Crux! Spes Unica!*: Suffering in the New Testament

When on one occasion Jesus was presented with a case of a man born blind, he was asked: "Who has sinned, this man or his parents, that he should be born blind?" The underlying assumption is that tragedies like being born blind must be the result of sin. Jesus took the opportunity to teach the capital lesson that sin and suffering may not necessarily have a causal link with respect to individual persons. He replied, "Neither this man nor his parents have sinned." Why then was he born blind? The answer is most enlightening: that the glory of God might be made manifest. We need not go now into how the sufferer sees the glory of God in his or her own predicament. But this answer of Jesus continues to be the perennial answer of the Christian to the dilemma of the just sufferer.

In recent times, the continent of Africa has been afflicted by the great tragedy of the spread of HIV/AIDS. For some time, the perception was rife that this disease was God's punishment on people of low moral character. This is still one of the reasons why stigmatization has remained a major problem in adequately addressing this great pandemic. People still ask the same old question: How did you get infected? Now of course we should know better. There are many infected by the virus through legitimate sexual activity, e.g. the innocent spouse of a careless husband or wife. There are also the cases of careless medical practices, not to speak of those infected while trying to help others.

The teaching of Jesus is reflected most graphically in the example of his own life, especially in his death on the cross. Here was a clear case of a just man suffering for no fault of his own. But it is also an expression of God's bringing his glory out of such suffering. John's Gospel presents the death of Jesus as his hour of glory. Jesus hangs on the cross so that, lifted up, he might draw all men and women to himself. The Johannine record of the passion story shows Jesus fully in charge of everything. Pilate would have no power over him unless it was given to him from above. Even his death was a deliberate surrendering of his spirit to the Father. By the cross, Jesus redeemed the world. That is why in our church, we sing in the liturgy of Good Friday: *Ave Crux, spes unica* ("O Cross, our only hope").

It is the cross of Calvary that gives a meaning to human suffering. That picture of the crucified Lord has become the center of our Christian faith. Paul insists very much on this, even though it was difficult for him to explain it to his audience. While the Greeks were looking for wisdom and the Jews seeking for signs, all Paul can give them is Jesus crucified, which is foolishness to the Greeks and a scandal for the Jews, but for those who believe, it is the wisdom and power of God. Paul's theology of the cross is profound and comprehensive. The Jewish nation was expecting the triumphant Messiah that would inaugurate the era of Israelite supremacy over the whole world. They were not expecting someone hanging on the cross like a criminal. That is why it was difficult to accept Jesus as the Messiah. When they asked him for a sign, he promised them the sign of Jonah, his rising from the dead after three days. The cross event will always be a scandal for those who expect a powerful demonstration of God's might. The cross shows us how the power of God is often expressed in the form of weakness and suffering. The Greeks, on their part, had no provisions in their philosophical system for a God that hangs on a cross. It was for them absolute foolishness. When Paul spoke to the intellectuals of the Aeropause in Athens, they listened with polite boredom and ended up dismissing him with, "We shall hear you another time" (Acts 17:32).

The cross and all that it means continues to challenge our system of human reasoning. It just does not make sense for God to allow his Son to hang on the cross. No wonder efforts have been made on several occasions to actually rewrite the story, beginning from some of the earliest apocryphal accounts to the Islamic version seeking to protect the prophet of God from undeserved punishment. But all such attempts will always remain futile. We cannot improve on God's plan. For Paul, it is precisely this Jesus crucified who is for those who believe the power and the wisdom of God. Faith gives us access to the power of the cross and light to see the wisdom of God in surrendering his Son for our sake. "For God so loved the world that he gave his only Son, so that everyone who believes in him may ... have eternal life" (John 3:16).

4. The Church and Suffering

The cross of Christ is therefore the very center of the Christian faith. Indeed it is the most powerful symbol of our religion. Jesus himself defined discipleship in terms of the cross: "If any want to become my followers, let them deny themselves and take up their cross daily and follow me" (Luke 9:23). Taking up the cross means nothing if it does not mean accepting suffering – and death if need be – for the sake of the kingdom. This has been the experience of the church from the beginning. The martyrs who suffered and died for their faith in Jesus were indeed "witnesses" to the cross of Christ. They, of course, contemplated the cross in the light of the resurrection and of a vivid conviction about the glorification of Christ and his imminent second coming. Paul says it all: "I consider that the sufferings of this present time are not worth comparing with the glory" (Rom. 8:18) that is reserved for those who love God. This is why the martyrs were eager to face death as the gateway to the glory of the resurrection. For them martyrdom was victory. The story of Ignatius of Antioch is very instructive in this regard, as he practically begged the Roman brethren to do nothing that would stop his mortal appointment with the lions of the coliseum. That is why the martyrs, in Christian iconography, are presented as carrying palm branches as symbols of victory.

Martyrdom did not have to lead to physical death. Many suffered untold hardship, witnessing to their faith, those whom we normally referred to as confessors throughout the history of the church, up to the present. There have always been martyrs and confessors who happily accept all manner of suffering for the sake of the Lord Jesus. In fact, the twentieth century is said to have been the century with the greatest number of martyrs. The age of martyrs has not ended at all.

We should note that sometimes the reasons for martyrdom are often unclear. Sometimes there is a mixed agenda at play, especially from the point of view of the persecutor. The Roman emperors and their agents killed many Christians for political reasons rather than religious. By their refusal to conform to the official religious practices of the empire, Christians were seen as subversive elements in the state. Sometimes, too, religious persecution is inflicted for religious reasons by rival religious organizations. Even in our days, there are still instances of this. This shows the need for clarity in situations of presumed religious persecution. The church will always need to constantly assure herself that she is really carrying the cross of the Lord Jesus Christ, and not some other cross.

5. *Fuga Crucis*

It is natural to try to avoid suffering, but it is not Christian. When the Lord Jesus informed his disciples about his impending suffering and death and resurrection, Peter, the head of the apostles, remonstrated with him: "Lord that must not happen to you." Peter had good intentions. He could not imagine his Lord and master undergoing such terrible pains. The response of the Lord was "Get behind me, Satan." Jesus saw in Peter's reaction the efforts of the Evil One to divert him from his mission. He further remarked to Peter, "You are thinking not as God thinks but as human beings do" (Matt. 16:21–23). During the passion we are told that almost all his disciples abandoned him and took refuge in safer places. Even Peter, who did not run away, "followed afar off" and denied the Lord when the threat to himself became real (Matt. 26:58, 69–75).

The denial of martyrdom is a constant temptation for the church of God. There are records during the persecutions in the early church of many who apostatized in order to avoid the pains of martyrdom. Church history tells us of the different categories of apostates, ranging from those who actually denied their faith and sacrificed to the idols to those who merely allowed the persecutors to believe that they had done so, by simply signing a document to that effect. In each case, it was still a question of reluctance to accept the cross.

On a different note, the history of the church also includes great temptations to build a kingdom for Christ in this world, contrary to his assertion, "My kingdom is not of this world" (John 18:36). The temptation of triumphalism has always been with the church all through the ages. We recall here the examples of questionable collaboration or collusion for power between church leaders and civil authorities, between popes and emperors, between kings and bishops, often leading to a situation where the church loses the sign of the cross. In fact, where the church becomes politically powerful, it often has difficulty proclaiming the clear message of the gospel of Christ. Almost invariably, wherever the church is "married" to civil powers, it is often the civil powers that use the church, and not the other way round. The church has therefore to be constantly on her guard not to allow anything to stand in the way of her ability to freely and coherently preach the gospel. This is not to say that she should constantly seek to antagonize civil authorities. Indeed there is the need to accompany them, like *Mater et Magister* (Mother and Teacher).

Today there are other ways in which the church might be tempted to run from the cross. There is the pressure on the church to adopt contemporary fashions, especially in the area of social morality. The recent contemporary debate within and between the churches about issues of sexual morality like contraception, abortion, divorce, and homosexuality are cases in point. Whatever position we take on these matters, we need to assure ourselves that we are not offering the gospel *a bon marche*, at a cheap price. Christianity without the cross cannot be genuine. Another phenomenon that needs to be watched carefully is the emphasis on prosperity and material well-being in certain churches, which rely heavily on miracles and visions. It is difficult to understand those who tell their followers "Believe in Jesus, and everything will go well with you." What I see from the gospels is quite different. Unfortunately, such a message is very attractive and it does often attract large crowds. Many go all over the place looking for miracles, seeking to throw away the cross that God has placed on their shoulders. While we are not denying the reality of miracles and the fact that the Lord Jesus has come to carry away our pains, we cannot seriously sustain the concept of the church of God that is there only to save people from physical pains and difficulties.

6. Redemptive Suffering

If suffering and pain are necessary dimensions of the life of the church, it is precisely because she is the continuation of Christ who redeemed us through his suffering and death. Catholic theology, especially since the Second Vatican Council, at times speaks of the church as a "sacrament" of salvation. By this we mean that the church is a sign and an instrument of what Jesus is all about. In the church, by the grace of Jesus, humanity is helped to make sense of life's inevitable suffering. Living in solidarity with those who suffer, the church shares their lot and thereby lightens their burdens.

At the same time, the church never stops caring for those who suffer, offering healing where there are wounds and witnessing to the loving care of the Lord Jesus himself. That is why the church will always be involved in programs of health institutions or helping those who are in physical and emotional distress of whatever form. The Lord Jesus proclaimed in the synagogue of Nazareth, following the prophesy of Isaiah, that he had come to feed the hungry, give sight to the blind, liberate those who are captives, and generally proclaim the Lord's year of favor, especially to the poor (Luke 4:14ff.). It goes without saying therefore that the church must never put herself in a situation where she inflicts pain on people, either directly or indirectly, be it by commission or by omission. We need to be constantly on our guard never to be the cause of pain for anyone.

Yet after we have done all we can, there will always be pain and suffering in the church and in the world around us. This is all the more reason why we should always be seen to be carrying the good news that no one needs to suffer in vain. In particular, the suffering of an innocent person can always be redemptive, if accepted with the right spirit.

7. Conclusion

Throughout this chapter I have been speaking of "the church" in general. While I acknowledge the non-negligible differences among the various traditions within the wide range of communities that go under the name of Christian, I believe our topic is one of those about which it is easiest for us to speak one language. This has been demonstrated by the fruitful ecumenical experiences of the churches in South Africa under Apartheid, or of Christians persecuted by the German Nazis. Suffering is a reality common to all humanity and therefore to all Christian traditions. The world of our day is more and more looking at the church as one entity and has great expectations of those of us who claim to have the redeeming message of Christ. Suffering is a powerful point of contact where the church can impact on the world of our day and make the message of Christ relevant and effective. There are already too many agents of the evil one wreaking havoc and causing pain in the world. The church should have its hands full responding to the needs of our world, which is very much in need of the salvation of the Lord Jesus Christ.

Section III

THE MIDDLE EAST

6

Persecution of Christians in the Muslim World

PATRICK SOOKHDEO

In the post-communist era, Islam has emerged as a main persecutor of Christians around the world. Christians have been suffering to varying degrees under Islam since its inception, but at the start of the twenty-first century, persecution of Christians by Muslims seems to be on the increase across most of the Muslim world.

While most Muslim states have signed United Nations declarations on human rights and religious freedoms, they usually add caveats stating these are accepted as long as they do not contradict Islamic law. Shari'a however, is inherently discriminatory to non-Muslims, excluding them from any position of power in the state and ensuring their subservience to Islam. Most Muslims accept it as natural that non-Muslims should face restrictions on their right to manifest their religion, especially in public. Most Muslims also accept it as natural that Muslims should face restrictions on their individual right to choose their faith. Shari'a strongly influences the thinking and behavior of most Muslims, even when it is not the only law of the land or not mentioned in legislation at all.

Contrary to internationally accepted norms of human rights and religious freedoms, various Muslim states place limits on Christian public worship and on Christian outreach to Muslims. There are no reciprocal limits on Muslim public worship or on Muslim proselytization efforts. In some areas, Christian places of worship are closed or destroyed with impunity, physical attacks on Christians are perpetrated. Christians are arrested and tortured, expelled from their homes and villages, and forced into exile. Christians are discriminated against in political representation, education, and employment.

Christians face a variety of situations and attitudes in Muslim-majority countries. The experience of Christians in stable moderate states like Jordan is quite different from that of Christians in Islamist Iran, in Wahhabi Saudi Arabia, or in Islamist Sudan.

Western media and governments often seem to ignore the plight of Christians being persecuted in Muslim states. This may be a result of their endeavors to maintain good relations with oil-rich Muslim states and their concern not to upset their own increasingly large and vocal Muslim minorities. Non-radical Muslims in the West hardly ever raise their voices to condemn atrocities carried out against Christians in the name of Islam. It is imperative that Christians in the West know the truth on this issue, speak out in public about it, help their suffering fellow-Christians, and demand action to stop such persecution.

1. Christians in Muslim-Majority Societies

1.1 Ancient Christian churches

These ancient churches survive from the pre-Islamic New Testament and early church eras mainly in the Middle East. They include the Coptic, Ethiopian, Syrian/Jacobite, Assyrian/Chaldean, Armenian, Maronite, Greek Orthodox, and Greek Catholic churches. After the Islamic conquest of their majority Christian lands, they were tolerated as second-class *dhimmi* subjects of the dominant Muslim state, living under severe limitations. They are still marginalized and face various restrictions today. As a result, many are emigrating to the West, and the proportion of Christians in the population of their countries is diminishing fast.

1.2 Modern national churches

These are the fruit of modern-day missionary efforts (Roman Catholic and Protestant) in the last 350 years – especially in sub-Saharan Africa, the Indian subcontinent, and Indonesia. The background of these church members is mostly animist religions,

Hinduism, and Buddhism. They face growing attacks by militant Islamist groups today.

1.3 Converts from Islam

A growing number of Christians in Muslim countries today come from an Islamic background. The largest such group is in Indonesia, but there are growing groups in Algeria, Iran and other lands. These are the most vulnerable Christians, as under Shari'a law they are considered apostates from Islam, deserving the death sentence.

1.4 Expatriate Christian workers

Working especially in oil-rich Saudi Arabia and the Arab Gulf states, expatriate Christian workers originate mainly from Southeast Asia and Asia-Pacific countries. Others come from Africa, Arab lands, and the West. These people are not citizens, have lesser rights, and are very dependent on the goodwill of the authorities for permission to reside and work. Open Christian worship is often restricted; in Saudi Arabia, for example, no Christian worship or symbols are allowed at all. These Christians can face quick arrest, imprisonment, and deportation for the practice of their faith.

2. Root Causes of Persecution

The first generation of Muslims was an endangered minority in the non-Muslim world it set out to conquer. This created a sense of defensiveness and fear of being overwhelmed by the conquered communities that persist today in spite of centuries of Muslim dominance. Aggressive mistrust of non-Muslims has carried down over the generations. Even in modern secular Muslim states, Islam and Shari'a have such a hold on public perceptions that attitudes of contempt and practices of discrimination against Christians and other non-Muslims are accepted as normal.

2.1 Traditional Muslim attitudes to dhimmis

Christians ruled by Muslims had the legal status of *dhimmis*, tolerated and given limited protection of person and property in return for submitting to Muslim rule. However, their status was that of subordinate inferior minorities, outside the full community of the theocratic Islamic state. Shari'a accords only limited communal rights to non-Muslim minorities who must live strictly within the limits it sets. Discrimination on grounds of religion is inherent in Shari'a, which cannot integrate modern concepts of individual religious freedom. *Dhimmis* had no political rights and had to humbly accept their subordinate place in the Islamic state. They were marginalized and shut out from power. Subjugation and humiliation were expressed in the payment of the poll tax (*jizya*), and in appropriate humble behavior toward Muslims.

Behind these restrictions lay the conviction that Muslims are unquestionably far superior to all other religious groups. Only Muslims can exercise political rule. The God-willed relationship between Muslims and *dhimmi* communities is that of dominant versus subordinate, expressed in the subservience and public humiliation of the *dhimmis* who are seen as weak and shameful. Contempt to all *dhimmis,* including Christians, is an expression of the God-decreed superiority of Islam.

Shari'a restrictions on *dhimmis* included the prohibition of public displays of Christian symbols. They were required to dress in distinctive fashion so as not to be mistaken for Muslims. *Dhimmis* were not allowed to carry arms, have public positions over Muslims, or insult Islam in any way. They could not give evidence in court against Muslims and were not permitted to marry Muslim women. They could not build new churches except by special permission from the head of state. These Shari'a restrictions still influence public and government attitudes to Christians even in states with secular constitutions.

According to Shari'a, all non-Muslims are potentially subject to violent jihad, which becomes operative when they break the terms of their *dhimmi* covenant by seeking equality with Muslims, by being arrogant towards Muslims, or by conspiring with the enemies of Islam.

These attitudes have been inculcated into the general Muslim psyche over centuries of Islamic dominance. Christian demands for a secular state with equal rights for all citizens regardless of religion are seen by many Muslims as a rebellion against God's law and a breaking of the *dhimmi*-protection pact, opening the way for persecution and violence.

2.2 *The rising power of Islamism*

The rise of secular and socialist forms of nationalism at the end of the colonial period brought some temporary reprieve from traditional Muslim hostility. There were great hopes of forging new national identities across religious and ethnic divides. Early gains, however, were soon lost in the growing tide of Islamism that revived the deep hatred of Muslims for the Christian West. This in turn fuelled the hatred of Muslim populations against the local Christians in their midst. Islamism redefined Christians as not being protected "people of the book," but rejecters of Islam, pact breakers, or even infidels. Christians are now charged with being western collaborators, western spies and a fifth column for the West in the heart of Islam. Conspiracy theories abound that turn Christians into scapegoats.

These attitudes result in the erosion of hard-won freedoms from the colonial- and independence-era past. Discrimination, persecution and attacks by armed jihadist militias on Christians are on the increase in many Muslim states.

The Islamist program includes the following:

1. The full Islamization of Muslim-majority states by destabilizing secular regimes and replacing them with Islamic state systems based on Shari'a. Iran and Sudan are examples of countries where this has already taken place. Algeria and Egypt are examples of countries where violent attempts have so far been thwarted, but the danger remains.

2. The implementation of Shari'a. There is a widespread and often violent agitation for this in most Muslim states and in countries with large Muslim minorities, especially in the Third World. The call for the imposition of Shari'a heralds a return to the traditional *dhimmi* status of Christians

and the end of their equality as citizens before the law. Once introduced, Shari'a ensures the dominance of Islam over non-Muslims, who quickly lose their equal status and become second-rate citizens in their own countries.

3. Destabilizing the border areas of Islam to expand the domain of Islam. This is carried out by radical Islamist movements, supported by Muslim oil-rich states supplying funds, recruits, and safe havens. Examples include the Philippines, Thailand, Nigeria, Sudan, Indonesia, and Côte d'Ivoire. Rebellions are fomented among Muslim minorities. Attacks are initiated against Christians in regions with Christian majorities. Christian minorities are attacked, ethnically cleansed, or forcibly Islamized. The call for jihad in these border areas results in much emotional support across the Muslim world, and volunteers and finances pour in to support the Holy Cause. The borders of unbelief are constantly being rolled back in favor of Islam.

3. Christian Responses to Pressures

Christians in Muslim lands face an identity crisis as they seek to be loyal to their nations while facing persecution by dominant Islam. Christian attempts to influence internal politics or to seek western pressure on their governments often backfire, as they "prove" to Muslims that Christians are arrogant, forget their rightful subservient place in Muslim societies, are western collaborators, and must be taught a lesson. These dilemmas cause many Christians to try and emigrate to the West. Others passively accept their fate, and some convert to Islam to escape it.

4. Sources of Persecution

4.1 The state

In some countries it is the state and its organs that persecute Christians through unjust laws, restrictions on church activities, arbitrary arrest, torture, and imprisonment. An extreme example is Saudi Arabia where all non-Muslim religious practice is banned. In several Muslim states such as Saudi Arabia, Qatar, Iran, and Sudan, the law specifies the death sentence for a Muslim who converts to another religion such as Christianity. In Sudan, the Islamic government for decades pursued a ruthless policy of Arabizing and Islamizing the mainly non-Muslim and non-Arab south, resulting in millions of southerners, including Christians, being killed, and millions being internally displaced. In Iran, the government has severely restricted the activities of Protestants, closing several churches and Bible Society. Churches are forbidden to hold services in Farsi, the national language. Several Christian leaders have been abducted and killed, apparently by the secret services, and one convert from Islam has been executed.

4.2 Radical Islamist groups

In some states, vocal Islamists are pressuring governments to become more Islamic, implement Shari'a, and take a more negative stance towards Christians. Armed radical Islamist militias raid and attack Christians to reinstate Muslim superiority and dominance in all areas. In Indonesia, Egypt, Pakistan, and other states, this has been an ongoing and intensifying process. Governments are often unwilling to defend their Christian citizens because of the powerful influence of radical Islamists.

4.3 Communal and mob violence

Following incitement by radical preachers, mob violence has repeatedly erupted against Christians in various states where Christians had previously lived in relative peace with their Muslim neighbors. This has happened in Nigeria, Indonesia, and Egypt, among others.

4.4 The family

For converts from Islam to Christianity, their own close relatives are often a major source of persecution, which can range from eviction from the home to physical violence and even murder.

Usually there is a combination of elements working together to worsen the persecution of Christians. Traditional ingrained attitudes of contempt to Christians are widespread, opening the way for covert and open cooperation between political leaders, radical Islamists, and rabid anti-Christian preachers.

5. Types and Stages of Persecution

5.1 *Disinformation*

Disinformation about Christianity is widespread in the media and in mosques. Articles, radio and TV broadcasts, sermons and pamphlets often parody the Christian faith and rob Christians of their good reputation. Offensive language and insults about Christians are often heard in public discourse. This includes repetition of traditional Muslim views of Christians as contemptible, impure, unbelievers, and second-class citizens. Unfounded accusations of bribing Muslims to convert them to Christianity, or of Christians being agents of western powers, are accepted as fact by a Muslim public, influenced by centuries of negative Muslim attitudes to Christianity. Disinformation creates mistrust and ill will, and it paves the way for institutionalized discrimination.

5.2 *Discrimination*

Public opinion constantly fed with disinformation results in discrimination against Christians, which relegates them to second-class citizenship status with inferior legal, social, political, and economic rights compared to the Muslim majority. Discrimination is widespread and practiced in education, employment, the judicial system, and allocation of resources. Official and unofficial bureaucratic hurdles are placed before Christians seeking their constitutional rights. The inbuilt bias of the judicial systems in most Muslim states makes appeals and complaints ineffective and often counterproductive.

Christians often find it difficult to get jobs in the civil service, security forces, and higher education. Christians may be excluded from the political system, following the generally accepted Islamic concept that non-Muslims must never have authority over Muslims. Christians often do not get merited promotion. Some state constitutions reserve the highest offices for Muslims. Legal discrimination based on Shari'a means that in some states the witness of a Christian in court is worth less than that of a Muslim, and compensation accorded by courts is less for Christians than for Muslims. Blasphemy and apostasy laws are sometimes used to threaten Christians with the death penalty or long terms of imprisonment.

In some states linguistic discrimination is used against Christians. In Iran it is not allowed to conduct Christian services in the national language, Farsi. In Malaysia, there were legal efforts to forbid Christians the use of the word for God and several other religious terms in the national language, Bahasa Malaysia, which were to be reserved only for use by Muslims.

5.3 Outright persecution

The effects of disinformation and discrimination are cumulative and mean that persecution can be practiced without public outcry or opposition. Persecution is expressed by repression and violence.

5.4 Repression

In many Muslim states it is difficult or impossible to repair churches or to build new ones. Churches may be closed down. Christian schools, hospitals, clinics, and orphanages may be obstructed by nationalization or by bureaucracy and legal hurdles. It might be difficult or impossible to buy land to build churches or Christian institutions. Christians often face threats, intimidation, loss of employment, and other forms of harassment.

5.5 *Violence*

In certain contexts, violence is perpetrated on Christians by organized raids of shootings, killings, and property destruction. These raids may be implemented by Islamist extremists, security forces, paramilitaries, and by mobs incited by preachers. Christians are killed and wounded; Christian churches, schools, clinics, and homes are burnt down or bulldozed; Christian property is looted. Christians are arbitrarily arrested, beaten, jailed, and tortured. These violent activities aim at humiliating Christians, turning them into an oppressed underclass, at ethnically cleansing areas of high Christian concentration, and at forcing Christians to emigrate.

6. Some Examples of Persecution[1]

6.1 *Indonesia*

Following independence, an inclusive Pancasila state philosophy established a fairly tolerant modern state identity. However, as Suharto's grip on power diminished in the 1990s, he used conservative Islam against the demands for democracy and human rights. This fueled an Islamic revival and the growth of radical Islamist groups demanding an Islamic state under Shari'a. Islamist militias were formed such as Laskar Jihad and Jema'a Islamiyya.

The loss of mainly Christian East Timor (1999–2002) was a source of deep shame to the Muslim population and to the security forces in Indonesia. It generated a desire for revenge against the West that had supported East Timor's demands for independence. Indonesian Christians were accused of separatist sentiments, secularism, and of being allies of the Christian West against Muslim Indonesia.

Central Sulawesi, the Malukus, and Papua have been infiltrated by thousands of radical militias including foreign mujahidin. Militant Islamists have engaged in jihad and ethnic cleansing against Christian regions. Laskar Jihad, Jema'a Islamiyya, and other militants attacked Christian villages and churches, resulting in destruction, murder, ethnic cleansing, rape, and forced conversions.

The military and police forces in these regions were often complicit in violence against Christians. In the Malukus, from 1999 to 2002, anti-Christian violence resulted in at least 10,000 Christians killed and 500,000 displaced. In Central Sulawesi, from 1998 to 2002, violence resulted in 2,500 Christians killed and 50,000 displaced.[2] A peace accord in 2002 disarmed the Christians but not the jihadists. Tensions and sporadic violence have continued. In both regions Christian churches, institutions, and whole villages were destroyed. Forcible conversions of Christians to Islam, including forced circumcisions were carried out, and Christian women were raped.

6.2 Nigeria

In modern Nigeria, Muslims and Christians are almost equal in number, but unevenly distributed. There are three belts: the Muslim-majority north, the Christian-majority south, and the middle belt where Christians and Muslims are equally distributed. Ethnic, religious, and regional differences combine to form an explosive mixture.

Northern Nigeria has a history of Muslim jihads and caliphates (Sokoto, Borno). Modern Nigerian politics has been mainly dominated by Muslims since the 1960s. The military dictatorship, consisting mainly of northern Muslim officers, manipulated Islam to retain power and started the Islamization process.

The rapid spread of Christianity and the election of a Christian, Olusegun Obasanjo, to the presidency in 1999 caused Muslims to fear losing their supremacy. This was coupled with a growing Islamist infiltration that further radicalized the Muslim population. The imposition of full Shari'a in northern and central Nigerian states (Zamfara first in 1999, now twelve states), was seen as license to discriminate against Christians. There has been much inflammatory preaching resulting in mob violence and riots. Many Christians were killed and injured. Christian churches, property, and villages were destroyed, and there has been an internal displacement of Christians. Muslim leaders stated that Shari'a would not apply to non-Muslims, but in reality gender segregation, Islamic dress, and other Islamic practices are being forced on them. Shari'a effectively turned northern Christians into second-rate, marginalized citizens.

During Obasanjo's first four years in office (1999–2003) over 10,000 people, mainly Christians, were killed in the anti-Christian violence.[3]

6.3 Egypt

Historically Islam was the religion of state and the Christian Copts (10–16 percent of the population) were *dhimmis*, who see their history as a long martyrdom under Islam. From the end of the nineteenth century to the 1920s a consensus emerged around a secular-liberal national identity. Christians were heavily involved in the freedom struggle against the British. This was the Golden Age for the Copts. The consensus soon broke due to the rise of pan-Arabism and Islamism; Islam became central to the Egyptian national identity, and the Copts were marginalized, even though the constitution offered theoretical equality.

Islamists saw Copts as allied to the imperialist West and to western plots against Islam. Demands for equality were seen as breaking the *dhimmi* pact, constituting an arrogant attitude that must be punished. Copts have also been accused of harboring separatist sentiments.

Coptic trust lands were confiscated by Nasser and not returned when Islamic trust lands were returned to Muslim endowments, but were instead then seized by the Ministry of Islamic Affairs. Christians face great difficulties in obtaining permits to repair and build churches; until 1999 presidential approval was needed. Issuing repair permits has now devolved to local governments, which often obstruct the process through bureaucratic hurdles. Islam is taught in all state schools to all pupils, but Christianity cannot be taught to Christian children. Textbooks denigrate Christianity. Coptic teachers cannot teach Arabic. No Christian university is allowed. Government media widely disseminates Islam, including messages disparaging Christianity, but hardly includes any Christian message. There is an asymmetry in conversions – Copts are encouraged to convert to Islam, but Muslims who convert to Christianity face harassment and severe persecution.

Copts are restricted in admission to the military, police, medical schools, and high public office; there no Christian governors, ambassadors, or presidents of universities.

There has been a rising tide of violence by radical Islamists against Copts: riots, destruction of property, killings, abductions, and forced conversions. Since 1990, over 1,300 Copts have been killed in Egypt by Muslims.[4]

6.4 Saudi Arabia

The Saudi government enforces Wahhabi Islam to the exclusion of all others. It denies religious freedom to non-Muslims and vigorously enforces prohibitions against their public expression. Abuses are extensive and affect every aspect of an individual's life. No church buildings are allowed in Saudi Arabia. Foreign clergy are not allowed into the country. As an example, no priests are allowed to minister to the religious needs of over 600,000 Filipino workers, 90 percent of whom are Catholic. Christians are forced to conduct their activities in secret to escape detection by the religious police (*muttawa'*). Bibles and crosses may be confiscated, particularly Bibles in the Arabic language. Christians are prohibited from any form of public worship. Private worship is often condoned nowadays, but sometimes leads to persecution. House church leaders and believers have been harassed, arrested, abused, beaten by religious police, imprisoned, and finally deported. Filipino, Ethiopian, and other developing-world Christians are especially targeted, as their governments are seen as too weak to protect them. In the summer of 2001 there was a crackdown in Jeddah on a loose network of private Christian "home fellowships." All were arrested, detained without charge, and confined to harsh prison conditions and repeated interrogations. All were deported by March 2002 after months in prison.[5]

6.5 Sudan

Of Sudan's thirty million people, 65 percent are Muslim, living mainly in the north and speaking Arabic. Twenty-three percent are Christian, and the remainder animists. Christians and animists live mainly in the south and central parts of Sudan. Following independence, central governments dominated by the Arab-Muslim elite increasingly tried to Arabize and Islamize the mainly African Christian and animist south. This led to the civil war that has been raging since 1983 following attempts to apply Shari'a in the south, which caused southerners to rebel.

The 1989 coup resulted in an Islamist regime that declared a jihad against its opponents in the south, intensifying the fighting and the suffering of the non-Muslim population. It is estimated that the civil war has caused the death of two to three million people and led to the displacement of a further four to five million.[6] Vast areas of the south and of the Nuba Mountains have been devastated, villages razed and burnt down and their inhabitants killed, injured, or forced to flee. Many atrocities have been reported, including the ethnic cleansing of the Nuba Mountain population, aerial bombardment of civilians and of humanitarian facilities, deliberate denial of international assistance, and the abduction and enslavement of women and children as well as widespread rape. Large refugee camps have sprouted around the capital, Khartoum, where southerners, mainly Christians, live in the most primitive accommodations with almost no state or municipal services.

While the recently signed peace treaties bring hope for a better future, only time will tell whether they will be really implemented.

6.6 Pakistan

The Islamic Republic of Pakistan was founded in 1947 as a home-land for the Muslims of the Indian subcontinent. The Christian community numbers some three percent of the population and is mainly descended from lower castes of Hindus converted to Christianity. They form the poorest class and do menial jobs. Eighty percent of bonded laborers in Pakistan are Christian. Poverty and discrimination restrict their access to education, employment, and to justice in the courts.

The notorious "Blasphemy Law" decrees death for anyone who even accidentally "defiles" the name of Muhammad, and life imprisonment for anyone who desecrates a copy of the

Qur'an. This law has been abused by Muslims seeking to settle personal grudges against Christians. There is no penalty for false accusations of blasphemy, and law courts have a tendency to believe Muslims rather than Christians. Many Christians have been accused of blasphemy, imprisoned for years awaiting judgment, and condemned to death. Some were finally released on appeal to higher courts.[7]

Following the American attack on Afghanistan in 2001, armed militant Islamists have attacked churches and other Christian institutions and murdered many Christians, including women and children. In the year 2002 alone, more than forty Christians were killed and more than one hundred injured in such attacks.[8]

These brief descriptions demonstrate the apparent increase of persecution of Christians in much of the Muslim world. Such treatment of Christians in these Muslim-majority countries deserves the attention and thoughtful concerted action of human rights efforts worldwide, as well as the aid and prayers of the Christian church.

Endnotes

[1] Editors' note: Throughout this chapter, Patrick Sookhdeo draws upon "The Persecuted Church" Lausanne Occasional Paper No. 32 (no city: Lausanne Committee for World Evangelization, 2005), 17–23, which was produced by the Issue Group on this topic at the 2004 Forum for World Evangelization in Pattaya, Thailand, September 29 – October 5, 2004. While the whole Issue Group participated in its preparation, Patrick Sookhdeo was the primary writer of this Lausanne Occasional Paper.

[2] United States Commission On International Religious Freedom Report On Indonesia, May 2002, http://www.uscirf.gov (viewed October 21, 2003); Maluku, Global Security.org, http://www.globalsecurity.org/military/world/war/maluku.htm (viewed September 9, 2005); Human Rights Watch, Indonesia, 14.9 (C), December 2002, http://www.hrw.org/reports/2002/indonesia/indonesia1102.pdf (viewed September 9, 2005); Ian Freestone, Maluku Support Project, Jihad in Central Sulawesi, 4/12/01, Radio National Perspective, http://www.abc.net.au/rn/talks/perspective/stories/s432309.htm (viewed September 9, 2005); Jeff M. Sellers, "Religious Cleansing: What you can do to help persecuted Christians in Indonesia," *Christianity Today* 47:4 (April 15, 2003), 98, http://www.christianitytoday.com/ct/2003/004/27.98.html (viewed September 9, 2005).

3 Obed Minchakpu, "Eye for an Eye for an Eye – Are Nigeria's deadly religious riots really about religion?", *Christianity Today*, July 2004; Aminu Abubakar, ReliefWeb, "Christian-Muslim violence displaces 2,000: Nigerian Red Cross", Source: Agence France-Presse, June 11, 2004; "The Talibanization Of Nigeria: Radical Islam, Extremist Shari'a Law And Religious Freedom", http://freedomhouse.org/religion/pdfdocs/Nigeria%20Report.pdf (viewed September 9, 2005); Annual Report Of The United States Commission On International Religious Freedom May 2005, http://www.uscirf.gov/countries/publications/currentreport/2005annualRpt.pdf#page=123 (viewed September 9, 2005).

4 "End Human Rights Abuses against Copts in Egypt", Petition to The UN Secretary, US Congress, United Nations High Commissioner for Human Rights, http://www.petitiononline.com/coptic/petition.html, viewed September 12, 2005; Jeff. M. Sellers, "Heightened Hostilities: What you can do to help persecuted Christians in Egypt," *Christianity Today* 46:13 (December 9, 2002), 58, http://www.christianitytoday.com/ct/2002/013/36.58.html (viewed September 12, 2002).

5 Julie Stahl, "Saudi Arabia Cracks Down On Christians In Jeddah", CNSNews.com, Jerusalem Bureau Chief , August 2, 2001, http://www.cnsnews.com/ViewForeignBureaus.asp?Page=//ForeignBureaus//archive//200108//For20010802g.html (viewed September 9, 2005); Julie Stahl, "Christians Jailed In Saudi Arabia Ask for US Help", CNSNews.com, Jerusalem Bureau Chief, September 7, 2001, http://www.cnsnews.com/ViewForeignBureaus.asp?Page=/ForeignBureaus/archive/200109/For20010907d.html (viewed September 9, 2005).

6 United States Commission On International Religious Freedom Report On Sudan, April 2002, http://www.uscirf.gov (viewed September 9, 2005); "About 6 million people internally displaced in Sudan (2005)", Global IDP, Sudan, http://www.db.idpproject.org/Sites/IdpProjectDb/idpSurvey.nsf/wViewCountries/E8DA1C451E4B4EF2C12568E7004CDE81 (viewed September 12, 2005).

7 "Pakistani Christian on Death Row Released after Appeal to Supreme Court", *Christian Solidarity Worldwide*, August 15, 2002; "Blasphemy Laws and Intellectual Freedom in Pakistan," *South Asian Voice* (August 2002), http://india_resource.tripod.cpm/ifpakistan.html, viewed October 21, 2002; "SC acquits blasphemy accused", *DAWN*, Internet edition, August 16, 2002, http://www.dawn.com/2002/08/16/top11.htm (viewed October 21, 2002); "Christian minorities in Pakistan: little freedom and rising Islamic pressure", AsiaNews.it (September 30, 2004), http://www.asianews.it/view.php?l=en&art=1583 (viewed September 9, 2005); "Anti-blasphemy law: harassment and violence for all religions alike", AsiaNews.it (September 30, 2004), http://www.asianews.it/view.php?l=en&art=1582 (viewed September 9, 2005).

8 "Seven Killed in Pakistan Shooting", Associated Press, Wednesday, September 25, 2002, http://www.foxnews.com/story/0,2933,64006,00.html

(viewed September 9, 2005; "18 March 2003 Update From HCJB World Radio" (Mission Network News/Assist), http://jmm.aaa.net.au/articles/10773.htm (viewed September 12, 2005); Barbara G. Baker, "Terrorists attack Pakistani church service", Human Rights Without Frontiers Int. http://www.hrwf.net/html/pakistan2002.HTM (viewed September 12, 2005).

7

An Orthodox Response to Persecution
The Situation in the Middle East

DESPINA D. PRASSAS

As anyone knows who picks up a newspaper or listens to the news on the radio or television, our world can be a dangerous place in which to live. And within our world, the church, in particular, is not immune from the danger that surrounds it. Jesus' own prophetic words in Matthew 5:11–12 guarantee that suffering will take place among Christians: "Blessed are you when people revile you and persecute you and utter all kinds of evil against you falsely on my account. Rejoice and be glad, for your reward is great in heaven, for in the same way they persecuted the prophets who were before you" (NOAB). Persecution of the Christian church has been a defining characteristic throughout the last 2,000 years, and the Christian churches of today are no different.

From the earliest centuries of Christianity, the followers of Jesus have been persecuted.[1] These persecutions have taken many forms, from sporadic, localized persecutions characterized by the first-century Roman emperor, Nero, to the well-organized, comprehensive persecutions of Diocletian that took place in the late third and early fourth centuries. While there are always reasons for the persecution, the persecution cannot ever be justified, except perhaps through the words in Paul's first letter to Timothy, "all who desire to live a godly life in Christ Jesus will be persecuted" (1 Tim. 3:12). By living a godly life, the Christian is assured persecution. It stands to reason then that when the church is the church, when the church engages in the mission of the gospel of Jesus Christ, she, too, is assured of persecution.

I would like to share with you some of the experiences of the Orthodox Church in the Middle East, and specifically how the Orthodox Church is responding to the persecution facing all Christians in the Middle East. As a reminder, I am not a citizen of a Middle Eastern nation, but am looking at this topic from the perspective of an Orthodox Christian living in the USA.

The Middle East is a particularly dangerous place to live these days, and that danger is not simply physical, but perhaps in a more damaging way, the danger is spiritual. Therefore, I will also share with you the some of the spiritual weapons with which the Orthodox Church equips its faithful, and how these weapons are the greatest source of protection against the debilitating spiritual warfare that is taking place in the Holy Land.

With the Muslim incursions that began in the seventh century, the persecution of Christians across in the Middle East and across Africa became an ongoing reality, taking on a variety of forms. As the Arab tribes swept across Persian lands into northern Africa, they left crumbling churches and ruins of monasteries in their wake. Throughout the history of these ongoing persecutions, the church made all efforts to maintain good relations with their persecutors, and have survived until this day. But for many Christian churches in the Middle East, specifically the Orthodox churches, which are the largest of the Christian churches, the persecution continues.

In Egypt, from the reports of the international media, the Coptic Orthodox Church has experienced persecution at the hands of specific, non-government-related groups.[2] The events of August 1998, when two Christians were murdered in the village of Al Kosheh in the diocese of El-Belliana, as well as the subsequent arrest of individuals who are Christians suspected of murdering the two Christians, stunned the international Christian community. The suspects were tortured, humiliated, and insulted, and the officers responsible were reported to have blasphemed Christianity and the cross. Men, women, and children were tortured in order to force someone to confess to the crime. When the local bishop and several priests interceded on the behalf of the people, they were arrested for inciting trouble.

A year later, following an argument between a merchant and a customer, in the same village of Al Kosheh, Christian-owned homes and shops were looted, destroyed, and then burned. The following day, killing began. Twenty people were killed, and the bodies of two among the group were burned. The Copts shut themselves up in their homes, and Pope Shenouda III, the leader of the Coptic Orthodox Church, was contacted the following day. He sent two bishops to the area who were escorted by a government official. The bishops and the Egyptian official surveyed the village and found the bodies of eleven who had been killed, and eight bodies in a nearby field. Another body was found, that of a man who had been shot and left for dead.

The violence spread from Al Kosheh to the surrounding villages, and one church (St. George's in Awlad Touq) was looted and destroyed.[3]

In response, the international community voiced its concerns. The Egyptian government makes concerted efforts to keep the peace between the Christians and Muslims. The political leaders have good relations with the church leaders. But the persecution continues in a much more subtle form, that of discrimination.[4] There are reports that Christians in Egypt are treated as second-class citizens, denied certain jobs, and given lower salaries. There is an unspoken understanding that if a Muslim man marries a Christian woman, she will become Muslim.[5]

How has the Coptic Orthodox Church responded to these events? Pope Shenouda released a report in November of 1998 outlining the result of the preliminary investigations that took place following the events. The pope worked with the Minister of Interior Affairs and was told that the office of the Attorney General was continuing the investigation. In the report, the pope expresses his dissatisfaction with the way in which the event was dramatized in the media, and calls the media reports "extremely exaggerated." He states that the matter should come to an end, and that an escalation would not prove beneficial. He specifically rejects any foreign interference in the affairs of the people of Egypt, and concludes by asking that any more provocation is not welcome.[6] Yet there was an article published in the *Al Kiraza* magazine on January 21, 2000 entitled "Our Martyrs in Al-Kosheh."[7] This article makes an impassioned plea for the truth, suggesting that there may have been a cover-up of the incidents that occurred there and that that cover-up will not resolve any problems, but lead to greater difficulties in the future.

This incident provides a useful example of how Christians respond to persecution. The initial response by the members of the Christian community was to contact their church leader. Two bishops, as representatives of the pope, were sent to investigate the situation and then report back to the pope. They traveled with a government official, and so the government authorities were involved from the beginning of the investigation. The Minister of Internal Affairs became involved in the investigation, and this was at the request of the pope. Perhaps, most significantly, the pope's concern was to keep the incident contained and let the proper authorities investigate the event. He specifically speaks out against any external involvement, namely, the activities of the international media, and cautions against responses from the international community. Pope Shenouda believes efforts should be directed to bringing matters to an end rather than provoking further action.

Bishop Seraphim of Los Angeles, writing on the incident that occurred in Al Kosheh, includes an exhortation to pray for those who have suffered and asks God to "grant the people of Egypt the strength and endurance to face these afflictions."[8]

These efforts on the part of the Coptic Orthodox Church are multifaceted:

1. The involvement of the church leaders.
2. The investigation of the events.
3. The involvement of secular authorities.
4. Prayer for those who are suffering.
5. The discouragement of external involvement, namely, those who are responding to reports of the events but who may not have any firsthand knowledge of the events.
6. The decision on the part of the church leaders to bring the incident to a close.

Pope Shenouda's response may have shocked international observers. As a person from a western nation, the pope's words of caution with regard to external involvement would be met with skepticism and raise some questions: is it possible someone is threatening him? How will the pope answer the questions of the family members regarding the incident? Yet Pope Shenouda is approaching this problem from a different perspective. He is approaching the problem having a clear understanding of the teachings of the Orthodox Church, namely, the place of persecution in the life of the church, or, more specifically, the place of suffering in the life of a Christian.

Suffering is an integral part of life. The questions raised by the book of Job with regard to suffering are many, and confusing to many Christians. It is much easier, especially in western society, to believe that God rewards those who are good and punishes those who are bad. The notion that bad things may happen to good people is something most Christians do not want to hear.

According to the teaching of the Orthodox Church, there are three main sources of suffering: suffering of the body and soul as the result of the persecution of others; suffering from sickness and disease; and suffering in spirit because of the sins of the world. One has the choice of how to address any type of suffering: either one accepts the suffering and transforms it into the way of salvation for oneself and others, or one rebels and rejects the suffering and is defeated by it, and in the end, "curses God and dies" (Job 2:9–10), as Job was tempted to do by his wife.

Yet Christians are told to "count it all joy" when they "meet various trials" (Jas. 1:2), and they should rejoice "that they were counted worthy to suffer dishonor for the name" of Jesus Christ (Acts 5:41).

The model for Christian suffering is found in Paul, who endured almost every type of suffering, as he describes in 2 Corinthians 4:8–10, "We are afflicted in every way, but not crushed; perplexed, but not driven to despair; persecuted, but not forsaken; struck down, but not destroyed; always carrying in the body the death of Jesus so that the life of Jesus may also be made visible in our bodies" (NRSV). He sees suffering in a unique way: "For just as the sufferings of Christ are abundant for us, so also our consolation is abundant through Christ" (2 Cor. 1:5, NRSV).

What Paul is saying throughout all these passages is that there is no suffering without redemption. Or as we Orthodox would put it, there is no crucifixion without resurrection. Likewise, there is no resurrection without crucifixion. Paul continues in the second letter to the Corinthians:

> So we do not lose heart. Even though our outer nature is wasting away, our inner nature is being renewed day by day. For this slight momentary affliction is preparing us for an eternal weight of glory beyond all measure, because we look not at what can be seen but at what cannot be seen; for what can be seen is temporary, but what cannot be seen is eternal (2 Cor. 4:16–18).

Or in other words, we look toward the kingdom of God, and through our suffering are being born into that kingdom. "So we are always confident" (2 Cor. 5:6).

St. Isaac the Syrian, a seventh-century monk, wrote of suffering as a great gift, and that it should be accepted joyously.[9] The person who experiences suffering has become worthy to be a partaker of the sufferings of the prophets and apostles who also suffered for the sake of the gospel. St. Isaac the Syrian concludes that if you do not have any difficulties, you should not rejoice; and when the difficulties come, do not consider them to be something foreign to God. If one wishes to follow in the footsteps of the saints, you must endure suffering.[10]

But the most grievous suffering does not take place in the flesh but in the spirit. The love and mercy of God, both for all of humankind and the entire *cosmos,* is the great gift that has been and continues to be rejected by the world which God loves. The refusal on the part of humanity for this divine gift is the greatest type of suffering.

True suffering takes place when one suffers over the sins of our fellow human beings. The great saints of the church were those who suffered for others. According to St. Isaac the Syrian, "if they [the saints] were cast into fire ten times per day for the sake of their love for man, even that would seem to them to be too little."[11] He was known to weep for others, for the entire creation, and even for the devil himself. To have a deep love for all others is to enter into the greatest form of suffering. This is the love of Christ.

How is it we look toward the kingdom of God in the face of persecution? The Orthodox Peace Fellowship is an association of Orthodox believers that works to apply the principles of the gospel to situations of division and conflict, whether in the home, the parish, the community, the workplace, our particular nation, or between nations. This group has been dedicated to providing resources for Orthodox and other Christians for engaging in peaceful resolutions to difficulties.

Daniel Lieuwen, a member of the Orthodox Peace Fellowship, in an article entitled "The Persecution of Christians Worldwide," outlines how to respond if one finds oneself in a situation of persecution.[12] He suggests:

1. Understanding the details of what is happening.

2. Praying, specifically for the persecutors that God will change their hearts; he also suggests praying for all people so that they will not become weary but remain courageous and steadfast.

3. The inclusion of petitions specifically for those engaged in suffering that can be recited during the liturgical services. I have been to several churches where this happens on a regular basis.

4. Organizing prayer vigils, specifically in front of embassies and consulates.

5. Writing letters of protest to governments and legislators.

6. Boycotting products produced in countries where the persecution is taking place.

7. Educating one's community with regard to the persecution of Christians.

8. Providing aid to suffering communities.

These suggestions are not in any way prioritized as I have presented them. But they begin to provide both spiritual and practical tools for understanding and helping those under persecution.

Lastly, I would like to mention one more important way in which the Orthodox Church addresses the subject of persecution. One of the greatest gifts of the ecumenical movement has been the relationships that have developed as a result of the renewed efforts for the Christian churches to come together. Through these relationships and networks, the churches have been in a much better position to respond to persecution. While there are exceptions, with regard to the Middle East, specifically the Occupied Palestinian Territory, the persecution that has been inflicted upon one church has affected all the churches. The destruction of olive trees, the closure of hospitals, the blockades at military checkpoints, the decreased access by humanitarian groups to those in need, and the construction of the walls and fences within the Occupied Territories isolating farmers from their crops, has affected all people, Palestinians and Christians.

But in the midst of these problems, perhaps one source of comfort for the Christians is that their leaders are speaking with one voice. The closing statement of the Middle East Council of Churches' Eighth General Assembly held in December 2003 has church leaders and representatives calling upon international, regional, and local councils and church organizations to "demand of world decision-makers to end the Israeli occupation of Palestinian lands."[13] The effort on the part of church leaders to come to one mind and one voice regarding the persecution is a sign of hope for the Christians in the Middle East.

The World Council of Churches (WCC) has added its voice to those of the Middle East church leaders,[14] and the WCC's Commission of the Churches on International Affairs interceded on the part of the churches in the Middle East at the 57th session of the United Nations High Commission on Human Rights when it met in Geneva in 2001.[15] The WCC has also initiated an Ecumenical Accompaniment Programme in Palestine and Israel (EAPPI) to receive direct reports from observers on the situation in the Occupied Territories and to work in conjunction with other peace groups in the area.[16]

The outcry against the US-led war in Iraq was even louder. We find statements by heads of churches in the Middle East,[17] the church leaders in Teheran,[18] and an individual appeal by the

Patriarch of Antioch, Ignatius IV (the church is based in Syria). Orthodox leaders from around the world spoke out: Ecumenical Patriarch Bartholomew I, Patriarch Alexis II of Moscow and All Russia, Patriarch Petros VII of Alexandria and All Africa, Catholicos-Patriarch Elijah II of All Georgia, Metropolitan Amfilohije of Montenegro, representing the Serbian Orthodox Church, the Holy Synod of the Church of Greece, Orthodox Bishops in Germany, the Standing Conference of Canonical Orthodox Bishops in the Americas, SYNDESMOS – the world federation of Orthodox youth, Orthodox Christians in Britain, and the Orthodox Peace Fellowship in North America.

Church leaders and groups from around the world added their voices, including Rowan Williams, the Archbishop of Canterbury,[19] leaders of the Superior Order of US Catholics, the Evangelical Lutheran Church in America Presiding Bishop Hanson, as well as the opinions expressed in a press release of the National Council of Churches, USA.[20]

In our world today, Christian leaders are developing an awareness of what is happening to the members of other churches, and developing a desire to provide assistance. This may be unprecedented in the history of Christianity. In the end when it comes to the issue of persecution within the Christian church, perhaps, St. Isaac the Syrian notwithstanding, all we can really say is "Lord, have mercy!"

Endnotes

[1] Some sources to consult regarding early Christian persecution: H. Musurillo (ed.), *The Acts of the Christian Martyrs,* texts with English translation (Oxford Early Christian Texts; Oxford: Clarendon, 1972); G. Lanata, *Gli Atti dei martiri come documenti processuali* (Milan: Giuliana, 1973); W. H. C. Frend, *Marytrdom and Persecution in the Early Church* (Oxford: Blackwell, 1965); G. E. M. de St-Croix, "Why Were the Early Christians Persecuted?" *Past and Present* 26 (1963), 6–38; C. Delvoye, *Les Persécutions contre les Chrétiens dans l'Empire romain* (Brussels: no publisher, 1967); T. D. Barnes, "Pre-Decian Acta Martyrum," *Journal of Theological Studies* 19 (1968), 509–31; "Persecutions," in *Encyclopaedia of the Early Church* (Oxford: Oxford University Press, 1992), 2:671–74.

2 I will discuss the Coptic Orthodox Church in Egypt, though technically this church is located in North Africa, not the Middle East. The Orthodox Church in the Occupied Territories (Palestine) is also under persecution, as are all the Christian churches in that area. The discussion of the churches in the Occupied Territories is a complex one; there is the persecution on the part of the Israeli authorities of all the Palestinian people in the Occupied Territories, and then there is also persecution at the hands of the Palestinian Muslims. For information on these complex issues, see *Middle East Digest,* Nov/Dec 1997; *Time,* April 23, 1990; *The Jerusalem Post,* May 2, 1991 and May 6, 1994; *The Times,* London, Dec 22, 1997. For specific information regarding the status of the Palestinians in the Occupied Territories, see *To the International Development Committee enquiry on Development Assistance and the Occupied Palestinian Territories,* Christian Aid (September 2003).

3 Much of this information can be found on the website of the Coptic Orthodox Church, http://www.antonius.org/docs/library/news (viewed January 25, 2004). Descriptions of the situation of the Coptic Orthodox Church can also be found in the online resource, *The Peace Encyclopedia,* http://www.yahoodi.com/peace/ (viewed January 25, 2004), specifically the section on "Christians in the Middle East." This section http://www.yahoodi.com/peace/christians.html (viewed January 25, 2004) in the *Peace Encyclopedia* provides general information about the persecution of Christians in the Middle East.

4 Cf. *Religion Today,* July 7, 2000, HRWF International Secretariat (July 12, 2000) http://www.hrwf.net (viewed January 25, 2004); email: info@hrwf.net. A former government official in Egypt is breaking the silence about official discrimination against Christians: Christians "suffer bad dealings," former Interior Ministry official Muhammad Al Ghanam, a Muslim, told *Religion Today* in a telephone conversation from Egypt. He said his phone line is tapped and that he is being followed by government agents. "Christians suffer twice," Ghanam said. Egyptian authorities sometimes inflict human rights abuses such as illegal detention and torture, but the Christians are singled out for discrimination because of their faith, he said. "They are in a bad situation and they really need help."

5 The human rights advocacy group, Human Rights Without Frontiers, has chronicled many of the incidents regarding infringement of the rights of Coptic Orthodox Christians; see http://www.hrwf.net/html/egypt2000.html#_top (viewed January 25, 2004).

6 From the *Report by Pope Shenouda II concerning events in El-Kosheh,* November 5, 1998.

7 Cf. http://www.antonius.org/docs/library/news/al_kosheh.htm (viewed January 25, 2004).

8 Cf. "We Pray for the Suffering of our Brothers in El-Belliana, Egypt," from *Copt Net,* found on the Coptic Orthodox Church website

http://www.antonius.org/docs/library/news/raid_bypolice_
elbelliana.htm (viewed January 25, 2004).

[9] Homily 59, *The Ascetical Homilies of St. Isaac the Syrian*, translated by the Holy
Transfiguration Monastery (Boston: Holy Transfiguration Monastery, 1984),
289.

[10] Ibid., 290.

[11] Quoted from St. Isaac the Syrian's *Mystical Treatises*, A. J. Wensinck
(ed.), found at http://www.oca.org/pages/orth_chri/Orthodox-Faith/
Spirituality/Suffering.html (viewed January 25, 2004).

[12] These suggestions are found at http://www.incommunion.org/Lieuwen.htm
(viewed January 25, 2004).

[13] Cf. http://www.mecchurches.org/posandpress/news.asp?id=157 (viewed
January 25, 2004).

[14] Cf. *Statement on the Ecumenical Response to the Israeli-Palestinian Conflict in
the Holy Land*, Adopted September 2, 2002 by the WCC Central Committee,
Geneva, Switzerland. This text can be found at http://www.wcc-coe.org/
wcc/what/international/palestine/cc2002statement.html (viewed January
25, 2004).

[15] Cf. http://www.wcc-coe.org/wcc/news/press/01/06pu.html (viewed
January 25, 2004).

[16] The WCC website has a link to the EAPPI program.

[17] The texts of the following statements mentioned can be found on the
Orthodox Peace Fellowship websites http://www.incommunion.org/
resources/iraqwar.htm and http://www.incommunion.org/resources/
iraq.asp (both viewed January 25, 2004).

[18] The group's statement can be found at http://www.mecchurches.org/
posandpress/news.asp?id=163 (viewed January 25, 2004)

[19] Excerpts from his petition to the British Prime Minister, Tony Blair, can
be found at http://www.washington-report.org/archives/november02/
0211080.html (viewed January 25, 2004).

[20] http://www.mecchurches.org/newsreport/vol15_1/voice.asp (viewed
January 25, 2004).

Section IV

CENTRAL AND EASTERN EUROPE

8

Persecution of the Romanian Church in the Twentieth Century

An Historical and Theological Perspective

IOAN F. TIPEI

1. Introduction

The experience of suffering is part and parcel of the history of the Romanian people. For more than 500 years Romania was continuously subjugated and oppressed by two foreign empires: the Ottoman Empire and the Austro-Hungarian Empire. The freedom acquired at the beginning of the twentieth century (1918) through the Great Unification of Transylvania with the rest of the country did not last very long because, when the lots were cast in the aftermath of the Second World War, Romania found itself once again given away to a dominating power, worse than any previous oppressor. Under the rule of Soviet and then domestic communism, the Romanian people faced the climax of all that is described by words like humiliation, dehumanization, oppression.

The sufferings mentioned affected the lives of millions not only in terms of civil liberties and elementary human rights but also in terms of their religious experience. In the first part of this paper we will present a brief overview of the persecutions endured by the churches of Romania in the twentieth century. Then, in the second part, we will attempt to produce a theology of suffering that emerges from the experience of suffering and persecution endured by the churches of Romania.

2. Persecutions of the Romanian Christians in the Twentieth Century: Historical Overview

2.1 *Persecution of Romanian Christians before the Second World War*

Many Romanians remember the period between the two world wars as the best period of the twentieth century in the sense that it was a time of prosperity and freedom. It was, probably, the most prosperous period in over 500 years. Enjoying full freedom now in all three provinces of Romania, the Orthodox Church consolidated her status as the National Church. Therefore, we cannot talk about persecution of regular Orthodox believers during this period. However, after the rise of the Lord's Army, an Orthodox awakening movement, due to personal conflicts between the Metropolitan of Ardeal (Transylvania) Nicolae Balan and the founder of the movement, priest Iosif Trifa, many adherents of the Lord's Army (known as "soldiers") felt persecuted by the Orthodox clergy. Father Trifa himself was eventually stripped of his credentials[1] by the Synod of the Orthodox Church, and the movement was officially dissolved.

This was also the period of Pentecostal beginnings in Romania. The first Pentecostal congregation was opened on September 10, 1922. The new movement functioned illegally between 1922 and 1950 when it was recognized by the communist government. For almost thirty years before communism, Pentecostals were harassed by the authorities and forced to meet at night or in the forests to avoid imprisonment and large fines.[2] Those who were caught assembled were beaten, fined, publicly humiliated, and sometimes imprisoned. For Stefan and Petra Ardelean of Graniceri, Arad, husband and wife (seventy-seven and seventy-four years old), the dust on their knees was enough evidence that they prayed. They were arrested and then condemned to one year and two months imprisonment, and the younger believers caught with them were sentenced to a two years imprisonment.[3] The case of the Pentecostals from Ilva Mare and Maieru is well known to the Romanian Pentecostals. They were forced to take turns pulling a wagon loaded with gravel, having their necks put in a yoke, like oxen, to the astonishment of the villagers. While pulling the wagon, they were whipped until they started to bleed and their bodies became black.[4] Referring to the incident, an article in a national newspaper read: "We are living in plain Middle Ages and some are still not happy. They want more. What exactly? Perhaps burning at the stake!"[5] There are only two recorded cases of Pentecostal martyrs during this period: The first is Partenie Pera of Lipova, Arad. The police caught him praying with other believers in Şoimuş, a nearby village. The soles of his feet were beaten with chains so badly that he died after two days in enormous pain. He left behind a wife and two minor children.[6] On September 17, 1942, another Pentecostal, Voicu Rusin of Lascar Catargiu village, was sentenced to twenty-five years of forced labor for refusing to leave the Pentecostal faith. He died in a prison cell in August 1944, during the bombardment.[7]

Between the two world wars, the Pentecostals of Romania suffered mostly at the hand of the Orthodox Church, because of their aggressive missionary activity.[8] Even though persecutions were conducted by local or central authorities, it was done either at the instigation of the Orthodox Church or in the name of Orthodoxy.[9] In a few cases Baptists would cooperate with the authorities against Pentecostals, nourishing grudges for the churches they lost as a result of their transfer to the Pentecostal side.

The worst time of all for the Romanian Pentecostals (and evangelicals) was the period 1940–44, under the rule of Antonescu, when all evangelical groups were declared illegal and their churches were closed. Hundreds of evangelicals were imprisoned.[10] They were forced to baptize their children in the Orthodox Church. Pastor Ungureanu, the secretary general of the Baptist Union, was constrained to transfer to Orthodoxy and was made a priest, to serve as an example for all Baptists.[11] In 1942 the Martial Court of Galaţi sentenced eighteen Pentecostal believers to heavy imprisonment (hard labor) for refusing to be baptized in the Orthodox Church. A priest was called into the prison and seventeen accepted baptism. They were acquitted, but the one who refused carried his sentence and died in the prison.[12] Because of the hard persecution, many Pentecostals transferred their membership to churches recognized by the government – Orthodox, Lutheran, etc. – but others spread out in the country where the Pentecostal phenomenon was not known and established new groups, especially in remote villages with no police forces.

2.2 Legalization but no freedom: The church under communism

2.2.1 General persecution of Christians in the 1950s and 1960s
Soon after the Second World War, the communists took over in Romania. Evangelicals resumed the practice of their faith and the Pentecostals received provisional recognition in 1946 and became legal in 1950 on the condition of loyalty towards the communist authorities. During the later years of the Stalinist period, the communist regime of Romania launched a campaign to indoctrinate the population with Marxist ideology, planning to eventually eradicate all forms of religion. At the beginning a strategy was devised by which the state would take control of all churches. The new regulations were transmitted mainly verbally because they were unconstitutional.[13]

Hundreds, possibly thousands, of Christians from all denominations were imprisoned as reactionary elements against the communist regime. The strategy of the communist regime was to use the church, the institution with the highest credibility, to convince the population that communism was the right way. Priests and pastors were asked to be informers of the secret police. A refusal meant imprisonment. Those who agreed to cooperate with communist authorities were rewarded with leadership positions in their own churches.[14] So many priests and ministers were corrupted by the regime that, at the Congress of All Religions held during the years of Stalinist occupation – Stalin who was guilty of genocide against Christians – was elected the Honorary President of the Congress.[15]

The first Orthodox martyr in the fifties was a priest by the name of Felea, from Arad, who, when asked to cooperate and be an informer said, "I pledged to Christ to defend the holy cause of the Church, so I will be loyal to this commitment."[16] During one of the following nights he was taken from his home, arrested, and two years of torture and interrogation followed until he died in the prison of Aiud, under a regime of extermination. Leaders of the "Lord's Army," Traian Dorz[17] and Sergiu Grossu,[18] were imprisoned with many other priests, especially Greco-Roman clergy (a Romanian Catholic Church that, during communism, was forced to join the Orthodox Church) for "illegal activity."[19]

While the religious persecution before the Second World War was mainly physical (beating, imprisonment, etc.), during the communist years it took devious forms by which Christians were tortured not only physically but also psychologically. The communists conceived of diabolical methods of intimidation and torture. For example, in the prison of Pitești, an Orthodox priest, brought almost to insanity by daily torture, was forced to administer the Eucharist with excrement and urine. When asked why he did it, he answered, "Please don't judge me! I suffered more than Christ did."[20] The psychological torture suffered by a man of God forced to commit such sacrilege is beyond the capacity of any description. Another example is the well-known Lutheran minister Richard Wurmbrand, who spent fourteen years in communist prisons and experienced enormous torture and pain. At his first detention, for more than eight years nobody at home knew whether he was alive or dead. Several years before he was released, secret police agents, pretending to be former prison mates of Wurmbrand, visited his wife to tell her that he was dead and that they assisted in his funeral.[21] This is the same Richard Wurmbrand who said that during torture, "the soul is the master of the body." Even when the physical pain was excruciating, says Wurmbrand, it felt remote, because the soul was in an intimate communion with God and remained untouched by what was happening to the body.[22]

2.2.2 *Persecution of evangelicals in the 1970s*

During this period, Christians outside the evangelical churches enjoyed relative freedom. There are not many cases of persecution recorded against the mainline churches. We can mention here the persecution of Pr. Gheorghe Calciu Dumitreasa for his sermons directed against the regime, the harassment of the Lord's Army and the demolishing of a significant number of churches, especially in the capital city of Bucharest.

After Iosif Ţon published his booklet *Cine îşi va pierde viaţa?* in 1973, a work that was sent to the Romanian communist authorities and to Kenston College in England, the evangelical churches regained their freedom to a great extent. Regulations that choked the church for the past two to three years were partially lifted in 1974. It was, however, difficult for the communists to accept a defeat. Soon they were relaunching their attacks, but this time aiming them at the individual rather than the church as an institution.

In 1975 Romania was represented at the Conference for Human Rights held in Helsinki. Pledging to observe the resolutions of this Conference and the Constitution of Romania, which granted each citizen full freedom to choose, practice, and change his or her religion, the communist regime of Romania ceased to attack the evangelical churches directly. But the persecution against evangelicals did not stop. It was directed now against the individual believer, taking the following forms: (a) Evangelical believers were identified at their workplace or school and were threatened with layoff or dismissal if they did not renounce their faith. Although they announced the real reasons for such dismissals, the authorities protected themselves by invoking other reasons in the official documents. (b) Heavy fines were applied to believers who were caught assembled in houses for prayer or Bible study, on the charge that they were disturbing the public order. Not all the police agents were thoroughly instructed about how to carry out the orders, and some filled in on receipt forms the real reasons for which they applied the fines.[23] (c) High school students were threatened that if they did not give up their faith their names would be given to all colleges and universities of Romania and would not be accepted for further education.[24] Many evangelical students were publicly humiliated by their own teachers and peers in an effort to discourage and destroy the faith they practiced. The present writer was countless times an object of such ridicule.

During the communist period, not a single case is known of an evangelical believer holding a leadership position in a village, town, city, school, factory, financial institution, etc. Those who held such a position and later became members of an evangelical church were immediately discharged.[25] A campaign was conducted in the mid-1970s against those evangelicals who held teaching positions in schools. Many teachers were fired in order to avoid any negative influence on the young people who were enrolled in a program of atheistic indoctrination.

Because of their connections with the West, evangelicals were perceived as dangerous people, spies for and agents of the capitalist world, people who undermined the regime and threatened the national unity. The regime managed to inculcate these ideas in the minds of most people, so that the "repenters," a derogatory label for evangelicals, were looked upon as medieval people, as the "husk" of the society. Denigration in newspapers, books, television programs, etc., together with pressures to transfer to the less offensive and dynamic Orthodox faith, were methods used by communists to discourage the practice of faith. In a document known as "The Call to the Truth," Iosif Ţon describes the persecutions of that period:

> Our persecution starts through the attitude of the authorities at all levels of the society towards us, the believers. All over the country, we are looked upon as enemies, as people belonging to a past which must be eradicated, as being anachronistic, undesirable. We are frequently told that we have no place here, that we are dangerous, that we destroy the unity of our nation, that we are agents for Capitalism, that we subvert the regime.[26]

2.2.3 *Other forms of persecution*

Other forms of persecution in the seventh decade of the twentieth century reflect the communist regime's tight control of the evangelical churches. The following lists these methods with brief comments:

1. The pastors of larger churches, especially district overseers, were forced to present a weekly report to the Regional Inspector for Religious Affairs (RIRA) about the church services of the previous Sunday.

2. To preach in a church from another town, a pastor needed the approval from the inspector or a letter of accreditation from his superiors. Special approval from the Department of Cults (a special office in the Ministry of Culture) was

needed for all foreign ministers who visited Romania and desired to preach in a church. For a short period, the pulpit of a local church was restricted to the pastor and a member of the pastoral team, namely people in good standing with the Department of Cults.

3. The lists of candidates for water baptism were approved by the RIRA. The first ones to be removed from the list were those who formerly belonged to the mainline churches or were atheists. This was a real challenge and a problem of conscience for the pastors because the command to baptize those who believe was given directly by the Lord. To respect the measures imposed by the regime meant a conflict of interests, an abandonment of the mandate given by the Lord Jesus himself (Matt. 28:19–20). There were situations when under the threat of losing their license, the Department of Cults required that the church would receive back as members, believers who were formerly excommunicated.[27]

4. The lists of candidates for any ministry in a local church (even laypersons on the pastoral council) needed to be approved by the RIRA.

5. All pastors had to be approved by the Department of Cults. Intellectuals and those perceived as hostile to the regime had no chance of being promoted to the ministry. The spiritual problem created by this measure was discussed by Iosif Ţon in one of his books.[28] To accept pastors who are imposed by the regime meant giving up the work of the Spirit and the Lordship of Christ in the church. The book is an appeal to all Baptists from Romania to refuse to accept the measures imposed by the communists. The acceptance or rejection of such measures was, according to Ţon, a test of loyalties. Were Baptists loyal to Caesar or to Christ?

6. The applicants to theological studies needed to be first approved by the Department of Cults. Those who were graduates of colleges and universities were automatically removed from the list.

7. The Department through its inspectors controlled the financial operations of local churches. The pastors were

required to ask approval to purchase cult objects, musical instruments, etc.[29] Building a new facility for the local church was practically impossible. While all building projects were stopped, the regime was engaged in a campaign to destroy many church buildings. The "reason" was the urbanization of the Romanian cities and towns. In this area, the Orthodox Church suffered more loss than any other church. In Bucharest alone they demolished or moved over twenty church buildings.

8. The Sunday school, a program rival to the indoctrination program of the government, was prohibited.

9. The Department of Cults dictated that each pastor must serve several churches, depending on their membership. This measure limited the number of approved ministers. The right of the deacons to administer Eucharist was revoked by the Department, so that the pastors (now regional pastors) were forced to run from one church to another and function as "administrators of the Eucharist."[30]

10. The government refused to authorize new local churches that satisfied all the legal requirements.

11. The government totally prohibited the printing of Bibles and severely controlled the printing of other religious literature.

12. Through the Department of Cults the government established the hours for church activities (including divine services) and prohibited any religious manifestation outside the church building, except for funerals.

We have mentioned the names of just a few of the priests and pastors who, in the face of the most atrocious persecution did not give in, but showed the most beautiful spirit a human being can show. Hundreds of them from all denominations were thrown in prison in the fifties. Many others took enormous risks in their stand for freedom of worship. Among the most prominent leaders during this period who fought for religious rights from inside the country we mention Orthodox priest Gheorghe Calciu Dumitreasa and evangelical ministers like Iosif Ton, Aurel Popescu, Paul

Nicolescu, Constantin Caraman, Silviu Cioată, Vasile Taloş, Vasile Brânzei.

At the other end of the spectrum, there were hundreds and perhaps thousands of priests and pastors who, especially in the years of Ceausescu's personality cult, stepped overboard in praising the regime, pledging loyalty, affirming that communism and Christianity are essentially similar, and acclaiming the government for the freedom of worship they enjoyed. This was true for simple priests and pastors and for national leaders of almost all denominations.[31]

2.3 *The outcome of the persecution on the Romanian church*

It was expected that the spiritual vacuum created during the long years of persecution against the church in Romania would trigger a significant and long-lasting revival after the fall of communism. Such spiritual revival announced itself from the first days of the new post-communist era when, overwhelmed by the astonishing changes, the multitudes promised to turn back to God. Unfortunately, the momentum did not last for a very long period. The vacuum was rapidly filled with a preoccupation especially for the new economic and entertainment opportunities created. Caught unprepared to handle the freedom brought by the revolution, Romania soon faced a real spiritual regress. Although remarkable progress has been made in new areas like social assistance, chaplaincy, home missions, missionary activity, theological education, etc., and some evangelical churches report an increase of their members, numbers and physical growth tell little about the real life of our churches. There is a lot of apathy reflected in a decrease in both church attendance and participation in the life of the church. The spiritual regress made by Romanian churches translated into apathy and moral decline seems to indicate that freedom is a more efficient sieve than persecution. Unlike persecution, which tends to fan one's passion for Christ, unlimited freedom comes with a package of alternatives that will accurately test one's priorities and the depth of one's faith. Some who had passed the test of persecution failed lamentably the test of freedom.

It was also expected that the past experience of suffering together at the hand of an atheistic regime would strengthen the ties between the churches of post-communist Romania. Some progress has been made here, especially in areas like theological education, translation of the Bible, and conferences on social issues.

For all churches in Romania, the long years of persecution shattered the trust of many Christians in their spiritual leaders. Since the great majority of ministers are still active after revolution, there is a lot of suspicion about their former collaboration with the secret police. To the present writer, as an evangelical, it is interesting to see how the mainline churches reconcile this lack of trust in their leaders with their view of the apostolic succession as the means by which not only is the apostolic tradition transmitted but also priestly grace.

Another outcome that emerges not only from the sad experience under communism but also from the long history of political domination of Romania is the reluctance of some evangelical churches to accept integration into larger Christian organizations. They fear being dominated again. But, on the other hand, Romanian Christians need the expertise of churches from the West in areas such as management and leadership. They also need substantial material help. The few who integrated with denominations from the United States have benefited immensely. Many evangelical leaders outside Romania find it difficult to reconcile their cry for help with the Romanian evangelicals' refusal to integrate.

Finally, at the emotional level, many Christians who suffered bitterly during communism received the power to forgive their oppressors and their brothers in Christ who contributed to their suffering. However, a general reconciliation is a remote aspiration and will not take place before the secret police files are published and those who sinned against the church or individual Christians assume responsibility for what they have done.

3. A Theology of Christian Persecution

The French philosopher Pascal expressed the reality of suffering in the following words: "Christ is in agony until the end of the world." Although risen and glorified, the eternal Son of God bears the suffering of the fallen world, and particularly of those who surrender their own suffering into his hands. Christian persecution is not a new experience of the church. It can be traced to the beginnings of Christianity. Jesus himself suffered at the hand of governments and dignitaries, and bore witness to the clash between God's kingdom on earth and temporal earthly kingdoms. He warned his followers that this tension would result in discrimination, hatred, physical harm, and even death. Jesus said, "No servant is greater than his master. If they persecuted me, they will persecute you also" (John 15:20; 16:1–4, 33).

The subject of suffering in general is too broad to be discussed in this paper. Therefore, our discussion will be limited to one aspect of the idea of suffering for the gospel, namely Christian persecution. It is a well-known fact that followers of Christ are persecuted all over the world simply for what they believe. It is estimated that Christians in over sixty countries face the realities of massacre, rape, torture, family division, harassment, detention, discrimination in education and employment, and even death. It is also estimated that more Christians were martyred in the twentieth century than in the other nineteen centuries combined.[32]

This section aims to present a theology of Christian persecution that springs out of the suffering experience of the Romanian church. Such theology includes a pragmatic definition of Christian persecution itself.

3.1 *A definition of Christian persecution*

The notion of "Christian persecution" refers strictly to the type of suffering that is inflicted upon Christians by others. From a pragmatic standpoint, it is not always easy to discern if a certain Christian is experiencing persecution or some other type of suffering. For example, we might not be too off-track in claiming that even in some western, democratic countries Christians experience some milder persecution, especially in the form of discrimination and limitation of their full expression of faith. Even when witnessing atrocities like arrest, torture, enslavement, and martyrdom, we cannot tell *a priori* if such extreme situations can be classified as "Christian persecution." We need to learn more about the circumstances that brought about the particular incidents. Therefore, we start our discussion by pointing out what Christian persecution is not.

The apostle Peter says in 1 Peter 4:15 that some people suffer because they are "troublesome meddlers." At first glance the meaning of the term appears to be rather obvious: A troublesome meddler describes the person who is always interested in everyone's business but his own. The term, however, requires closer examination to fully understand it in relation to our theme.

So often Christians suffer mild persecution entirely because of their own foolishness, because of something that is either in themselves or in what they are doing. But this is not Christian suffering. For example, many times we can create difficulties for ourselves that are quite unnecessary or can bring endless suffering upon ourselves because we have some rather foolish notion of witnessing and testifying. In his study on the Sermon on the Mount, Martyn Lloyd Jones says, "We are slow to realize the difference between prejudice and principle; and we are so slow to understand the difference between being offensive, in a natural sense, because of our particular make-up and temperament, and causing offence because we are righteous ... Fanaticism can lead to persecution; but fanaticism is never commended in the New Testament."[33] Christ's disciples did not look for trouble, but did what was right. When the state authority and the biblical principles conflict with one another, the Christian should follow the example of the apostles, who said, "We must obey God rather than men" (Acts 5:30).

There are some people who deceive themselves in believing that they suffer for righteousness' sake when, in reality, they are persecuted for a certain cause. It is true that the two notions can sometimes become one. Often people suffered and died both for righteousness' sake and for a cause. It is possible that Christians are discriminated against, are imprisoned and suffer terribly for religion, however, without suffering for righteousness' sake. Christian persecution is not always identical with one's suffering for his or her strong convictions. There is always this danger that people develop a spirit of martyrdom. In sticking to their own ideas, they almost court martyrdom. Without naming any particular Christian leader mentioned above, it is obvious that Romanian evangelicals (and perhaps mainline Christians too) have had amongst them people moved by such a spirit. Another noble cause is the activity of some anti-abortion groups. Making the government aware of the genocide, as some pro-life groups do, is one thing, but resorting to violent acts, is quite a different thing. Being "persecuted" for violent acts in the name of civil disobedience, expressed sometimes through violence and even murders, is not Christian persecution. Some Romanian Christians engaged themselves in a battle for human rights or religious rights, without being provoked by the communist government and, in doing that, attracted not only the attention of the authorities, but also reactions that negatively affected the lives of many other believers.

There are some people who confuse being persecuted because of righteousness with being persecuted for "religio-political" reasons. The term "political agitation" refers to a revolutionary activity that seeks to disrupt and interfere with the function of the existing government. If the term "troublesome meddlers" used by Peter is intended to also cover this sort of activity, then Peter is calling for Christians to live as good citizens in non-Christian, even hostile cultures. It must be said boldly and loudly that Christian faith is not essentially anti-communist, as many believe. On the contrary, the apostle Paul teaches the Roman Christians that "all authorities that exist have been established by God. Consequently, he who rebels against the authority is rebelling against what God has instituted" (Rom. 13:1–2). It is not uncommon that people suffer persecution for mixing their religion and politics. But this is not being persecuted because of their righteousness. To exemplify from the Romanian context, when countless Orthodox priests and monks were sympathizers of the "Iron Guard," a fascist society formed mainly of Orthodox fanatics, the persecution directed by the communist government against them was not Christian persecution *per se*.[34] In conclusion, suffering for political and social reasons might be a noble act, but the blessings spoken of by Jesus in the Sermon on the Mount (Matt. 5:10) do not apply to people involved in such activities.

What then is Christian persecution? In the Sermon on the Mount, Jesus blesses only those who suffer "for the sake of righteousness" (Matt. 5:10). Being righteous or practicing righteousness really means to be like Christ. Therefore, the term "Christian persecution" can be properly applied only to those who suffer for being like him.

3.2 Causes of persecution

In our attempt to find the causes for persecution from a human perspective, we look first to the persecutor. In most situations, the persecutor is another religion, another church, or some church leaders who have different views. Biblical examples abound! In the case of the apostles, the persecutor was the state religion through its representatives – high priests and theologians of that day (e.g. Saul the Pharisee). Romans were not very interested in the Christian religion, their only concern being the safety of their political domination. They got involved only when Jewish authorities alarmed them about the possibility of political destabilization caused by the new Christian religion.

Looking at Christian persecutions from a human perspective, in most cases believers are persecuted because they are looked upon as enemies. It is very important that, under any circumstances, the church not give any government or religious system reasons to believe that she has a hostile attitude towards the establishment. As mentioned above, the apostolic teaching on this issue is opposed to the view of many Christians who still believe it is a matter of faith to fight communism.

Christians are also persecuted because they are different. The righteous may not say anything to condemn the world, but there is an unspoken word of condemnation in what they are and what they do. So the world hates them and tries to find fault with them. This was the principle at work that determined the Jews to kill Jesus.

From God's perspective, evil exists, in part, not only because of the deeds of perpetrators but also because God is self-restrictive in this world.[35] Jesus announced to his disciples that persecution is *typical* rather than unusual:

Truly, truly, I say to you, unless a grain of wheat falls into the earth and dies, it remains by itself alone; but if it dies, it bears much fruit. He who loves his life loses it; and he who hates his life in this world shall keep it to life eternal. If anyone serves Me, let him follow Me; and where I am, there shall My servant also be; if anyone serves Me, the Father will honor him. (John 12:24–26)

Stephen's martyrdom follows the prophetic pattern Jesus taught his disciples. Stephen was falsely accused and brought before the council where he was given utterance and wisdom which none of his opponents could refute. It was not Stephen speaking; it was the Holy Spirit. It was the opportunity for his testimony. He was hated on account of Jesus' name and he was put to death. And yet, through his death he bore much fruit, for as Tertullian said, the blood of the martyrs is the seed of Christianity. Today in many parts of the world the *typical* pattern established by the Lord has become an *unusual* situation. Predictably, a sudden persecution would ravish many churches.

According to Bill Green, Christian suffering can only be properly understood and undertaken from a biblical view of eschatology.[36] He maintains that the opponents in 2 Corinthians appear to have been teaching that suffering in the Christian life was evidence of a lack of the presence of the Spirit, and thus Paul's apostleship was in question, since he obviously suffered wherever he went![37] The suffering of the Christian, says Paul, far from showing a lack of the power of the Spirit, on the contrary, is proof of one's unity with Christ. The very weakness of the Christian is the channel by which God manifests his grace and power, and so Paul says that he will boast in his weakness: "for when I am weak, then I am strong" (2 Cor. 12:10). By being transformed in spite of their weaknesses, Christians testify to the truth that "the all-surpassing power is from God, and not from us" (2 Cor. 4:7).

3.3 *The function of Christian persecution*

Suffering and martyrdom are ways used by God to accomplish his purposes with humankind. Through suffering and martyrdom,

God acts in two directions: (1) God accomplishes his purposes in history, and (2) the Christian is transformed.

3.3.1 *God accomplishes his purposes in history*

Through the suffering, torture, and martyrdom of Christ, God "showed us that suffering and self-sacrifice are his specific methods by which he solved the problem of rebellion, evil and human sin."[38] The children of God are called to solve the problems of this world through the same sacrificial love (*agape*) which expresses the nature of God. Jesus is still sending his disciples the same way he was sent by the Father, i.e. by the way of the cross. As representatives of Christ, God's children have to share the treatment Jesus received. Their cross does not always mean martyrdom, but it always implies suffering. There is no other way. It was Jesus who warned the disciples that in the world they would know sorrows, that if they did these things to him, how much more his disciples will suffer (2 Tim. 3:12). Martyrdom creates opportunities for the truth of God to triumph in the world. If personal suffering of the righteous is a means by which satan is defeated (e.g. Job) and God's name is glorified, so much more is accomplished through suffering for the sake of the gospel. It is a known fact that one role of suffering and persecution is to bring the church to unity, maturity, and growth.

3.3.2 *The redemptive nature of suffering: Sharing in the sufferings of Christ*

The apostle Paul says that God has set things up so that the suffering of his creation is redemptive. The whole creation is said to be groaning as in the pains of childbirth, straining toward the purposes for which God has designed it. It is not just the elect/chosen of creation who suffer redemptively; the whole creation suffers redemptively. The suffering of individual Christians is integral to the general suffering of the creation, known as "the groaning of the Creation" (Rom. 8:22–23).

According to Father John Breck, "suffering remains a mystery in the popular sense of the term precisely because we cannot explain – or explain away – its ultimate origin or meaning. This is precisely why it is suffering, and not simply pain, hurt or grief … It remains a crushing, perplexing, unexplainable and apparently unjust weight of anguish, loss and pain."[39] But for a Christian it is also a *mysterion*, notes Father Breck – it acquires a sacramental value:

> We are members of the Body of Christ. This is our most basic identity and it defines our most basic calling (Rom. 12; 1 Cor. 12). "If one member suffers," St. Paul tells us, "all suffer together" (1 Cor. 12:26). Yet the Head of the Body suffers as well. This means that whatever we experience is never experienced in isolation. We never suffer alone. Although other members of the Body may be oblivious to our suffering, Christ the Head bears it to the full. He drinks the cup of suffering – His own and ours – to the bitter dregs. We know that He even longs to assume our suffering, to assimilate it to His own, in order to transfigure it and ourselves into the image of His glory.[40]

According to Fr. Breck, all suffering endured by a Christian person can be transformed into a *mysterion* by a simple, sacramental gesture, accomplished through prayer, that is, to surrender it – whatever its cause, whatever its form – into the hands of the crucified one.[41] In our view, while all suffering of Christians may have a sacramental value, it is evident that suffering as *mysterion* applies first to Christian persecution. It is in suffering for being a Christian that one identifies him- or herself with the suffering of Christ. It is this suffering in which the Christian is asked to rejoice (Rom. 5:3–5).

Jesus did not suffer so that the church does not have to suffer anymore. On the contrary, it is through his suffering that the church could suffer *in his power and authority*, and thus overcome satan, thereby demonstrating God's wisdom through the church to the rulers and authorities in the heavenly places. This is one of God's purposes for the suffering of the church.

If the Christian's suffering together with all God's creation is redemptive, so much more is the Christian's suffering for Christ. Jesus himself said about Paul the apostle,

> He is a chosen instrument of Mine, to bear My name before the Gentiles and kings and the sons of Israel; for I will show him how much he must suffer for My name's sake. (Acts 9:15–16)

Our own salvation attests to the fact that Paul's suffering was redemptive. The salvation of others may one day attest to our willingness to suffer, as the apostle's did, so as to fill up the sufferings lacking in the Body of Christ:

> Now I rejoice in my sufferings for your sake, and in my flesh I do my share on behalf of His body (which is the church) in filling up that which is lacking in Christ's afflictions. (Col. 1:24)

Paul's suffering and ours is redemptive in the sense that it is God's channel by which his redemptive purposes in the world are accomplished. If Paul had a share of suffering to fulfil, we all have our own share. With a greater call to suffering comes a greater grace to endure. Since God has decided that additional worldly suffering is needed to fill up what he considers lacking in his affliction, there is nothing the church has to offer in this but her consent. Laying down our lives is for a redemptive purpose. A seed brings forth a hundredfold when it falls to the ground and dies. We are called to offer ourselves as living sacrifices, as sheep to be slaughtered. For precious in God's sight is the death of his saints. Clinging to our lives will cause us to lose them; laying our lives down will allow us to gain them. In this manner the church will crush satan underfoot. We must begin absorbing these truths of God, rather than the things of men, and begin moving toward this glorious destiny.

3.3.3 *Through suffering the Christian is transformed*
Through suffering and sacrificing one's own life in the work of God, character traits are produced that are transforming the child of God into the likeness of his Son.[42] Christ himself was made perfect through suffering (Heb. 2:10). When Christians suffer at the hand of those to whom they brings the saving truth, they share the fate of Christ who was crucified by those whom he came to save. Believers understand that, like Christ, they too have to pray for those who persecute them, forgive them, and bring them the saving truth.

According to the apostle Paul, persecutions and afflictions are methods used by God to purge, purify, and refine the Christian so that he/she might be made worthy of the kingdom of God:

> We ourselves speak proudly of you among the churches of God, for your perseverance and faith in the midst of all your persecutions and afflictions which you endure. This is a plain indication of God's righteous judgment so that you may be considered worthy of the kingdom of God, for which indeed you are suffering. (2 Thess. 1:2–5)

The Christian's suffering during persecution is a test of his or her loyalty to Christ and, thereby, of his or her worthiness to inherit the kingdom. The soteriological aspect of suffering and persecution is mentioned also by apostle Peter (1 Pet. 1:6–7; 4:12–13; 5:10), James (1:2–4), and in the Epistle to the Hebrews (2:10).

3.4 *The attitude of Christians in persecutions*

One's suffering during persecution affects not only the body, but the person as a whole. It touches especially the psychological dimension of the human being. When personal actions and decisions affect the lives of your family or the Christian community, it is not always easy to choose the right thing. One cannot know *a priori* how one will behave in suffering. After experiencing various forms of persecution, the apostle Paul said that *suffering for Christ is a grace* (Phil. 1:29). It is a grace only when the Christian comes out of it triumphantly! Precisely because suffering for Christ is a grace is it so difficult for us to predict how people will behave during persecution. The assurance that one will stand fast in suffering for Christ has to rest on a life of commitment prior to the outbreak of persecution. God will not give "the grace" of overcoming the trials to those who were "Christians of circumstances." "In order to overcome, the spirit must be nourished in order to free itself from the constraints of the human body," said Philip Yancey.[43] Even this sort of Christians may go sometimes through some collective type of persecution, but the history of the church has shown that, most likely, such Christians would renounce their faith or put it aside for a while, depending on the nature of persecution. As soon they do this, the persecution ceases for them and it also ceases to be a grace.

The apostle Peter exhorts Christians not only to accept persecution, but also to rejoice when it comes:

Beloved, do not be surprised at the fiery ordeal among you, which comes upon
you for your testing, as though some strange thing were happening to you;
but to the degree that you share the sufferings of Christ, keep on rejoicing;
so that also at the revelation of His glory, you may rejoice with exultation.
(1 Pet. 4:12–13)

Although the rejoicing in suffering goes against the human nature
of a person, the Christian has a special reason to rejoice: he or she
gets a share in the sufferings of Christ. The phrase "but to the
degree that you share the sufferings of Christ" used by the apostle
means that we are privileged, when persecuted for righteousness,
to enjoy the fellowship of our Lord's suffering. It is a grace that not
every Christian has. When Christ suffered, his eyes were fixed on
"the joy that was set before him" (Heb. 12:2). The text shows that
the grounds for rejoicing in suffering are outside the experience of
suffering. *Our rejoicing is not to be connected with the pain or difficulty
itself, but with the ramifications of it.*

In the midst of suffering, the Christian knows that he or she
is not alone. The One who initiated the suffering for the church
is constantly on the *via dolorosa*, alongside those who choose to
engage in this pilgrimage. The Christian must understand that
nothing will touch him or her on this journey, except that which is
allowed by our loving Father. If the sufferer does not see this, his
or her faith will be shaken in the times of trouble, and one will be
tempted to fall away, not trusting and understanding a God who
allows such things to bear on his children. It will indeed be God's
love, although perhaps not our short-term sentimental view of
it. The apostle Paul clearly understood this when he wrote to his
Roman fellow-Christians:

Who shall separate us from the love of Christ? Shall tribulation, or distress, or
persecution, or famine, or nakedness, or peril, or sword? Just as it is written,
"For Thy sake we are being put to death all day long; we were considered
as sheep to be slaughtered." But in all these things we overwhelmingly
conquer through Him who loved us. For I am convinced that neither death,
nor life, nor angels, nor principalities, nor things present, nor things to come,
nor powers, nor height, nor depth, nor any other created thing, shall be
able to separate us from the love of God, which is in Christ Jesus our Lord.
(Rom. 8:35–39)

4. Conclusion

Persecution should be looked upon as something that is allowed by God for two main reasons: as a means by which he accomplishes his purposes in the world and as a means by which the church in general or the individual Christian is tested, transformed, and made worthy of the kingdom of God. As the apostle Paul tells us in Romans 8:28, God can work out good in any and all circumstances. He can use cancer to confront someone with his or her own mortality and to bring that person to faith in Christ. But that does not mean we glorify cancer. Persecution is evil in all circumstances, even when it is used to fight a heresy. It is a sin on the part of persecutors that should be denounced. But, from the perspective of the persecuted, a Christian should not passively seek to die for Christ.[44] Death should be avoided so that the work of God is done in another place (Matt. 10:23). To take up your cross means to be prepared for whatever comes.[45]

If unavoidable, persecution is something that should be accepted for the collective and personal benefits that it brings. It is a known fact that persecution leads to church growth. In light of this reality, some Christians in the West ask themselves if they should really be working to stop persecution. The Bible also says that the poor will always be with us, but at the same time it urges Christians to give food to the hungry and clothes to the naked. Christians are clearly called to seek justice and to engage in acts of compassion (Zech. 7:9; Luke 11:42; Matt. 25). In following Christ's example, we are to show mercy to those who are suffering, especially to the household of faith (1 Cor. 12:26–27). While throughout history Christianity has grown tremendously after periods of persecution, we need to keep in mind that this is not always the case. The persecuted church is not always strong and pure, and persecution can lead to a church that is divided, demoralized, compromised, and embittered. Therefore, we must be careful not to romanticize persecution. The opinion of the present writer is that Christians around the world should attempt to stop the persecution of their brothers and sisters, without fearing that they are fighting against God. A failure in their attempt is only an indication that it was God's will for that particular group to suffer.

In the opinion of the present writer, while the persecutions suffered at the hand of the atheistic regime were beneficial to the churches of Romania in terms of spirituality and church growth, in other areas such as trust in the leaders, interdenominational relationships, leadership, sacrificial giving, and missionary zeal, they harmed the churches tremendously. Having said that, it is our conviction that, in the aftermath of the long and bitter communist domination, a long-awaited reconciliation, both intra- and interdenominational, is needed among Romanian Christians on a national scale. While a few high-ranking officials of the Orthodox Church admitted their culpability in collaborating with the communist regime against the interests of the Church and asked for forgiveness, none of the evangelical leaders followed their example.

We also believe that it is the call of the church in the West to continue assisting their brothers and sisters who were plagued for so long by communism especially in the area of education and leadership. This should be done not as an obligation, as some put it,[46] but out of Christian love, as members of the same body.

Endnotes

[1] He was restored post-mortem after the fall of communism, most likely under the pressure of the Oastea Domnului revival movement.

[2] Trandafir Sandru, *Trezirea Spirituală Penticostală din Romania* [*The Pentecostal Revival in Romania*] (Bucureşti: Editura Institutului Teologic Penticostal, 1997), 75.

[3] Ibid., 78f.

[4] Ibid., 84.

[5] Mihael Sevastos, Unidentified article, *Adevărul* 44 (November 21, 1931).

[6] Sandru, *Trezirea Spirituală*, 76; Petru Ardeu, *Scurt istoric penticostal* [*A Brief Pentecostal History*] (Arad, no publisher, 2002), 228; Ioan Ceuţă, *Mişcarea Penticostală în evenimente şi relatări ale secolului XX* [*The Pentecostal Movement: Events and Reports from the 20th Century*] (Bucureşti: Editura Lumina Evangheliei, 2002), 163.

[7] Sandru, *Trezirea Spirituală*, 78.

[8] The reverse situation is now taking place in a village in the Bistrita-Nasaud district where the predominant population is Pentecostal (over 90 percent). The Orthodox Church is planning to build a monastery right in the

middle of the village, but faces the opposition of the Pentecostal Church. The Pentecostals hold the same feelings toward them that the Orthodox nourished towards Pentecostals: that they are the owners of that place and won't give anything away.

⁹ The instigation of Orthodox priests is documented in books, official letters, and newspaper articles. They prove that the Jandarmeria (the police in charge of public order) was submissive to the Orthodox clergy. See Pr. Gheorghe Comşa, *Noua călăuză pentru cunoaşterea şi combaterea sectelor* [*A New Guide for Knowing and Fighting the Sects*] (Cernica: no publisher, 1925), 74, 75, 77; Sandru, *Trezirea Spirituală*, 74, 76, 77f., 79–81.

¹⁰ Report no. 68580 of December 18, 1942, sent by the Ministry of Culture and Religion to Marshall Antonescu, the ruler of Romania during the Second World War. Between 1940 and 1942, Marshall Antonescu was heavily influenced by the right-wing Iron Guard, a fanatically Orthodox and fascist group. See Richard Wurmbrand, *From Suffering to Triumph* (Grand Rapids, MI: Kregel, 1991), 26.

¹¹ Sandru, *Trezirea Spirituală*, 91.

¹² Constantin Cuciuc, *Religii care au fost interzise în Romania* [*Religions Outlawed in Romania*] (Bucureşti: Editura Gnosis, 2001), 81f.

¹³ Iosif Ţon, *Confruntări*, 19.

¹⁴ Nicolae Marini, *Istoria documentară a Oastei Domnului* (Bucureşti: Editura Societatea Evanghelică Română, 1999), 393.

¹⁵ R. Wurmbrand, *Strigătul bisericii prigonite* [*The Cry of the Persecuted Church*] (Bucureşti: Editura Stephanus, 1993), 16ff.

¹⁶ Marini, *Istoria documentară*, 383ff.

¹⁷ A well-known Christian poet and member of the Lord's Army who, under communism, was looked upon as the new leader of the movement.

¹⁸ Christian poet and writer, sentenced to twelve years imprisonment and hard labor for refusing to teach philosophy and for his "illegal" activity in the Lord's Army.

¹⁹ Marini, *Istoria documentară*, 390ff.

²⁰ Wurmbrand, *Strigătul bisericii prigonite*, 44.

²¹ Ibid., 41.

²² Ibid., 51. For many examples of priests and pastors tortured in communist prisons, see the following books by R. Wurmbrand: *Tortured for Christ* (Bartlesville, OK: Living Sacrifice Book Co., 1998); *From Suffering to Triumph* (Grand Rapids, MI: Kregel, 1993); and *In God's Underground* (London: Hodder & Stoughton, 1969).

²³ On one of these receipts it was written "because they prayed without being authorized" (Ţon, *Confruntări*, 125).

²⁴ Ibid., 129.

²⁵ Ibid., 130.

²⁶ Iosif Ţon, "Chemare la adevăr" [*A Call to the Truth*], radio broadcasting on Free Europe Radio station, April 2, 1977.

27 See the case of Simeria baptist church. Cf. Ţon, *Confruntări*, 73.
28 Iosif Ţon, "Cine-şi va pierde viaţa?" ["Who Will Lose His Life?"], included now in *Confruntări*, 11–77. See especially 65–69, 74.
29 Ţon, *Confruntări*, 71–72.
30 Ibid., 72.
31 As already mentioned, the highest position in the Orthodox Church was occupied twice by men chosen by the Communist Party. The second one, Patriarch Iustin Moisescu, who succeeded Iustinian Marina (already mentioned), was a layperson (school teacher) who was made Metropolitan of Ardeal (rom. Mitropolit) in four days. Shortly after this he was made Metropolitan of Moldavia and finally Patriarch. During his tenure, in Bucharest alone more than twenty churches were demolished. Cf. Marini, *Istoria documentară*, 393. Evangelicals are more reserved about discussing freely the corruption of their leaders than are the Orthodox, but it is a known fact that those who gave in and "played the game" of the communists were not just a few.
32 A. W. Pink, "The Problem of Persecution," online article at http://www.mountzion.org/fgb/Fall96/FgbF2-96.html (viewed January 2006).
33 Martyn Lloyd Jones, *The Sermon on the Mount* [Romanian. trans. *Predica de pe munte*] (Oradea: Cartea Crestină, 2002), 83.
34 For documents that attest the political involvement of many Orthodox priests with the Iron Guard, see C. Păiuşan and R. Ciuceanu, *Biserica Ortodoxă Română sub regimul comunist* Vol. 1 (Bucureşti: Institutul National pentru Studiul Totalitarismului, 2001).
35 John E. Thiel, *God, Evil, and Innocent Suffering: A Theological Reflection* (New York: Crossroad, 2002), 131.
36 Online article "Suffering and Eschatology," http://www.kerux.com/documents/KeruxV11N1A3.asp (viewed January 2006). See also his master's thesis "Suffering and Eschatology: A Critical Study of 2 Corinthians 4 with Particular Emphasis on the Relationship of Suffering and Eschatology in Paul," Calvin Seminary, May 1989.
37 See Scott Hafemann's published doctoral thesis, *Suffering and the Spirit* (Tübingen: J. C. B. Mohr, 1986).
38 Iosif Ţon, *Suferinţă, martiraj şi răsplătire în cer* (Oradea: Cartea Creştină, 1999), 449. A translation into Romanian of Iosif Ţon's 'Suffering, Martyrdom and Rewards in Heaven' (Ph.D. diss., Evangelical Theological Faculty of Haverlee, Belgium, 1999).
39 Fr. John Breck, "On the Mystery of Suffering," online article at http://www.christianity.com/partner/Article (viewed October 5, 2004).
40 Ibid.
41 Ibid.
42 Ţon, *Suferinţă, martiraj*, 446 şi urm.; Philip Yancey, *Where Is God When It Hurts?* (Romanian trans.; Grand Rapids, MI: Zondervan, 1977), 99–101.
43 Yancey, *Where Is God When It Hurts?* ch. 15 (p. 276 in the Romanian edition).

[44] The apostle Paul, when facing persecution from religious leaders for preaching the gospel, tried to avoid it by invoking his Roman citizenship and demanding a hearing before the political leaders in Rome.

[45] John White, *The Cost of Commitment* (Leicester: Inter-Varsity Press, 1971), 34–35.

[46] Richard Wurmbrand believed it was a moral responsibility of the West to make reparations to Eastern Christianity for the harmful decisions of the past. He said, "The tragedy of all captive nations is a burden on American and British Christianity. The Americans must know that they helped the Soviets to overpower our nation with a regime of crime and terror. They must straighten this out, by helping the subjugated peoples to come back to the light of Christ" (*Strigătul bisericii prigonite*, 15).

9

Anatomy of Suffering: Consequences of Persecutions in the Past for the Church in the Post-Soviet Era

VALDIS TERAUDKALNS

Painful experiences rooted in the collective memory of many people inhabiting post-Soviet social space are very much linked with oppression and persecution initiated by the Soviet authorities. Sufferings have been experienced not only by devoted Christians and political dissidents who did not fit in the framework constructed by Soviet ideology but also by ordinary people who otherwise did not constitute the ideological Other not tolerated by authoritarian regimes. In March 1949 about 13,504 families with a total of 42,322 persons were deported from Latvia.[1]

The suffering and alienation was so intense, people were ready to cling to any sign of hope, real or imagined, that could provide some sense of relief. For example, a myth circulated among believers that Lenin and his close coworkers had been more positive towards religion than functionaries who came to power after Lenin's death. This belief was also popularized during Gorbachev's years of perestroika in the 1980s when Soviet mass media talked about the "human face of socialism." After each political shift, many believers expected that maybe the time had come for freedom of religion. This mythology has some historical background coming from the period before the First World War when communists in the Russian Empire were still struggling to gain more influence and therefore were looking for allies who could help to create a broader political platform against the tsarist rule. It is no surprise, then, that the Second Congress of the Party of Social-Democrats of Russia (1903) accepted the resolution that called sectarians (a term then used by authorities and mass media for various religious minorities) a democratic movement that stands against the ruling power. Members of the party were encouraged to engage individuals in the ranks of the party who came from religious minorities.[2] But it changed when communists came to power. V. Bonch-Brujevich, who before the First World War acted as a promoter of cooperation with sectarians in a letter written in 1932, tried to explain these drastic changes employing the typical rhetoric of Stalin's period. Baptists, Mennonites, and Adventists are called "direct agents of international capitalism and bourgeois-fascist governments."[3]

Depending on the attitude of Soviet officials, religious groups in the USSR, including Latvia (then one of fifteen Soviet republics), could be classified in the following way:

1. Larger religious groups (Catholics, Orthodox, Lutherans, Baptists/evangelical Christians, etc.) that were registered and in a limited way allowed to have centralized structures. They also were used in Soviet propaganda campaigns to show the West that there was no religious persecution in the USSR.

2. Groups that were registered at the local level as congregations but for most of the time were not allowed any centralized structure. Seventh-day Adventists fall under this category because in 1960 their All-Union Centre in Moscow was closed, its archives and documents confiscated.[4]

3. Groups that were forced to unite with others without room left for any autonomy (Pentecostals, Methodists, etc.). A less-known example of this kind of discrimination is the dissolution of Catholic-Apostolic congregations (followers of the nineteenth-century Scottish minister, Edward Irving) in Latvia after the Second World War. In 1948, two remaining congregations in Riga and Liepaja reached an agreement with the Lutheran leadership about acceptance of these groups into the Lutheran Church, but even that was not acceptable to the Council for the Affairs of Religious Cults in the USSR, and congregations as entities were closed and their premises confiscated.[5]

4. Groups pushed underground (Jehovah's Witnesses, Christian Science, etc.). Jehovah's Witnesses were severely persecuted as a group that so consistently rejected the Soviet ideology. In 1951, according to the plan developed by the Soviet leadership, many Jehovah's Witnesses still left in freedom were sent to the Far East of the USSR. According to the official data, in 1956, 7,449 Jehovah's Witnesses lived in the regions of Irkutsk and Tomsk.[6]

Official policy differed from republic to republic. For example, Methodists in Estonia were allowed to continue their activities, but in Latvia, in 1948, they were united with Lutherans (in spite of the fact that in 1944 there were twenty-seven Latvian Methodist parishes and seventeen members of the clergy).[7] The legal status enjoyed by a religious group in one region did not stop the authorities in another region from denying that group its right to be registered. Lutherans in the Baltic republics were allowed to exist, but in Russia itself where many of them were ethnic Germans, they were persecuted and their church buildings were confiscated.

The Catholic Church in Latvia and Lithuania was large enough to be at least tolerated, but Catholics in Russia, being a rather small minority, were heavily oppressed. If at the beginning of the twentieth century there were more then 100 Catholic church buildings and chapels in Russia, at the beginning of Gorbachev's rule only two were left open – one in Moscow and one in St. Petersburg (then Leningrad).[8] Catholics in the Baltic area tried to help their co-believers in other Soviet republics by sending priests to serve parishes (e.g. in Ukraine and Armenia), as well as by offering training for candidates to the priesthood coming from other Soviet republics, but this work was restricted. Only in 1976 did the Catholic Seminary in Riga receive the status of "inter-republican" educational establishment. But even then there was only a limited number of study permits for students coming from other regions of the USSR.[9]

Sometimes in the forceful process of the unification of various religious groups there were clear signs of the involvement of local Soviet officials. For example, at the end of the forties, a period in

Latvia named by officials themselves as the "time of liquidating small sects,"[10] the Plenipotentiary of the Council for Affairs of Religious Cults in Latvia, Voldemars Seskens, expressed the idea of uniting Moravian Brethren with Orthodox (he probably knew about the conversion of some Latvian Moravians to Orthodoxy in the nineteenth century).[11] This idea was never realized, but the coupling of Protestant and Orthodox churches would have been an interesting project of ecumenism by force.

For Pentecostals the Soviet period was a continuation of the struggles for acceptance that they had in the tsar's times. Michael Bourdeaux (Keston Institute, Oxford) has rightly called Pentecostals "the Soviet denomination,"[12] because their identity was shaped and their numbers grew especially in the period of Soviet rule. They had only two options – to join Baptists / evangelical Christians (only at the end of the sixties were Pentecostal congregations allowed registration outside of existing denominational bodies, and until 1988 in the USSR 200 such congregations were registered)[13] or go underground. Many of them chose the second option. Pentecostals were under constant pressure from the offices of the Committee of the State Security (the fourth branch of the Fifth department of the Committee) organized in 1967 to fight groups and individuals labeled as ideological enemies.[14] They were constantly charged with conducting rites endangering health, violation of social order, attempts to emigrate, distribution of illegal literature, etc.

In the West, the heroic attempts of Pentecostals and some other groups to keep their identity have often been glorified as examples of resistance to the regime. However, such a perspective is one-sided because the mentality of all sides involved, both collaborationists and members of underground churches, were negatively affected by the situation. The weakness of collaborationists was the naïve belief that maximum cooperation with the state would mean more freedom of religion. In the face of the clash of two religions, in which one of them (communist ideology) enjoyed the benefits of the state, there was no peaceful solution possible. Another issue, not to be forgotten, is that collaborationists started to believe what their oppressors told them.[15] Actually, many people belonging to the post-war generation are now faced with the difficult moral and psychological issue of dealing with vanished ideals and expectations. As the Russian literary critic Lev Anninskij said:

> We were a generation of those who stayed alive and practically the last generation of those who believed that they will live in Communism … We are still walking as bald-headed idealists … We will die and our grandchildren will ask how we were able to keep this faith. Children are not asking it.[16]

The same can be said about people who believed the claims of the Cold War witch-hunters in the West. Traces of the Cold War mentality still have some impact on relationships between Latvians who, during the Soviet occupation, stayed in the USSR and those who emigrated. Some of those who stayed were of the opinion that the road of emigration was a deliberate choice of the easiest way, and that churches abroad, including ones established by emigrants, often turned their backs on churches under communist rule.[17] It is an emotionally charged issue because the two communities ("local" Latvians and emigrants) have formed differing social memories and there is no clear-cut answer to the question of what would be the best for Latvia – to stay or to leave? In any case, an individual's choice must be respected. Speaking about West–East relationships during the Cold War, we may understand the dilemmas faced by Western churches. "There was not much they could do … In order to be able to foster these contacts with the 'churches in the East,' the churches in the West needed to observe the code of conduct and rules of socialist speech."[18] Both political worlds – West and East – were so different that even prominent guests who travelled to the Soviet bloc together with advisors and carefully prepared details for their visit beforehand, made mistakes. One characteristic example is that of Billy Graham, who made several trips to Eastern Europe. Later in his memoirs the evangelist admits, "my intentions were good, but I naively thought going to the Soviet Union from the USA was as simple as going from the USA to the UK. Nor did I fully realize then the extent to which churches in such societies were forced to cooperate with the government authorities."[19]

On the other hand, we need to take into the picture the complex relationships within emigrant communities between "hard liners" who wanted to avoid any contacts with representatives of churches in the East, labeling them as agents of Soviet secret services, and "rebels" who tried to foster links with their homeland. Looking back now to that period, we can see that in spite of the fact that cultural contacts between emigrants and their former home countries were subject to Soviet propaganda and secret service activities, people benefited from these few open gates between two opposite political worlds.[20]

Today, emigrant churches have left these issues behind. That has happened not only because of radical political shifts, but also because of the fact that now their priority is survival. As admitted by the Dean of the Middle District of the Latvian Lutheran Church in the USA, Gunars Lazdinsh, the "lack of pastors and decreasing of church membership in all our parishes has pushed us to serious evaluation of our future."[21] Hopes that people in the new wave of emigration, which started after the collapse of the USSR and is caused by economic needs, will join Latvian churches abroad have not been fulfilled. "Importing" women who have graduated from a course in theological studies in Latvia and who do not have a place for pastoral ministry there because the largest Protestant group in Latvia, the Evangelical Lutheran Church, does not ordain women anymore,[22] can help to fill vacancies in emigrant parishes. But this solution will not solve the dilemma as such.

In the USSR, the problem of "catacomb believers" was like that of the early Christian Donatists. They developed a "complex of suffering," where the state of being persecuted is not simply a reality one faces, but it is also an indicator of a more mature spiritual level and is viewed by many as something that should be a characteristic of "true" believers. With the collapse of the Soviet Union and regained freedom, the question of the basis for Christian identity arose. Sufferings of the past still provided enough symbolic capital to serve as inspiration for many believers, but it did not solve the problem of relating to the world around them. Some Pentecostal and Baptist groups in the former USSR refused to register and to start cooperation with other Christian organizations, even when it became clear that such a legal status would not restrict their activities. For these groups, maintaining a countercultural stance became one of the markers of their identity.

There are other cases when glorification of martyrs overlaps with certain political sentiments, as in the case of the canonization of the last tsar, Nikolay II, which fits the framework of romantic sentiments towards the tsarist period in the mass and political culture of contemporary Russia. Another example of this simplified past is the canonization (in 2003) of the Latvian Orthodox Archbishop Janis Pommers, who under uncertain circumstances was killed in 1934, in the period of the First Republic. Besides the version that he died because of his faith and uncompromised stand against Communism, there are other views, like the one expressed by Latvian historian Aivars Stranga, who pointed to rumours about sexual misconduct of the archbishop and financial scandals in the church. Pommers had been active in the Russian right-wing monarchist organization "Sojuz russkovo naroda" (*Union of the Russian Nation*) that in tsarist times strongly insisted on an undivided empire and denied rights of self-governance to nations incorporated in the Russian Empire.[23] In his speeches from the period between the two world wars when he was elected to the Parliament of Latvia, one can also find anti-Semitic expressions.

What about dealing with this past is important for the future?

1. Placing Local Experiences in a Wider Context

We can easily become so focused on our own suffering that we do not see others living in even more painful situations. A long-term alienation from the wider world and exclusion from social-political life has erected obstacles to the creation of critical solidarity with those suffering in other parts of the world. But suffering has a creative potential that, if used in a proper way, can bring people closer to each other in a dialogue where differences are not silenced but respected. As noted by the Catholic theologian, Paul Knitter: "Suffering has a universality and immediacy that makes it the most suitable, and necessary, site for establishing common ground for interreligious dialogue."[24]

For Pentecostals of the former Soviet republics, an additional factor in the dominance of inward-looking perspectives has been the fact that in the period between the world wars and after the

Second World War, many of them were still going through the first phase of their history, one characterized by an apocalyptic mood. One of founders of the Pentecostal movement in Latvia, James Grevinsh, in his letter, published in 1930, expressed the view (according to him it was a conviction of many of his fellow believers) that 1930 would be the last year of peace in Europe.[25] During the Soviet period from time to time there were rumors circulating among Christians about a coming world catastrophe that would bring history to its end. Solidarity with the poor was seen not as a working project for today, but rather as an eschatological goal or purely spiritual perspective. Pentecostal hymnology showed it clearly:

> And weak and poor
> Who gain this power[26]
> Are becoming mighty in Christ.[27]

Of course, dynamic and vibrant spiritualities rising in the area during the past ten years and acquaintance with social issues in the world are bringing in new currents. Yet, the strategy of such a major Christian fundraiser as the Latvian Bible Society, which so far has had only local fundraising projects, shows that people are mainly open to local concerns. It is difficult to raise funds for international projects. If wider interests surface, they are predominantly related to the identification with the needs of one's own ethnic group. There are cases of Estonians helping remnants of small ethnic groups in Russia, which are part of the same Finnish-Ugric language group, or of people from Latvia going to Latvian villages in Russia. Such a situation is caused in part by the fact that many people who have lived for most of their lives in a culture where persons of a different colour are a rarity are inclined to racism. According to the recent Internet poll, 45 percent of respondents mentioned immigrants and 59 percent named people with dark skin among those subject to the highest levels of discrimination.[28] Surveys "On the Road to a Civil Society" done in 1997 and 2000 show that inhabitants of Latvia express the greatest distance towards people from the Caucasus, Kurds, Chinese, and people with dark-skinned.[29] A number of state offices and nongovernmental organizations have been involved in working out possible long-term solutions to this problem. On the other hand, Churches have been slow in providing a clear response.

2. Transformation of Tragic Experiences in the Past into Something Affirming and Oriented Toward the Future

Memoria passionis (memory of suffering) should not be neglected. It is part of what we are. Instead of following simplistic therapeutic techniques of popular psychology, we should learn to deal with the past. Not only Christ's sufferings but also the pain of the world, that is, all the inhabitants of our universe, has a theological meaning. As John Sobrino has observed:

> The crucified people have a strictly *theo-logical* potential. They give shape to faith in a God of the weak, because they themselves are weak. This God may be accepted or not, but if this God is accepted, the crucified peoples are the most suitable setting for faith in this God. . . . God was not only at one point on Jesus' cross reconciling the world but is still present in the crosses of history.[30]

Unfortunately, "prosperity theology" as a global phenomenon is easily crossing borders because it is designed as a set of universally applicable principles, and its festive character is favored by the younger generation of Pentecostals who are distancing themselves from the legalistic, world-denying countercultures of many classical Pentecostals in post-socialist countries.[31] But its ideology cannot help in healing memories of the past because forgetting or silencing is not a solution. The Christian community fulfils its mission only when it is neither a captive of the past nor a child ignorant of the past, but rather a fellowship of those who see God working in everything to bring all to him. Such a church is sensitive to the needs of others and considers human rights as part of the gospel, not as something designed by secularists. Apart from this view, former victims can easily become oppressors. Restorationist impulses of imposing a particular version of Christianity that some segments of the church believe to be an embodiment of the gospel can be observed in various Christian groups in post-socialist countries. In some cases Pentecostals have suffered by being excluded from this vision and have experienced the violation of their rights (there are many such examples in Russia), but there are also cases when they have been standing at the side of those in power. For example, in the last parliamentary elections in Latvia (2002), neo-Pentecostal groups were active in supporting the First Party, which also gained seats in the Parliament and became a member of the ruling coalition.[32]

These activities are a byproduct of a growing respectability and embracing of middle-class culture on the part of new charismatic churches. Among neo-Pentecostal activists are such publicly known figures as the former Minister of Economics and former Vice-Mayor of the city of Riga, Juris Lujans (Message of Joy Church), actress Maija Doveiko (Message of Joy Church), musician Raimonds Maskats (New Generation Church).[33] Neo-Pentecostals in general have not been very visible in politics. The new political elites are just as afraid as their predecessors were, that too close of an association with religious minorities can cause them to lose votes.[34] The question remains whether some of the current policies aimed at imposing Christian values on others can be considered really Christian in their nature.[35] We also need to take into account the fact that dominion theologies of some neo-Pentecostal circles with their concept of a "new world order"[36] are misused by members of militant anti-cult movements who misquote them as a sign of the revolt of new religious movements against state and public order. However, it should be stressed that it is an exaggeration to speak about a possible takeover by any kind of right-wing group, religious or secular, in the near future. In the present situation, when behind politics stand pragmatic business interests, the deeds of political groups that call themselves conservative are not always consistent with their claims. As noticed by observers, the rhetoric of traditional values is used, but it is not always clear what is meant by the term.[37] The First Party was criticized by members of the mass media for using patriarchal slogans in its election campaign,[38] but in its program the party states that it "stands for the strengthening of woman's role in Latvia."[39] This political group also nominated as a candidate for the newly established position of the Special Tasks Minister for Social Integration the liberal-minded Nils Muiznieks, who was accepted in spite of opposition from some partners of the coalition who disapproved of his views.[40] We also need to remember that religion, like politics, in post-socialist countries is a diverse phenomenon, and various groups within churches are responding differently to the new social reality.

One example of this new situation appears when two churches from one confessional family stand against each other because of their responses to the social reality. This took place when the contrasting perspectives of the Anglican parish of Riga and parish of the Charismatic Episcopal Church addressed themselves to the subject of the first gay pride day in Riga, in the summer of 2005. The event provided an opportunity for the parish of the Charismatic Episcopal Church to present itself and its conservative position in the public arena, as a "traditional" church standing side by side with other churches that condemned the event. For the Anglican parish of Riga, it was an opportunity to make clear its self-understanding that it stands for the rights of the marginalized as part of its Christian witness in a secular world. Such controversies raise questions to interdenominational relationships that often diplomatically keep silence on ethical concerns, but instead, focus on dogmatic and general social issues. For a long time ethics have become the point where various Christian traditions often depart and, therefore, these issues cannot be ignored. These issues are not entirely foreign to members of the Pentecostal/charismatic movement as well.[41]

3. Correction of Simplified Black-and-White Histories

Christian faith does not function in abstract, ahistorical space. Our theologies are based in certain historical contexts to which we are all attached. Globalization has intensified the mingling of these contexts, blurring boundaries among them, but still it does not destroy the localities and collective memories of people inhabiting them. Christians should not undermine the positive aspects of Marxist philosophy even if this may be a difficult acknowledgment for Eastern European believers who have experienced the results of a simplified and vulgarized version of Marxism. It would be difficult to deny the fact that the Stalinism-Leninism practiced in the USSR was just as responsible for the massacre of many people during the Second World War as the Nazi regime. But at the same time it should not overshadow the fact that to modern Christian theology Marxism serves as a reminder of the inescapable intermingling of the socio-political and religious dimensions of life. "[The] Marxist discovery is the discovery of the world as a historical project, and of human beings as the agents of their history. Here Marxism touches and develops another basic theme of Christianity, namely, history."[42] Theological hermeneutics should not reduce the biblical plurality to a single abstract principle presented as the core of Christianity (like the Protestant slogan "justification by faith") acting in ahistorical space. Instead it should constantly think of a meaning-producing triangle "biblical text – reader – social environment," positioned in the present historical reality.

This is a common problem not only for religious groups in post-socialist countries, but also for the population of these territories in general. The Soviet period often has been depicted only in negative terms,[43] and dealing with the past in the name of finding the truth has became a political project which serves the needs of political actors but does not take into account the complexity of the situation. A similar tendency is to activate negative memories from the past to justify certain contemporary policies in the eyes of society. For example, in the conflict between the Catholic Gymnasium situated in Aglona (a place of pilgrimage for many Catholics) and the secular boarding school in the same village, Cardinal Janis Pujats said that "a school led by militant atheists is an insult to thousands of Christians."[44] Many people still remember children in Soviet schools being indoctrinated into atheism. However, in modern times, secular education, even if separated from the church, is not aimed at challenging faith but in providing information on a general social and historical framework in which religion functions.

Religious life in Latvia has escaped sharp conflicts experienced in some other countries like Romania. In Latvia the most intense conflict between collaborationists and reformists in the church happened in the second part of the 1980s when some Lutheran pastors formed a group that stood in opposition to Archbishop Eriks Mesters, who was obedient to Soviet policies. But already in 1989 the synod elected his successor, Karlis Gailitis, who started a new period in the history of the Latvian Lutheran Church. The Orthodox Church, which in many countries has gone through continuous fragmentation, has stayed united except for the small splinter group called the Autonomous True Orthodox Church of Latvia, the diocese (eparchy) of The Russian Orthodox Autonomous Church.[45] This group is still unregistered and it will not be able to gain legal status in the near future because an agreement between the state and the Orthodox Church of Latvia (signed in 2004), which states that no organization can use the name "Orthodox" except an institution belonging to the "official" Orthodox Church.[46]

In spite of the relative calmness of the situation, the work of those who led churches during years of oppression is subject to different interpretations. We must admit that there is no escape from this plurality of histories because selection of facts is based on the life experiences and standpoints of the compilers of such histories, be they "official" histories produced by the establishment or from some other oral or written histories.

Groups like the Pentecostals have a history of being marginalized by other denominations. Soviet rule used existing tensions for its purposes. For example, in 1962 in Daugavpils (Latvia) there was a trial of some Pentecostals who established an illegal group, and one of the witnesses called by the court was a Baptist who said that Pentecostals are under trial not because of their convictions but because of their health-damaging rituals.[47] On the other hand, Pentecostals often have proselytised among Baptists, and it has laid an additional burden on the relationship between these two Protestant groups. It is not easy to avoid tensions in a situation where two groups are aiming at the same relatively small target audience.

In history, boundaries between both groups – Baptists and Pentecostals – often have not been clear-cut, and local Baptist churches have risen from various streams. For example, the origins of the small countryside church in Zalenieki (its work was stopped after deportations in 1949) can be traced back to the efforts of the interdenominational "Christian Endeavours" and preaching of such well-known inter-war Pentecostal preachers as J. Gevinsh and V. Strazdinsh.[48] Baptist revivalists have often used Pentecostal rhetoric in speaking about a new Pentecost, Baptism in the Spirit, etc.[49] For their part Pentecostals have taken on board many hymns used by Baptists. Both traditions have departed in their ways but there is a lot of common heritage to be rediscovered.

Pentecostals are now going through the steps of slowly getting more involved in ecumenical relations. The presence of like-minded charismatics from the "historic" churches in interdenominational organizations is making the process of accommodation of former "untouchables," easier. For religious groups, the process of getting more established and losing the characteristics of an apocalyptic community also means a growing interest in history to prove that the group is not new. This is not too far from the next step of looking for common roots, which unites that group with others.[50]

Suffering has been experienced by all religious groups in the former Soviet Union, just as now new freedoms and new challenges are part of daily life. The same can be said about divisions between Russian-speaking and Latvian- (Lithuanian-, Estonian-, etc.) speaking communities. With the rebirth of nationalism, at the end of the 1980s and the beginning of the 1990s, there has been a common trend in public discourse to depict some as oppressors and others as victims. But, in fact, the Russian population has also experienced tremendous losses during Soviet rule. Even if, continuing Russification policies of the former absolutist regime, the symbolic world of tsarist times since Stalin's time were transformed according to the canons of Soviet ideology (including the images and figures of the tsarist period, e.g. famous army leaders), these tendencies cannot be attributed to the Russian nation as a whole.

Today the ethnic integration of two communities divided by language is hampered not only by the unrealistic, populist claims of some Latvian politicians ("Russians go home") but also by the fact that the political orientation of the local Russian community is towards the past. It is expressed in such cultural events as the continuing celebration of International Women's Day on March 8 [Latvians celebrate the Family (Mother's) Sunday instead], Victory Day on the May 9 (a festival from the Soviet calendar dedicated to the victory over Nazi Germany), etc. Similarly, the journalist Alexander Shabanov, a Russian, claims that local Russian identity "is not Russian or Slavonic but rather Soviet and totalitarian."[51] From being an ethnic minority a better understanding of other minorities does not always follow.

Recently a study undertaken by the Baltic Institute of Social Sciences showed that Islamophobic views demanding even the forbidding of Islam were especially prevalent among the Russian-speaking population of Riga.[52] As an example of good practice, we should mention a bilingual socio-political internet site www.dialogi.lv, which has on its team, people of various ethnic groups and which fosters a reconciliation process. It has also organized and published forums with the involvement of theologians.

We should have a realistic vision of the future. Suffering should not be left in the vanishing shades of the past. "Participation in the apostolic mission of Christ leads inevitably into tribulation, contradiction and suffering."[53] However, for the church the question is not only how to deal with sufferings in the past but also how to take the responsibility of being not *for* others (this well-known phrase of Dietrich Bonhoeffer's has a patronizing flavor) but *with* others. It is a dangerous responsibility because we can be easily misunderstood and even rejected, thus becoming martyrs of our age in the wider sense of this word.[54] But if we want to live out the gospel there is no other path for us to take.

Endnotes

[1] H. Strods, "Latvijas cilveku izvedeji 1949. gada 25. marta," *Latvijas Vesture* 1 (1999), 68.

[2] V. D. Bonch-Brujevich, *Izbrannije sochinenija* (ed. N. A. Smirnov; Moskva: Izdatelstvo Akademii Nauk SSSR, 1959), T. 1, 21.

[3] Ibid., 378.

[4] E. Cernevskis, *Adventes kustiba Latvija* (Riga: Patmos, 1998), 42.

5   J. Talonen, *Church under the Pressure of Stalinism* (Helsinki: Societas Historica Finlandiae Septentrionalis, 1997), 242.

6   N. Gills, "Cels uz atzisanu: Jehovas liecinieki Latvija 20. gadsimta," *Religiski-filozofiski Raksti* 8 (2003), 292.

7   Talonen, *Church under the Pressure of Stalinism*, 234–38.

8   A. Barmin, "Katolichestvo v sovremennoi Rossii," *Logos* 50, (1995), 123.

9   H. Strods, *Latvijas katolu baznicas vesture 1075–1995* (Riga: author's publication, 1996), 320.

10 The phrase used by the Plenipotentiary of the Council of Affairs for Religious Cults in Latvia, Julijs Restbergs. See LVA (State Archive of Latvia), 101. f., 21. apr., 73. l., 28. lp. (standard Latvian abbreviations are used to help potential researchers).

11 A. Bergmanis, "Bralu draudzes Latvija pec II Pasaules kara," *MLB Zinotajs* (March 1996), 2.

12 M. Bourdeaux, *Gorbachev, Glastnotj and the Gospel* (London: Hodder & Stoughton, 1990), 129.

13 I. Jefimov, *Sovremennoje Harizmaticheskoje dvizhenije sektanstva* (Moskva, 1998), 268.

14 I. Zalite, "LPSR VDK uzbuve un galvenie darba virzieni (1980–1991. g.)," *Latvijas Vesture* 1 (1999), 115–16.

15 The phrase "believers are genuine patriots of their homeland and Soviet power" (Beseda s mitropolitom Krutickim i Kolomenskim Juvenalijem, *Na puti k svobode sovesti*, sost. D.J. Furman, o. Mark (Smirnov) [Moskva: Progress, 1989], 116), a claim made by Orthodox Metropolitan Juvenalij at the end of the Soviet period, is one example of such deformation of consciousness.

16 I. Skulte, "Paaudze, kura Vacieti zinaja visi," *Forums* 49 (2003), 2–3.

17 In his memoirs Latvian Lutheran theologian Roberts Feldmanis is quoted as saying, "Pastors gave over churches [to Soviets] by leaving them. They put their hope to distant, free countries. They turned their eyes to America, Sweden. And we heard nothing of them." A. Gaide, "Sarunas ar profesoru Robertu Feldmani", *Cela Biedrs* 9 (2003), 138.

18 G. Stricker, "Glaube in der 2. Welt Institute: A Religious Research Center in Zollikon Near Zurich," *Religion in Eastern Europe* 23.3 (2003), 29.

19 Billy Graham, *Just As I Am* (San Francisco, CA: Harper Collins / Grand Rapids, MI: Zondervan, 1997), 380.

20 In Latvia there are only a few studies on relationships between emigrants and those who remained in Soviet Latvia. See, for example, the analytical article written by Atis Lejinsh (emigrant Latvian, now the Director of the Latvian Institute of International Affairs): A. Lejins, "Kurs bija kakis, kurs pele?" *Diena* 212 (2004), 15.

21 G. Lazdins, "Vidienas apgabals," *Baznicas gadagramata 2004. gadam* (Riga: Klints, 2003), 273.

22 Problems related to the place of women in the church were discussed recently in an international conference in Riga (August 22, 2005) organized

by the Association of Lutheran Women Theologians in Latvia to celebrate thirty years since the first ordination of a woman in the Latvian Lutheran Church.

23 A. J. Stranga, "Pommera slepkavibai ir vesturisks fons," *Diena* 235 (2003), 2.

24 P. Knitter, *One Earth, Many Religions: Multifaith Dialogue and Global Responsibility* (Maryknoll, NY: Orbis, 1995), 15.

25 *Trust* 29.5/6 (1930), 24.

26 Pentecostal experience is meant here.

27 *Atmodas dziesmas* (Riga: Atmoda, 1939⁴), 182.

28 "Aptaujas par neiecietibu Latvija rezultati"; http://www.politika.lv (viewed December 12, 2003).

29 *Cultural Diversity and Tolerance in Latvia* (Riga, Secretariat of the Special Tasks Minister for Social Integration, 2003), 18–19.

30 J. Sobrino, "Our World: Cruelty and Compassion," *Concilium* 1 (2003), 21.

31 However, the boundaries between classical Pentecostals and neo-Pentecostals are not so distinct anymore. There are many classical Pentecostal churches that have abandoned the closed identities of their forefathers. See V. Teraudkalns, "New Charismatic Churches in Latvia as Examples of Postmodern Religious Subculture," *International Review of Mission* 90.359 (2001), 444–54.

32 The First Party of Latvia gained ten seats in Parliament. However, in January 2004 it left the coalition. Shortly after that, in February, the government led by Einars Repse from the New Era Party resigned after being in power for fifteen months. The First Party was part of a restructured ruling coalition, thus also securing places in the new government.

33 I. Springe, "Pie Dieva netradicionali," *Sestdiena* (September 2003, 20–26), 26.

34 For example, mass media criticized the Special Tasks Minister for Social Integration, Nils Muiznieks, for a public speech in the worship service of the neo-Pentecostal church "New Generation," where he praised that church as the best. S. Benfelde, "Ministrs ignore Satversmi un pelna punktus velesanam," *Nedela* 38, (2004), 14.

35 The Ministry of Education and Science in Latvia has accepted the plan that starting from September 2004 parents will be obliged to choose on behalf of their children between Christian instruction compiled by four denominations (Pentecostals are not among them) or secular ethics. Instruction in the Christian faith is already offered in schools but it is limited only to some denominations. This plan has stirred up debate, and many experts have objected to it as giving privileges to some religious groups ("Jauna izglitibas politika apdraud valsts un baznicas noskirtibu"; http://www.delfi.lv [viewed November 27, 2003]).

36 These theologies very quickly are becoming voices of Western neo-liberalism and imperialism. See, for example, pastor of the New Generation Church, Riga, A. Ledjajev's glorification of George Bush's politics as an example

of Christian government (A.Ledjajev, "Novij mirovoj porjadok" http://www.gospel.lv/point/NewWorld.htm [viewed October 11, 2005]).

37 V. Belokons, Konservativisms – mits vai realitate musdienu Latvija, *Diena* 27 (2003), 2.

38 The saying "no sooner said than done" that was used by the First Party is translated in Latvian as "man and word."

39 http://www.lpp.lv (viewed October 11, 2005).

40 For example, deputy Peteris Tabuns (of the "For Fatherland and Freedom" party), employing traditional right-wing argument of threats to the Latvian language, characterized Nils Muiznieks' opinion as "leftist cosmopolitism;" http://www.saeima.lv/steno/2002_8/st_021121/st2111.htm (viewed October 11, 2005).

41 See, for example, the predominantly gay Potter's Hose Fellowship Church, a Pentecostal and predominantly gay church in Florida (USA). Its pastor, Robert Morgan, once a licensed minister with the United Pentecostal Church International, co-founded the Fellowship of Reconciling Pentecostals International; http://www.rpifellowship.com (viewed October 11, 2005).

42 J. B. Metz, "Political Theology: A New Paradigm of Theology," in L. S. Rouner (ed.), *Civil Religion and Political Theology* (Notre Dame, IN: University of Notre Dame Press, 1986), 146–47.

43 In spite of negative feelings about the Soviet period, according to the poll done in 2004, 63 percent of the population in Latvia think that fifteen years ago they were better off economically ("Lielaka dala sabiedribas uzskata, ka padomju laikos dzivojusi labak"; http://www.delfi.lv [viewed August 19, 2004]). This perception is the result of another socio-political extreme: neo-liberalism.

44 S. Benfelde, "Krusta kars par bernu dveselem vai veletaju balsim," *Nedela* 36 (2004), 10. Some days before the beginning of the new school year, the Ministry of Science and Education stopped financing the boarding school and started to support the Catholic school in the same area.

45 According to the agency "Vertograd," which provides news about Orthodox separatists, this group in Latvia has fourteen parishes, and like others it tries to connect its short history with times that have more symbolic capital by considering itself a successor of the pre-war Latvian Orthodox Church; http://www.vertograd.ru/txt/03/08/378.html (viewed October 11, 2005).

46 http://www.mk.gov.lv/site/files/5/514.doc (viewed October 11, 2005). Agreements signed with other churches do not have such strict terms.

47 LVA-1448.f. – 1.apr.-166.l.- 43.-50. lpp.

48 A. Skuburs, "Par Jani Dresku un Zalenieku draudzi," *Darbabiedrs* 1 (1991), 71–75.

49 See also similar tendencies in Great Britain in I. M. Randall, "The myth of the Missing Spirituality: Spirituality among English Baptists in the Early Twentieth Century," in P. E. Thompson and A. R. Cross (eds.), *Recycling the Past or Researching History* (Milton Keynes: Paternoster, 2005), 111–14.

50 Interest in church tradition and liturgy has stimulated the establishment of the local branch of the Charismatic Episcopal Church (its headquarters are in the USA). However, it should be admitted that so far in Latvia it is not a widespread movement, but the result of the recent individual faith journey of former Methodist Minister, Ints Danielsons.

51 A. Sabanovs, "Latvijas krievi, kadi mes esam?" *Diena* 141, (2002), 2.

52 *Etniska tolerance un Latvijas sabiedribas integracija* (Riga: Baltijas Socialo Zinatnu instituts, 2004), 28.

53 J. Moltmann, *The Church in the Power of the Spirit* (New York, London: Harper & Row, 1977), 361.

54 In his writings, the American Pentecostal theologian Cecil M. Robeck, Jr. has reminded us of different forms of martyrdom: "those who are called upon to give up something else by virtue of what they do, things like position, reputation, prestige, or even acceptance within their own Christian communities." See, C. M. Robeck, Jr., "When Being a 'Martyr' Is Not Enough: Catholics and Pentecostals," *PNEUMA: The Journal of the Society for Pentecostal Studies* 21.1 (1999), 5.

10

Martyria and *Koinonia*

Theological Reflections on Some Aspects of the History of Poland

DARIUSZ MIKOLAJ CUPIAL

1. Introduction

As we can see clearly in the Bible, especially in the Old Testament, God has been exhorting people through their history: "Now all these things happened to them by way of example, and they were described in writing to be a lesson for us." (1 Cor. 10:11). In the New Testament, Jesus Christ promised the gift of the Holy Spirit to the apostles: "But the Paraclete, the Holy Spirit, whom the Father will send in my name, will teach you everything and remind you of all I have said to you" (John 14:26). This promise concerns not only the apostles but also all their successors as well as all the believers that will be led by the Spirit.

"If you love me you will keep my commandments. I shall ask the Father, and He will give you another Paraclete to be with you forever, the Spirit of truth" (John 14:15–17). The Second Vatican Council referred to that Scripture passage when it addressed the issue of reading, understanding, and explaining the signs of the times. "To carry out such a task, the Church has always had the duty of scrutinizing the signs of the times and of interpreting them in the light of the gospel … We must therefore recognize and understand the world in which we live, its explanations, its longings, and its often dramatic characteristics" (*Gaudeum et Spes* 4). This quotation is the starting point for my further reflection.

2. *Martyria* – The Response of Faith

An explanation of the word *martyria* will be very helpful while we reflect on the topic of the suffering church. The biblical Greek term *martyria* means both "one who gives witness" and "martyrdom." I believe this explains well the essential attitude of a Christian towards suffering, persecution, and oppression.

Some western theologians see two basic periods in the history of the church: an era of martyrdom (*martyrs*) and an era of moral ordeal (*confessor*). According to this concept, these two eras are successive. I must admit that we can notice them throughout Poland's history. But rather than being successive, they were experienced at the same time and were soon followed by a third period. This third period is an era of sanctification of earthly things. The martyrs of our history offered up their lives to defend Christian moral values. The confessors suffered for the truth. And then there was also a struggle to remain faithful to the gospel and the church in society, culture, politics, and all other earthly things (Christian as *homo vivens, practicing*).[1]

Martyria is one of the most essential elements for the vitality of the church in every age. Because of this, the church becomes alive, growing and expressing herself as community – *koinonia*. The church is alive when all her members live out three basic activities: *martyria, diakonia, leiturgia*. A deeper understanding of the word *martyria* draws our eyes to Christ. How did Jesus witness? The book of Revelation describes him as "the faithful witness" (Rev. 1:5). Christ is a witness to the Father. We need to remember how Jesus testified in order to understand in what ways we should be witnessing to God. Christ, being the Word of the Father, witnesses through:

- his words;
- his deeds;
- his attitude and whole life.

And the most complete witness of Christ was revealed on the cross.

3. *Deus Vincit* – God Has Conquered

Polish people accepted and embraced the gospel over 1,000 years ago. Their history is both fascinating and tragic. There are moments of great victory and glory as well as moments of painful failure. This nation has contributed greatly to the heritage of the church with many witnesses and martyrs, starting with St. Stanislaw and ending with St. Maximilian and Fr. Jerzy Popieluszko. It was in Poland that Nicolas Kopernikus published a book that changed the view of the world. It was also in Poland that Pawel Wlodkowic developed an innovative idea of human rights, and the great first woman chemist, Maria Curie-Sklodowska, started her research on radioactive elements. A long time before the concept of the European Union was born, a union was signed in the Polish town of Lublin that brought together different nations and peoples on the basis of partnership and equality – *unitas in pluralitate* (unity in diversity). This happened in the sixteenth century.

Later, when almost the whole of Europe was plunged in terror from the Inquisition and religious wars, Poland appeared to be an oasis of tolerance and freedom for Protestants, Jews, and even Muslims. A Catholic king of Poland who faced a lot of pressure ordering him to limit such freedom replied: "I'm not a ruler of my people's conscience." Poland was called by some historians a country without a stake or gallows. This kind of approach throughout the history of Poland sheds light on the way in which the gospel message penetrated social life. It was very different from the *quius regio eius religio* (the ruler dictates the religion of the people) principle that became a foundation of religious policy in other countries.

The "Magna Charta" of Polish history was the proclamation of the May 3, 1791 constitution that was the very first in Europe, and the second in the world just after the American constitution.

During the course of history, God gave Poland rulers and leaders who stood up to defend the nation, freedom, and Christianity. These were King Jan Sobieski III, Tadeusz Kosciuszko, and Jozef Pilsudski, just to mention a few. All historians – believers and nonbelievers (among them Norman Davies) – have described the battle of Warsaw in 1920 as one of the few historical events that shaped the fortunes of the modern world.[2] Polish troops led by Marsal Pilsudski faced the Soviet Red Army and stopped its march towards Europe in what was later called "the miracle by the Vistual River."

Earlier in her history, Poland had served in defense of the far eastern frontier of Christianity, standing in the way of Mongolian and Turkish expansions. In the year 1683 near Vienna, the Polish King Jan Sobieski III broke the power of the Ottoman Empire. The king faced a very difficult decision. He had two options: to protect the country from the north (Prussia) or to help Europe face the threat of Islam reaching her doorsteps. Jan Sobieski III chose the latter and went south to fight for Christian Europe. After the victory, he sent a letter to the Pope sharing his sense of God's intervention in the midst of the challenge: "*venimus, vidimus, Deus vincit,*" he said.[3]

4. *Non Possimus*[4]

The Polish nation suffered some painful defeats as well as its glorious victories. The last few centuries have seen many of these. At the end of the eighteenth century, three neighboring countries struck Poland, and as a result the country was under partition until 1918. It was an act of terrible harm and violation of international law. Poland was no longer included on the world's map. One of the famous Polish poets, Adam Mickiewicz, said that the homeland's freedom can be compared to health – its value is only appreciated properly when it has been taken away. In the midst of this suffering, there was hope and conviction not to give in. Being left alone and not understood by the international community as well as by the Holy See, the Polish church tried to bring moral and spiritual renewal to the nation. At the same time, God raised up great poets who also served as prophets and theologians, a few of the most significant being Adam Mickiewicz, Juliusz Slowacki, and Kamil Cyprian Norwid. They would encourage and comfort the people, teaching them that the time of suffering is also a time of messianic testimony. They thought that a nation can suffer also on behalf of other nations, just as one person can suffer for others. If the suffering is accepted in the spirit of *martyria* (witness), it will then give birth to a new dimension of community with God and humanity (*koinonia*). The suffering at the time of partition brought about a real explosion of new religious congregations that, remaining anonymous for the foreign regimes, penetrated the secular structure of education, industry, etc. They had a tremendous influence on that society, for example, fostering charitable works. This movement can be compared to the American Salvation Army. The gift of freedom came back to Poland after the First World War in 1918.

The next period worth mentioning started in the year 1939. British historian Norman Davies described it as the Polish Golgotha. Poland was the only country on the continent that never agreed to collaborate with the Nazis.[5] The nation paid with her blood by facing two deadly enemies, the Soviets and the Nazis, like the unfair battle of David who took on a giant Goliath. During the Second World War the Polish nation lost a quarter of its population in trying to fulfil its commitment to the alliance. Polish troops fought in Tobruk, Africa; Monte Cassino, Italy; Arnhem, Holland; and Great Britain. The sacrifice of blood did not hurt as much as the betrayal of the Allies in 1939, 1944, and 1945 when the Yalta Pact that submitted Poland to Soviet tyranny was signed. That led to another painful period. It started just after the war when more than two million people were driven out of their homes in the Eastern borderland since one third of the Polish territory came under Soviet administration. The suffering of the thousands of innocent people, doomed to torment and death, was to last some forty years longer.

5. *Unde Malum?*[6]

Many have asked, why do we suffer? The same question transcribed into Polish history can be formulated, why was it that so much hatred was directed towards a nation that has never been a major threat to its neighbors? The answer to this question cannot be solely found through a humanistic perspective. The key to understanding the suffering of a person or the suffering

of a group of people called a community or society can only be
discovered in the Christological dimension of faith. John Paul II,
during his first visit to Warsaw as pope, said, "It is not possible
to understand this nation [Poland] which had such a wonderful,
but at the same time terribly difficult past – without Christ"
(June 2, 1979).[7]

Jesus, the most innocent among the offspring of humans, has
taken all our suffering onto himself. But his salvation applies also
to the world, the cosmos, and the whole of humanity. The mystery
of suffering cannot be understood without the insight that comes
from the heroism of the Christian faith. If Christ alone suffered
and was afraid of passion and death, crying out, "My God, my
God, why have you forsaken me?" (Ps. 22:1; Matt. 27:45), this
means that suffering is included in the human condition. This is
why we can say that every human being's suffering has a share
in Christ's suffering (see Col. 1:24). A leading Polish theologian,
Abp Alfons Nossol, thinks that suffering makes sense only from
a Christological view: "Taking the example of Christ, we need to
follow him and know that love can direct suffering in such a way
that it ultimately becomes an expression of saving, redeeming and
humanizing love."[8]

6. Hope is Dead – Long Live Hope

For real hope to be strong and victorious, it must be purified
and stripped from any illusory (pseudo-)hope. One can say that
the Polish Church has gone through this process of purification
(*katarsis*) during the last several years. What have we learned from
this? The church marked by suffering is a community of deeper
relationship with God (*koinonia* in its vertical dimension). Meister
Eckhart said that Christians very often look at God in a way people
sometimes look at a cow. A cow is loveable because it gives us
milk, butter, and cheese. If God is unconditional love, he is then
worthy of being loved by us in the same way. Applying the same
principle, we can say that a greater amount of unconditional love
is required in the relationships between churches (*koinonia* in its
horizontal dimension).

The church as the body of Christ and *communio sanctorum*, grows like a living organism, and she no longer makes a distinction between active and passive members (teachers and listeners), as was thought after the Tridentine Council. Quoting the famous Polish poet Cyprian Kamil Norwid, one can say that a diamond has emerged from ashes. Likewise, the Polish Nobel Lauriat Czeslaw Milosz wrote unforgettable words in a poem on the monument of the three crosses in Gdansk in memory of those who died during the labor strikes in 1970.[9] Suffering accepted and embraced with faith has released a certain type of persistent testimony – *martyria*, which then in turn has given birth to the new community – *koinonia*, called "Solidarity." The bloodless revolution of the Solidarity movement led by Lech Walesa has been a completely new phenomenon in modern civil (or social) history. It is worth mentioning the profound impact that several preachers and theologians have had on the essence of this phenomenon. Among them are Cardinal Karol Wojtyla (the late Pope John Paul II), the legendary primate of Poland Cardinal Stefan Wyszynski, Professor Father Jozef Tischner, Father Jerzy Popieluszko, and Professor Father Franciszek Blachnicki.[10]

7. The So-Called Polish Liberation Theology

What is quite interesting is that that theology of suffering has never been quite developed in Poland. What was really developed was a theology of liberation. The main person behind it was a former prisoner of the Auschwitz Nazi death camp Franciszek Blachnicki, who was also the founder of the massive renewal movement called Light and Life (Oasis) as well as a few other associations and ministries.[11] His theology of liberty has been centered around the Lord's assurance "the truth will set you free" (John 8:32). The mission statement of one of Fr. Blachinicki's ministries says:

> Truth sets man free only if he has accepted it freely and submitted his life to be a subject of this truth. Fear stands in the way of accepting the truth; therefore, freedom from fear is a condition for liberation through truth. One

can be set free from fear only by entering into a father-son relationship with God. A person who becomes a son will not be a slave any longer. The way to liberation is to go through the experience of the cross.[12]

The liberation of humankind appears to be a central issue of the so-called free West. In this way, the experience of Eastern Christians can be of importance for solving issues in western society. Looking at the East could help the western world deepen an understanding of the gift of freedom and its implications. The Christian vision of liberty gains an integral dimension only when it is related to the truth. John Paul II has drawn our attention to the eighth commandment: "A man is free to speak untruth but he is not entirely free if he does not speak the truth."

Ultimately, the central issue is always the problem concerning humankind. If we say that communism was an anthropological catastrophe, we must also remember that the lack of a proper understanding (view) of humankind and freedom can become a source of social, economical, and political crisis in our times.

Endnotes

[1] Czesław Bartnik, "Najnowsze dzieje Kosciola w Polsce," in *Swiadectwo Kosciola Katolickiego w systemie totalitarnym Europy srodkowo-wszhodniej* (Lublin: no publisher, 1994), 45–46.

[2] Norman Davies, *God's Playground: A History of Poland* (Oxford: Clarendon, 1981).

[3] "We came, we saw, God conquered."

[4] "We cannot." See Acts 4:20.

[5] Professor of History Tomasz Strzembosz's research shows the unique and unheard of anywhere else in the world phenomenon of the Polish Underground State (PPP). Nazi terror occupied the territory of Poland and forced all the government departments to close down. In fact, all these state functions (the president, senate, parliament, judiciary, military, and primarily education) were secretly functioning in Warsaw and all of Poland. For example, over a million children and youth graduated from secret schools in Poland during the Second World War since the Nazi regime dissolved formal education.

[6] "Why suffering?"

[7] *Jan Pawel II w Polsce 1979, 1983, 1987* (Warszawa: 1989), 37.

8   Abp Alfons Nossol, "Z Czym w jutro chrześcijańskiej Europy?" in Bartnik, *Swiadectwo Kosciola,* 89–104.

9   You, who wronged a simple man,
    Bursting into laughter at the crime,
    And kept a crowd of fools around you,
    Mixing good and evil to blur the line,
    Though everyone bowed down before you,
    Saying Virtue and Wisdom lit your way,
    Striking gold medals in your honour,
    And glad to have survived another day,
    Do not feel safe. The poet remembers.
    You can slay him, but another is always born …
    The words are written down, the deed, the date.
    You would have done better with a winter's dawn,
    A rope, and a branch bent down beneath your weight.
    Czeslaw Milosz, quoted in Mary Craig, *The Crystal Spirit* (London: Hodder & Stoughton, 1986). See also Czeslaw Milosz, *The Captive Mind,* quoted in J. A. C. Brown, *Techniques of Persuasion* (Baltimore, MD: Pelican Books, 1964).

10 See John Lester and Pierre Spoerri, *Rediscovering Freedom* (London and Ottawa: Grosvenor, 1992).

11 See Grazyna Sikorska, *Light and Life: Renewal in Poland* (London: Collins, 1989); Tom Noe, *Into the Lion's Den* (South Bend, IN: Greenlawn Press, 1994); Dariusz M. Cupial, "Renewal among Catholics in Poland," *PNEUMA: The Journal of the Society for Pentecostal Studies* 16.2 (Fall 1994), 227–31; Dariusz Cupial, *Na drodze ewanglizacji i ekumenii: Ruch Swiatlo-Zycie w sluzbie jednosci chrzescian* (Lublin: Katolickiego Uniwersytetu Lubelskiego, 1996).

12 Franciszek Blachnicki, *Prawda – Krzyz – Wyzwolenie* (Carlsberg, Germany: Maximilianum, 1984), 139.

Section V

ASIA

11

God and Caesar

Church and State Relationships in Communist China

BOB (XIQIU) FU

1. Introduction

Due to spiritual, historical, and ideological reasons, Christianity has not played a crucial role in many of the atheist countries in which communism dominates. Mainland China is typical of the countries in which the Christian faith has been oppressed, then tolerated. Ironically in 1996, the Chinese Communist Party (CCP) even required the churches to "talk politics." Under this pattern of church and state relations, the responses of two types of churches in China embodied different attitudes toward God and Caesar. At stake was how much to submit to God and how much to Caesar. What are the different roles that the Three-self Patriotic Movement (TSPM) churches and the house churches have been playing under these two schemes of church-state relationship? Why do the house churches refuse to register with the government and join the TSPM?

2. Why Are Christians Oppressed in China?

2.1 Spiritual reasons

Scripture consistently reveals to us that "Every one who wants to live a godly life in Christ Jesus will be persecuted"(2 Tim. 3:12). Jesus also told his disciples they will be persecuted and hated and even put to death because of his name (Matt. 24:9; Luke 21:12).

Moreover, the apostle Peter warned: "do not be surprised at the painful trial you are suffering" (2 Pet. 4:12) because "your enemy the devil prowls around like a roaring lion looking for someone to devour" (1 Pet. 5:8).

Nevertheless, through oppression the children of God experience the transforming power in the suffering of Christ. This is how they know what it means to have fellowship with the suffering of Christ and to experience the power of his resurrection (Phil. 3:19–11). As a result, their faith can be strengthened, their churches purified, and their relationship with Christ deepened. Furthermore, if God could use Nebuchadnezzar the king of Babylon as his servant (Jer. 27:6), then he can use the persecution of Communists all the more, to revive his churches and to manifest to the persecutors his sovereignty by the rapid growth of his churches.

Throughout all of church history, God reveals the truth that the more persecution there is, the more revival there will be, and the more pressure there is, the more believers there will be.

2.2 Historical reasons

Although the first Protestant missionary, Robert Morrison (from the London Missionary Society), reached Canton in 1807, Christianity did not play a very crucial role in Chinese society; it was oppressed more often than welcomed. One of the historical reasons is that, to many Chinese, the gospel came into China along with the forces of western colonial pressure. This impression was strengthened especially when China lost the Second Opium War in 1858, as a result of which the unequal Treaty of Tianjin in 1860 was signed. This treaty included a "toleration clause" that granted foreign missionaries the right to share the Christian faith in China. This contributed greatly to the Chinese mindset of regarding Christianity as a foreign religion (Yang Jiao), which invaded the territory of traditional Chinese.

When Communism emerged after 1919, its constant propaganda led to the outbreak of the anti-Christian movement in 1922, which was later revived and spread throughout the whole of China. Christianity was criticized and accused of being the arm of western imperialism. In response, some Chinese church leaders started to establish Chinese indigenous churches, which later were used to initiate the so-called Three-self Movement after the Communist Party of China gained power in 1949. Professor Eric O. Hanson, in his book *Catholic Politics in China and Korea,* noted that the Chinese politico-religious culture strongly reinforces ideological and nationalistic antipathies toward the church, and the Chinese Communist government simply continues the traditional Chinese state religious policy of seeking to penetrate, regulate, and control any institutional religious activities.[1] The CCP has pursued social control of religion more strongly than ever before because of its greater reliance on popular political mobilization.[2]

2.3 Ideological reasons

According to Marxism, "religion is the opium of the people" and the product of false human interpretation of natural power. However, it will gradually disappear with the development of social and technological sciences as humanity gains more power over nature. Based on such an assessment, the CCP, on the one hand, declares that theism is an ideology forever opposed to Marxism. Yet, on the other hand, it admits that religion has its inevitable space in people's heart, even in the period of socialism, and it cannot be eliminated by administrative force, although the CCP did attempt but failed to destroy it during the Cultural Revolution (1966–76). This failure caused the party to raise special concerns about religion, especially after the collapse of the former Soviet Union and Eastern European communist countries in 1989; the CCP concluded that Christianity, including Catholicism, played a very "bad" role in subverting these countries. (I have seen some of the secret documents that make this conclusion evident.) Hence, the CCP started a tight controlling policy implementing different systems in the name of "making religion compatible with socialist society."[3]

According to an official in the Religious Affairs Bureau (RAB; a governmental department in charge of all the religious patriotic organizations through which the Communist Party carries out its religious policy), "compatible" means that religion is subordinate to socialism.[4] That is to say, some religious doctrines and ethical teachings must be used to promote socialist construction after the religions have been reformed; all negative elements of religion must be gotten rid of; and each religion must be under the direction of the CCP. In a word, "the legal existence of the religious complexities totally depends upon the leadership's cooperation with and the acceptance of the government, and the government holds the final right to choose the partnership."[5] More concretely, the result of being "compatible" with socialism is that only certain "patriotic" religious professionals (with preaching certificates issued by the CCP) are allowed to teach the ideals of love and a sacrificial spirit instead of teaching from the Bible about the Great Commission, redemption, the last day, and spiritual warfare. In addition, their activities are confined to certain times and certain designated places. These are the churches under the leadership of the Three-self Patriotic Movement (TSPM: self-supporting, self-governing, and self-propagating) and its permitted meeting points. It was established in 1954 by a few Protestant liberal leaders, headed by Wu Yaozong, and is used to help the CCP carry out its religious policy, which primarily was to cut off the churches in China from their western mother churches. (Actually, the TSPM gradually became a political tool with religious clothes.) It is forbidden, of course, to preach the gospel to young successors of socialism under eighteen years of age.

3. How Much to Submit to God and How Much to Caesar: The Church and State Relationship in China

3.1 *The pattern of state supremacy over all religions*

The traditional pattern for the relationship between the church and state in China is the supremacy of the state over religion. In traditional China, the emperor held the highest power. Confucianism was regarded as the state orthodoxy from the seventh century onward till the collapse of the Qing Dynasty in 1911. Imperial rule and the Confucian view of the subjects' loyalty to the state went hand in hand and mutually reinforced one another. Confucian orthodoxy was transmitted and enforced through the educational system and the civil service examination system.

Today this pattern of state supremacy and official orthodoxy persists in China under a socialist totalitarian state. This means there is no such thing as separation of church and state as understood in the West. The church must operate under the religious policies of the CCP and under the legal ordinances of the state. The state has its own official orthodox, namely Marxism, Leninism, and the thought of Mao (after the fifteenth Chinese Communist Party Congress, the thought of Deng Xiaoping was also added), which the party seeks to propagate. All other ideologies and beliefs are considered heterodox.

World religions like Christianity, Catholicism, Buddhism, Taoism, and Islam are considered "heterodox" in relation to Marxist "orthodoxy," but are allowed to conduct their religious activities so long as such activities come under the supervision and control of the state. The apparatus of control include the United Front Work Department of the Party, the Religious Affairs Bureau of the state, and the "patriotic religious organizations." Church activities that are conducted within this sphere of control are called "normal religious activities" and are given legal status. The five major patriotic religious organizations are the Chinese Buddhist Association, Chinese Taoist Association, Chinese Islamic Association, Chinese Catholic Patriotic Association, and the Chinese Protestant Three-self Patriotic Movement.

Religious activities carried outside of state control, that is, outside the patriotic organizations, are not only considered heterodox in ideology, but also "illegal religious activities." Hence, these are subject to prosecution, a form of legalized persecution. House churches that refuse to register with the state, and hence conduct their activities outside Three-self Patriotic Movement (sphere of control), come under this category of "illegitimate religious activities," and some of the organized house churches that are active in evangelistic expansion are labeled "cultic groups." These have become the state's primary target of attack.

3.2 *China's religious policy*

The constitution of China declares that citizens of China shall enjoy freedom of religious belief. This is defined as "free to believe and free not to believe; free to believe in this religion or that religion", and within a religion, one is "free to choose his sectarian differences; and free to move from unbelief to beliefs and vice-versa." Freedom of religion, however, does not include freedom of propagation outside the approved places designated for religious activities, nor does it include the freedom to establish churches according to one's religious convictions.

The major document outlining China's religious policy is Document No. 19 issued by the Party Central in March of 1982. It was further reinforced by Document No. 6 issued by the State Council in February of 1991. In January of 1994 the State Council issued decrees No. 144 and 145, governing religious activities among foreigners in China (144) and the requirement of registration for unregistered religious groups (145). Subsequently there have been numerous legal ordinances enforcing the state requirement for registration. Since April 1996 the government has stepped up its effort to enforce registration and to terminate all religious activities not approved by registration. Though China declares to the world that she respects and protects freedom of religion, her actual religious policy as revealed in recent state ordinances and secret documents is one of administrative control over all religious activities – the Protestant church in particular – because of their rapid expansion in terms of the multiplication of itinerant evangelists and the founding of house churches throughout the country, two hills in this battle that the state has not been able to take.

4. The Place of TSPM Churches and House Churches under State Supremacy

4.1 *The place of the TSPM and the China Christian Council*

Within the above framework of church and state relations and China's religious policy, the only legitimate sphere for Christian activities is the Three-self Patriotic Movement as one of the "patriotic organizations." At the third Christian Conference held in Nanking in October 1980, a parallel ecclesiastical body called the China Christian Council was set up to handle church affairs such as church organization, theological education, and delegations visiting foreign countries. The Three-self Reform Movement was set up by the State in 1950 and formally organized in 1954 as the Three-self Patriotic Movement. Its function is to assist the government in implementing its religious policy. The TSPM reports to the Religious Affairs Bureau which approves registration, pastoral personnel appointment, leadership training, and financial oversight. For example, if in a registered TSPM church the pastor gets sick, a second person to preach in his place must be approved by the Religious Affairs Bureau (RAB). During this time, he must not preach when his assistant preaches. When he gets well and is able to preach, his assistant may not preach.

The TSPM committees are organized on the national level, the provincial level, the municipal level, and the prefectural level, which controls various churches within its domain. The TSPM has the responsibility of carrying out the state's religious policy, which may vary from regime to regime, and to inform the government (Religious Affairs Bureau) of "illegitimate religious activities" being conducted in their area. In this sense they are agents of control as informers. Most arrests of house church leaders are done through information provided by "progressive" TSPM officials.

4.2 The place of house churches in this scheme

House churches that have developed through itinerant evangelism or spontaneous growth of the church are considered illegal. They are now required to register with the Religious Affairs Bureau (RAB). One of the requirements for registration is that they must have a pastoral leader who is endorsed by the TSPM, which in turn seeks the approval of the RAB. Other requirements include a certain number of believers, organization of a church council, and adequate reason to show that a church is needed.

Usually when a house church registers with the RAB, it must join the TSPM. Although one RAB official stated that one does not have to join the TSPM when registering, this is not the usual practice. If a house church does not register with the RAB or join the TSPM, its leaders are warned of the consequences. If they refuse to comply, their worship services would be terminated, their leaders arrested and sent to labor camps or in some cases fined. During 1996–97 many church leaders were arrested for refusing to register and join the TSPM, the most well-known of which is Xu Yongze, who was arrested on March 16, 1997 and sentenced to ten years of imprisonment in early October. In Wenzhou, a church was blasted down in the closure procedure. This conflict between church and state is still going on in China today.

4.3 Why house churches do not register and refuse to join the TSPM

First, the alienation between the house churches and the TSPM has been deeply rooted in the history of the church in China since 1950. Christians in the 1950s witnessed how the government used the TSPM to destroy both the institutional church established by western missions and indigenous churches founded by Chinese believers. This was done through a series of political movements directed by the state and carried out through the agency of the TSPM, such as the accusation campaigns of 1951, the pressure to join the TSPM as evidence of patriotism during 1951–55, the anti-Hu Feng campaign when independent church leaders like Wang Ming-tao were arrested and imprisoned, and the pastoral reform movement during the Great Leap Forward Movement, when a good number of pastors unwilling to bow down to the absolute authority of the state were imprisoned for two decades. Many of the pastors were sent to prison during this period through the betrayal of TSPM pastors.

Even today in many cases TSPM pastors work as informants of house church activities to the government resulting in the latter's arrest and imprisonment. Thus, to the house churches, the TSPM is an agent of the government. House church leaders do not regard the TSPM and the China Christian Council (CCC) as authentic representatives of the Chinese church. Hence it is hard for them to be reconciled with their betrayers who are still betraying them.

Secondly, once a house church registers with the government and joins the TSPM, its activities are limited to Sunday worship. Even mid-week prayer meetings and fellowship groups in the believers' homes are forbidden. As a leader in the TSPM church he must enforce this requirement over his own flock, which an evangelical pastor finds it difficult to do. In his heart, he wants his church to grow. He wants the people to have their own Bible study groups. Once he joins the TSPM, he loses the freedom to pastor his flock according to the leading of the Holy Spirit. So he would rather suffer the consequences of arrest than to lose his spiritual freedom.

Thirdly, once a house church registers and joins the TSPM, it can no longer engage in evangelism outside the church building or designated places of worship. But house churches are committed to evangelism, and they have developed rather sophisticated systems of training itinerant evangelists and sending them to border provinces and neighboring provinces where the gospel has not been preached. If they join the TSPM, they would have to give up evangelism. Thus, the issue is whether to evangelize or not to evangelize. The laws of the land are clearly against such expansion of the church through evangelism. The house churches believe that in the matter of evangelism they would rather obey God than human authorities.

Finally, the most important reason why house churches refuse to register and join the TSPM is their belief in the Lordship of Christ over the church. "Who is the head of the church: Christ or the state?" they would ask. The TSPM accepts the state as the supreme authority of church affairs. Among the prohibitions issued by the state and repeated in "patriotic covenants" issued by the TSPM are (1) support the leadership of the CCP and uphold the ideology of Marxism, Leninism, and the thought of Mao Zedong; (2) faithfully implement the religious policy of the state by observing the above three designates; (3) refrain from evangelizing or baptizing those under eighteen; (4) when production and religious life conflicts give priority to production; (5) refrain from making contacts with overseas church groups; and (6) refrain from listening to gospel radio broadcasts from abroad or receiving Christian literature or tapes from abroad, etc. House churches are committed to obedience to Christ, and if such obedience brings suffering, they would rather "walk the pathway of the cross" than yield obedience to an atheistic state power that frustrates them from serving Christ.

5. Conclusion

In China there is "limited freedom of religious beliefs" and freedom of worship within the state approved churches. Those who worship and serve there accept the limitations imposed upon them by the state and try to serve God within the sphere of such limitations in exchange for legal standing and freedom from persecution.

House churches, which are committed to the sole headship of Christ in the church and to evangelism, must operate as illegal groups conducting so-called illegal religious activities, and consequently must suffer the administrative penalties inflicted by the state. State persecution and Christian suffering take place within this context of "illegality." Yet the majority of the house churches have chosen rather to suffer for Christ and his Word than to enjoy the grace given by an anti-Christian state. Thus, their history has been a history of suffering. Their growth takes place within a context of persecution. In this context they have waxed strong and experienced the power of God in revivals, and through their endeavors in pioneer evangelism China is being evangelized. For this they suffer consistent persecution, and perhaps because of it they continue to grow in number and in spiritual maturity. Through obedience, they have tasted the goodness and tender mercies of the Lord. They have seen the fruit of their obedience, and they are not willing to give up God's delight and blessing in exchange for a status of legitimacy granted by an anti-Christian state. Instead of withdrawing from persecution, house churches in central China are now rallying for Christian unity in preparation for a great expansion of the gospel in China and for world evangelism.

"I didn't preach anything about politics in our church, because I believe the separation of the church and state."

"I want you to know that you must talk politics everywhere."

This is a dialogue I had when questioned in jail last year by the PSB. It reflects the contradictory nature of the so-called three-self religious policy (self-governing, self-propagating, self-supporting). Although the CCP kept telling the people that it is carrying out a religious policy that requires the separation of church and state, everyone could see that it means a united relationship with socialism while cutting off the relationship with capitalism. As Dr. Edmund P. Clowney noted, "religion is tolerated when it supports the claims of the state, the Party, the institutional hierarchy."[6]

It is a great regret that some who live in the free western societies, even Christians, know very little – or refuse to know – about the mounting persecution toward Christians in the modern world. To them, the secular government, and the media elites, "political dissidents like the brave young man who stood in front the tank at Tiananmen Square are the credible heroes," as Dr. Michael Horowitz noted in his introduction to the book *Their Blood Cries Out*, "it's hard for them to believe that there are, in today's world, people willing to endure the same certain fate as the Tiananmen Square hero in order to quietly profess a Christian faith."[7]

To the western Christians, persecution seems "more suited to biblical texts and ancient Roman history than to evening newscasts, more a product of mission-board puffery than hard fact."[8] Why? Ignorance? Or bias? Maybe both. Dr. Paul Marshall, in "Peace at Any Price" writes that American Evangelicals tend to emphasize the seeking of inner peace while the mainline churches are busy with seeking outer and international peace by establishing friendships with all political powers, even with persecutors.[9] What a pity! As a former teacher in the Beijing Party School of the CCP, I really know the CCP is good at telling lies, making up stories, and deceiving people in the western world. With its so-called international united front policy, the CCP both sends the TSPM leaders abroad to spread the propaganda of its deceiving religious policy and invites important religious figures to visit China and to speak in the pulpit so that it may prove its "right" religious policy to the naive foreigners. The Lord God is sovereign over all!

Endnotes

[1] Eric O. Hanson, *Catholic Politics in China and Korea* (New York: Orbis, 1980), 112.

[2] Ibid.

[3] *People's Daily,* March 14, 1996.

[4] *Zong Jiao Gong Zuo Tong Xun,* March 1996, 31.

[5] Bishop Ding, *Ding,* 15.88 (August 1995).

[6] Edmund P. Clowney, *Called to the Ministry* (Phillipsburg, NJ: Presbyterian and Reformed Publishing, 1964), 18.

[7] Paul Marshall with Lela Gilbert, *Their Blood Cries Out: The Worldwide Tragedy of Modern Christians Who Are Dying for Their Faith* (Dallas, TX: Word, 1997), 99.

[8] Ibid.

[9] Ibid., 149.

12

Human Rights Violations and the Church in Myanmar

CHIN KHUA KHAI

Myanmar, known as Burma before 1989, is an ancient nation on the Indochina peninsula. Until recently, its political and religious development has been relatively insulated from its neighbors. It is recognized internationally as one of the nations suffering most from human rights violations. The human rights violations have affected the church in many ways.

1. Country Background

With an area of 261,226 square miles (676,577 square kilometers), Myanmar shares its long border with the most populated countries in the world – China on the northeast, India on the northwest, and Bangladesh on the west. It also shares borders with Laos on the east and Thailand on the southeast. Its long southern coastal plain stretches along the Bay of Bengal and the Andaman Sea. Its tropical climate has three seasons: summer (March–May), the rainy season (June–October), and winter (November–February). Its main resources include agriculture, forestry, mining, fishing, and textile products.

Myanmar, with an estimated population of 51,539,000 by the year 2000, is made up of 135 ethnic groups, speaking 106 languages. The eight major ethnic groups are Bamar (69 percent), Shan (8.5 percent), Kayin (6.2 percent), Rakhine (4.5 percent), Mon (2.4 percent), Chin (2.2 percent), Kachin (1.4 percent), and Kayah (0.4 percent). The population is 24.81 percent urban and 75.19 percent rural. The literacy rate is 66.5 percent. The major religions in Myanmar are Buddhism (89.4 percent), Christianity (4.9 percent), Islam (3.9 percent), Hindusm (0.5 percent), and Animism (1.2 percent). A small number practice Confucianism, Judaism, and Laipianism, a local religion.

The nation's political history can be divided according to the times of the monarchy (1044–1855), colonialism (1824–1947), parliamentary democracy (1948–62), and the socialist regime (1962–88). Foreign agents and missionaries were expelled in 1966, during the socialist regime. Since 1988, Myanmar has been under a military government (junta) called the "State Law and Order Restoration Council," which is now known as the "State Peace and Development Council."

2. Church Mission Agencies

Churches in Myanmar are indigenous and steadily growing. More than thirty denominations and some parachurch movements are carrying out mission tasks through three main streams: Catholic, Conciliar Protestant, and evangelical-Pentecostal.[1]

Portuguese traders introduced Roman Catholicism to Myanmar around 1500. A Franciscan priest arrived at Bago with the traders in 1554, but had no success in making converts of the local population. Evangelization began when the priests Calchi and Joseph Vittoni came to Thanlyin in 1721 and obtained permission from King Taninganwe (1714–83) for the propagation of the gospel. More converts came when the mission reached tribal and ethnic peoples. As the second largest denomination today, with an estimated 606,000 members, sixteen bishops, and 600 priests serving in twelve dioceses, the Catholic mission stream has primarily emphasized the Roman Catholic tradition. Ninety percent of the members come from the ethnic minorities. The Catholic Church, with its emphasis on social work, has experienced a steady growth.

The Conciliar mission is a joint effort of eleven mainline Protestant churches united as the Myanmar Council of Churches, under the World Council of Churches. The Regional Council for

Burma was formed in 1914, renamed the Burma Christian Council in 1949, and became the Burma Council of Churches in 1975. Protestant Christianity was introduced into Myanmar first by the English Baptist missionaries James Chater, Richard Mardon, and Felix Carey in 1807, followed by the American Baptist missionaries Adoniram and Ann Judson in 1813. Today, the Myanmar Baptist Convention is the largest denomination with 1,079,000 communicants, including families and children. Missionaries from other traditions than Baptist followed subsequently and reached the tribes and ethnic groups. Indigenous churches are now sending home missionaries through their mission societies and boards. Evangelistic efforts since the 1970s, such as "Chins for Christ in One Century" and "Kachin Gideon Band, 3/330," have shown the most dynamic growth. The Conciliar mission stream emphasizes ecumenicity, development, and theological education.

Under the evangelical-Pentecostal stream, there are seventeen denominations and some parachurch movements, ranging in persuasion from fundamentalist to charismatic. The Myanmar Evangelical Christian Fellowship was organized in 1984. The Assemblies of God, the fastest growing (and third largest) denomination with a membership of 84,158 in the year 2000, began in 1931 and has a strong mission emphasis. All other denominations have come into existence as the result of renewal, evangelism, and church planting.

The renewal movement among the Zomi Chin during the last three decades has resulted in many mission programs across cultures. A number of parachurch movements such as Campus Crusade, Witnessing for Christ, Every Home for Christ, God's Trio Partners, Gospel for the Nation, and Laymen Mission Society, all help to fulfil the evangelistic mandate. Churches in the Evangelical-Pentecostal mission stream emphasize evangelism, renewal, church planting, and theological education.

Besides these church and parachurch elements, the Myanmar Bible Society, Christian Literature Society, and Myanmar Blind Mission Fellowship all work independently under their own mission boards.

3. Human Rights Violations in Myanmar

The term "human rights" is still fresh and foreign to the people in Myanmar. Commoners know nothing about it. The generals of the military junta criticize the concept as a political tool of western nations being held over small countries like Myanmar. After fifty years of independence, the people of Myanmar are still struggling for freedom from colonialism, disorganized social and political structures, and fear and uncertainty about their future.

The idea of human rights actually has a long developmental history. The early stages are seen in the English Bill of Rights (Magna Carta) in 1215, the American Declaration of Rights (Virginia Bill of Rights) 1776, and the French Declaration of Rights in 1789. It had been systematized, crystallized, and declared universally first by the League of Nations, and finalized by the United Nations in 1948.[2] The "Universal Declaration of Human Rights" proclaims that "every individual and every organ of society" should strive to promote the basic rights and freedoms to which all human beings regardless of race, nationality or religion are entitled. Specifically, Article 2 addresses the rights of everyone without distinction of any kind, stating:

> Everyone is entitled to all the rights and freedoms set forth in this Declaration, without distinction of any kind, such as race, color, sex, language, religion, political or other opinion, national or social origin, property, birth or other status. Furthermore, no distinction shall be made on the basis of the political, jurisdictional or international status of the country or territory to which a person belongs, whether it be independent, trust, non-self-governing or under any other limitation of sovereignty.

Article 18 addresses freedom of religion, stating,

> Everyone has the right to freedom of thought, conscience and religion; this right includes freedom to change his religion or belief, and freedom, either alone or in community with other and in public or private, to manifest his religion or belief in teaching, practice, worship and observance.[3]

Sadly, Myanmar is recorded as a country most violating human rights. Persecution and torture for political opinions or religious belief and practices are commonly reported. Racial discrimination, marginalized intolerance, limited freedom of expression, threats to religious freedom, socio-economic pressure, abuse, and rape are issues constantly being addressed. The church, being made up of many ethnic groups, is suffering from human rights violations. The causes of these violations have been rooted in national history, but are propagated most recently through the severe repressions of the socialist regime as well as the military junta now in power. I will examine and present the current issues in light of the "Universal Declaration of Human Rights."

4. Religious Pressure and Violations of Freedom of Worship

Christians are greatly suffering from the pressure of the dominant group, the Buddhists. They are always treated as a minority group with fewer privileges in spite of the granting of freedom of worship. Christianity has always been considered an inextricable part of colonization and a western cultural form of worship. This has been an obstacle to its acceptance in the local communities.

History shows that the Christian movement has always been mistakenly considered foreign domination. During colonial rule and even after national independence, Christians were accused of loving their country less, though they patriotically served the country and were involved in building the nation. Nationalism and Buddhism were bracketed together, with a slogan, "A good Myanma is a good Buddhist." This attitude rendered many loyal Christian leaders more or less inactive in their Christian faith and practice even today.

In reality, like all other religions, Buddhism was imported to the country in the eleventh century. It is undeniable that it has taken root in the culture and social life of the majority of Myanma people. The number of Buddhists and their influence is so strong that most religious festivals and social affairs are always connected with Buddhist religious observances. The country itself is known to be the land of pagodas (the Buddhist houses of worship). In the plains, pagodas are seen in all directions – north, south, east, and west. After the six Buddhist revivals during the 1950s, the prime minister, U Nu, declared Buddhism a state religion in 1961, which resulted in a changed situation in which Christians and other religious groups were unsatisfied with the government.

In order to strengthen socialism, the military regime, under the leadership of General Ne Win, in 1962, withdrew the recognition of Buddhism as the state religion and decreed that all religions would be equally respected. The establishment of the one-party system in 1964 obligated all groups, including religious and nonreligious organizations, to register with the authorities. Christian schools, hospitals, and institutions were nationalized in 1965–66. Since 1962, missionaries had been refused renewal of their residence permits, resulting in the expulsion of all 375 missionaries in 1966.[4] The edict, still in effect today, severely limits any permanent missions program by nonnationals. Though visitors and tourists are issued visas, their residency and travel are strictly limited.

The military government has been widely accused of violating religious freedoms. Civilians are massacred, villages are burned, churches are destroyed, Christian pastors are tortured, and public testimonies and the media often report forced relocations. The military government denies such uncivilized behavior, recognizing it as a violation of human rights. They claim that all religions are peacefully coexisting and flourishing in the nation. The Human Rights Watch Group, in their visit to the country in 1998, remarked on the possibility of all religions and ethnic groups living and working freely together. The truth was hidden from them.

The Oslo-based Democratic Voice of Burma Radio once reported that the State Peace and Development Council (SPDC) army had ordered that Christians in Chin State not hold Christmas celebrations.[5]

The fact is that the authorities make things harder among the tribes and ethnic groups where the majority are Christian, Muslim, or any other non-Buddhist religion. Any religious ceremony or activity requires permission from the authorities, and evangelistic rallies are not allowed. Many pastors have been tortured and jailed for their testimony; some have been killed; and many have been run out of the country, seeking asylum elsewhere.

Crosses planted on tops of mountains have been cut or pulled down and burned. In 1995, soldiers cut and burned the cross believers had posted on top of Kennedy Peak in northern Chin

State as a symbol of their faith. The Buddhists then built a pagoda on that same site. They also cut and burned the cross above the town of Tedim. These incidents have been repeated in many other places in the country.

In urban cities and the plains areas where Buddhists are dominant, no one dares to oppose or complain about their activities. Cash donations for reinforcing monastery projects are collected from all households whether they are Christian, Muslim, or any other religious group. Christians do not dare to refuse them. Many house churches have been forced to close.

Moreover, Christians are uneasy working under government employment. Promotion to a higher rank in the military is specifically restricted in the case of Christians. It is promised only if a person changes his religion to Buddhist. Christians are watched suspiciously. These events have commonly occurred during the past ten years, though the Human Rights Watch groups have not noticed.

Limited Christian publications are allowed by permission of the authorities, only after being censored. When publication is permitted, the label must read: "Circulated only within the church." This label highly controls both the marketing and spread of the Christian message. The socialist regime once allowed the printing of 10,000 copies of the Bible in Myanmar. Christian books and literature are rarely seen in bookstores.

The government totally controls the media, including all radio and television programs. Neither Christians nor any other non-Buddhist religion are allowed to make religious broadcasts. In contrast, the daily media programs often launch and advertise Buddhist activities. The TV news often depicts the generals in their visits to monasteries with offerings. Media listeners and viewers always complain about how boring the programming is and emphasize the danger of its diminishing their spiritual walk.

5. Violation of the Rights of Minorities

The political thrust of the minority ethnic groups in Myanmar since independence can be best understood as a struggle for identity, solidarity, and human rights. They have always felt their living and working privileges were being limited under the political pressures of the majority and the authorities. Since the majority of Christian members come from the smaller ethnic groups, mainly Kayin, Chin, and Kachin (the Shan and the Rakhaing are Buddhist), conflicts between the government and the ethnic groups have always affected the church.

Myanmar (Burma) obtained independence from British colonial rule on January 4, 1948. General Aungsan, the architect of independence, incorporated the small pre-British independent kingdoms of Shan, Karenni, Kachin, and Chin into the independent state of Myanmar. He envisioned and formulated minority rights in his statement entitled "Defense of Burma January 30, 1945." This agreement says:

> They [the minority people] must be given a proper place in the State. They must have their political, economic, and social rights defined and accorded. They must have employment. They must have their own right of representation. They must have equal opportunity in all spheres of the State. There must be no racial or religious discrimination. Any books, songs, signs, symbols, names, etc., which foster such ideas must be officially banned. And we must carry out special uplift work amongst them so that they can be brought to our level and finally to the world level together with us.[6]

The Aungsan–Atlee agreement concerning Myanmar's future (independence) was signed on January 27, 1947 and the Panglong Agreement by Aungsan and Frontier Areas leaders on February 12, 1947. The agreements express the frontier area leaders' desire to work together with the Burman leadership to attain freedom, and the acceptance of the former document recognizes the rights, autonomy, and territorial integrity of the non-Burman peoples.[7]

In spite of independence, insurgents arose in the countryside, and fighting with the government army has continued since 1949. The Burma Communist Party and the ethnic insurgents, such as the Kayin National Union, the Kachin Independent Army, the Shan, Lahus, and Kayah (Karenni), and the underground all resist the government and claim their own autonomy.

Independent Burma continued a parliamentary system of government. Nevertheless, the ethnic groups always felt neglected and despised, constantly pressured in the areas of socio-economic and political life. Projects were always delayed and progress was slow. Worse than this, U Nu endorsed Buddhism as the national religion in 1960 and discriminated against minorities' rights in all respects. This aroused greater disappointment, even anger and hatred, against the government among many nationalist and ethnic groups. The government lost its credibility and many nationalists began to actively oppose it.

Meanwhile, the parliamentary democratic regime was ended by a military coup on March 2, 1962. The military government then was named the Revolutionary Council of the Republic of the Union of Burma, with Ne Win as the chairman. In July 1962, the new administrative body, a one-party system, was formed and called the Burma Socialist Program Party (BSPP). The principle doctrine was the "Burmese Way to Socialism." Institutions and private properties were nationalized. Foreigners were sent back to their own countries and missionaries were sent home.

The Socialist regime has offered free education and free health services to all people, which has benefited the common classes. Schools for formal education and health assistance services were extended to many rural towns and villages. As a consequence, many young people could enter universities and colleges and take civil service exams. And all people could get basic health care. Yet the low quality of care and a lack of supplies for both educational and medical services have not improved after thirty years of reign. The Rangoon Arts and Sciences University, once one of the best in Southeast Asia, became a poor low-rated school suffering from thirty years of socialist disregard.

The pro-democracy movement in 1988 began when party chairman Ne Win announced free elections, looking toward democracy. Students, monks, and the masses joined together in protest marching, demanding changes in the government system through these free elections. It resulted in retaliation by the military in a coup on September 18 with large numbers of people being massacred. The military government, known as the State Law and Order Restoration Council (SLORC), promised the country political freedom but never followed through on the promise. The National League for Democracy (NLD) leader, Aung San Suu Kyi, won the election in 1990 with a landslide victory. However, power was not handed over to the newly elected civilians. Instead, the junta arrested and jailed many of the political leaders, and the NLD leader Aung San Suu Kyi was placed under house arrest. Released in 1995, Suu Kyi was given freedom to travel. However, the attempt to assassinate her during one of her tours of the provinces in upper Myanmar on May 30, 2003 caused shock and anxiety nationwide. Once again, she has been placed under house arrest. Throughout this political turmoil, many political leaders fled the country to avoid potential arrest. The civil rights of the people are being ignored, and authoritarians rule the country.

Since 1988, colleges and universities have been closed from time to time due to the political instability. Many young people have dropped out of school to avoid the mounting political and social pressures. The number of jobless grows higher every year. As a consequence, many young people have turned to undesirable means of livelihood, while others seek asylum in other countries. Today, an estimated 600,000 to 700,000 Myanmar refugees and those seeking asylum are living in the neighboring countries. Many of these are Christians.

The junta extended their military strength and built military camps at all frontier areas among the ethnic people groups. With the presence of the army in the midst of the people, personal conflicts between civilians and soldiers often erupt. Most often the ethnic rebels are identified as Christian, giving a negative label to the church. There are numerous reports about forced labor, portering, and rape. Rape itself has been used as a weapon of war against the rebellious areas. Soldiers are even promised a promotion if they marry local ethnic women, whatever consequences ensue. They do this, and divorce later.

Richard Lugar wrote in the *Bangkok Post* about military extension and expenses:

> The generals have killed thousands of democracy supporters since the student protests in 1988 and waged war on ethnic insurgents. To tighten their grip on the population, over the past 15 years they have doubled the size of the military, which now consumes 40 percent of the budget, at the expense of spending on health and education. Consequently, hundreds of thousands of their citizens have died as a

result of the broken-down health care system. The generals who run the country are notorious for their widespread use of forced labour, which the International Labour Organisation calls "a contemporary form of slavery." (October 5, 2003)

Civilians have been killed or tortured and put in jail on mere suspicion. In 1997, a group of soldiers confronted a school teacher on his way to the village where he worked. They asked him a question he could not answer. Instantly a soldier shot him in the leg. He lost his leg, but no compensation was ever paid. Incidents of this kind often occur in the frontier. Many more have been tortured and killed. Amnesty International has identified many similar cases. Lady Caroline wrote about the ethnic cleansing in *Christianity Today*:

> The SPDC has been systematically attacking villages of the Karen and Karenni people, rounding them up for forced labor and for use as human mine sweepers, killing those who do not comply or who are too weak to serve. Others are sent to relocation camps, which are little better than death camps. They believe death is inevitable from disease (there is no medical care), or from contaminated food (they claim that the Burmese authorities mix sand with the meager rations).[8]

Another report says:

> Women are raped during forced labor assignments, they are raped while farming, they are raped in their own homes and raped also when they are trying to flee to Thailand ... Aside from the fact that rapes are happening across ethnic boundaries, our report also showed that rape is happening on a widespread basis and is not the result of rogue groups or an occasional unruly soldier.[9]

The actions of soldiers are tyrannical, regressive, suppressive, discriminatory, uncivilized, and hostile.

The Human Rights Watch has noted Myanmar as having the greatest number of child soldiers in the world.[10] The government strongly denies this. According to its by-laws, no one under eighteen may be accepted for military service. In practice, many teenage boys have been inducted into military training and service. It is certain, however, that the government did not force these youth, but persuaded them into the military.

The ethnic national leaders were dissatisfied with the SPDC, excluding them from the recent political road map. After several peace talks with the ethnic rebels and visits by United Nations representatives because of political issues and human right violations, even in trying to negotiate with the opposition parties, the junta is still an authoritarian controller, driven by selfish desire. A former western diplomat indicates that the regime still feels very insecure and vulnerable to a range of external and internal threats. Their policies and actions not only oppress their own citizens but also threaten neighboring countries, the Asian communities, and the world at large. One commentator wrote:

> The military regime's policies threaten the peace and security of Southeast Asia in a number of ways: violent reactions to tensions on its borders with Thailand and Bangladesh, internal human rights abuses that embarrass ASEAN, economic mismanagement resulting in mass movements of people across its borders, civil war causing the flight of hundreds of thousands of villagers into neighboring countries, and a thriving drug industry that puts the people of neighboring countries and countries around the world at risk both of drug addiction and HIV infection.[11]

Civilians have no means of speaking their feelings or asserting their rights when faced with a gun barrel. The minorities live fearfully, unable to predict their fate, and always longing for freedom and peace.

6. The Pressure of Economic Shortage

Economic shortage has greatly affected the people in all areas of life – physical, moral, and spiritual. It has affected the church too. Churches are economically poor, so Christian ministers never receive adequate material support. Many small churches cannot pay their pastors a salary. Thus the ministers and their families have struggled for their daily living. Many urban churches do not have property for their buildings. They conduct worship services in rented houses. Many Christian workers do not have proper training, as they have not been able to afford the cost of education. Educated people have no desire to be full-time Christian ministers because of the low pay. Churches are unable to take advantage of modern facilities. In the midst of such turmoil, the church struggles not only for survival but also for growth. The church has been suffering the impact of all this over many years.

Since the socialist regime, the shortage of food and other products along with inflation have greatly stressed the livelihood of the common people. The country has ceased to be one of the world's major rice-exporting nations. The nationalization of land, the internal and external trade in rice and other major products, the cultivators' obligation to a specific purchase and delivery system, the cooperative movement of rice production – none of these systems worked the way the government expected. Farmers, unable to survive on the low government prices paid for rice, have left the land. The peasants have suffered severely from the rocketing market prices.

The socialist economic system could not supply or maintain the quality of factories, roads, transportation, electricity, or institutions. Oil, gas, and spare parts were rare and expensive. Dr. Nu Nu Yin, a specialist on business and industrial economics, conducted a survey of 132 manufacturing firms in Burma in 1997. She cites low-level technology, insufficient machinery, and shortages of spare parts and neglect of maintenance procedures as reasons for poor rates of production. Inefficiency is further compounded by the regime's failure to nurture human resources through education, training, and basic research.[12] According to the *Britannica 1989 Year Book*:

> The Burmese political and economic situation reached a new low in 1987, just four decades after independence. Twenty-five years of the Burmese Road to Socialism … brought the country – once the richest in Southeast Asia – to an unprecedented level of poverty and isolation from the outside world.[13]

Many cities and towns could not get sufficient electricity or water supplies. *Britannica* notes: "The political turmoil had crippled an economy already on a rapid downward trend. Factories halted production, transportation was paralyzed, and foreign currency reserves were virtually nil."[14]

The regime led the country into chaos in all areas of life. Most of the population lives in extreme poverty. In the 1960s a high-school teacher could feed his family sufficiently and also support a university student. In the 1970s and 1980s he or she could just barely survive with a family. Today, his or her salary lasts for only a week. How they survive is a question hard to answer. People work merely to survive.

The SLORC transformed the socialist economic system into a market-oriented economy in 1988. It enacted the Foreign Investment Law and has accepted 100 percent foreign capital investment as well as joint ventures. By 1997, $6,242.76 million (American) was invested in the country. Sell centers were opened to the public where American dollars or Myanmar kyats could be used. This has brought about some progress in the economic system. However, no significant change has prevailed. One analyst has noted:

> Shortages of capital and the lack of foreign currency are two obstacles to the development of industry. Low production standards are also affecting industrial growth and the development of new export markets ... Lack of technology is a significant factor in Burma's stunted industrial growth ... Observers point out that Burma's technological level is poised at the mechanical stage, and that the country has yet to enter the electronic age ... "Many infrastructure projects are for political and security purposes, not for enhancing business," notes an economics lecturer at Rangoon University. Consequently the government has been unable to support local entrepreneurs and private industries.[15]

Corruption in society persists, the inflation rate is higher year after year, and deterioration in political and social life is unpredictable. The black market has always been powerful against the government's economic system. It is said, "In Myanmar, you get nothing legally while you can get everything illegally." This means that what is not possible with the government, is possible through the black market or bribery. In the midst of this corruption, the common people and the ordinary workers, who comprise the majority of the citizens, suffer the most.

A recent economic boycott and the sanctions imposed by the EEU and the USA against the junta's human rights abuses have resulted in the closing of companies and factories. Many foreign companies have withdrawn their investments not only because of the impact of the boycott, but also because of the discomfort of working with the junta. One report says:

> On the outskirts of Rangoon, several private garment firms with fewer than 100 employees are shutting down, explains the editor of a business journal in the capital. Signed into law on July 29, 2003, America's severe sanctions will likely eliminate hundreds of thousands of jobs. The ban on imports threatens to cripple Burma's entire labour-intensive garment industry. Even the big manufacturers are buckling under the weight of US pressure. "We are almost dying. The future for our business looks so bleak," says a South Korean manager from Myanmar Daewoo International in Rangoon, on the condition of anonymity.[16]

As a result, many workers have been laid off. When people have nowhere to turn for their survival, they throw themselves into all kinds of immorality and unjust gain. Sadly, moral corruption is everywhere in Myanmar society today. The political instability, the economic failures, and many other factors have affected the moral character of the people, bringing social disorder and chaos. The practice of law is minimal, and it does not rule or influence society. People live, act, and decide only according to their religious convictions. In many cases, those who tell the truth are considered troublemakers.

One characteristic of this corruption is bribery. Bribery, also known as "give and take," drives the whole system of social relations between authorities and customers, between the haves and the have-nots. As mentioned, what is not possible legally is possible illegally through bribery. It is practiced in offices, in school, with the police and customs officials. Teachers take bribes from students for good grades in their exams. Officers take bribes from staff members for favors in the workplace. Office staff take bribes from customers for issuing documents and papers in a timely manner. Physicians in hospitals take bribes to provide better care. Jailors take bribes from prisoners for better care or outright release. Bribery is seen even in the courts where law condemns but bribery annuls. It is practiced in all social institutions throughout the country. Surprisingly, even the generals take bribes. Suu Kyi has unveiled it in her book *Freedom from Fear*: "Under totalitarian socialism, official policies with little relevance to actual needs had placed Burma in an economic and administrative limbo where government bribery and evasion of regulations were the indispensable lubricant to keep the wheels of everyday life turning."[17]

Christians find it difficult to live and work in this environment. But they have no way to avoid it because all the systems are managed this way. During my visit to Myanmar in December 2002, I bought my roundtrip air ticket from Yangon to Kale on the black market, sold by those who work at the Myanmar Air Corporation. It was not obtained at the sales counter; instead I gave a sum of money to the manager to get it. I found no other way to obtain it.

There is no respect for human life; soldiers without a value for human life do not hesitate to shoot and kill anyone for any reason, or without reason. Automobile drivers care nothing about the lives of the people who cross the street, and consequently pedestrians are at risk of life and limb. This lack of value affects all areas of life.

7. Conclusion

Despite the painful repressions, the church in Myanmar is growing. All churches report steady growth numerically, spiritually, and geographically. Evangelism and inland mission efforts thrive in spreading the gospel to all people groups in the country. The "3/300 Gideon Band" from Kachin Baptist Church, "The Chin for Christ in One Century," and "The Karen for Christ" are efforts to disciple their own people groups in this generation. The renewal movement has resulted in large-scale evangelism, cross-cultural missions, and church planting, with the Pentecostals most benefiting from the resurgence. The charismatic gifts help cross and penetrate social and cultural barriers. Many new Bible schools have been established during the past twenty years. Our sufferings produce perseverance; perseverance, character; and character, hope (Rom. 5:3). Christians in Myanmar must continue to live as good citizens and contribute their full allegiance, loyalty, and hearty service to the country.

Efforts to bring peace and democracy to the country continue. The nonviolent movement leader Suu Kyi has put a lot of effort into bringing forth peaceful democracy. The UNO has sent representatives time after time to negotiate between the junta and other parties and to stop the junta from violating human rights. The ASEAN community pressured the junta to loosen their tightening grip on the people. However, none of these attempts has brought significant results thus far. The UN Human Rights envoy Paulo Segio Pinheiro has confessed that his dialogue with the junta has not made progress as expected: "I am very sad that until now there are several hundreds of prisoners who continue in prison. But if I don't see any development in the situation, I will be obliged to revise my commitment to this mandate."[18]

It is time for the church, the body of Christ, to obligate themselves to peacemaking. Peacemaking is of Christ. He brought "peace" to the world and he promoted peacemaking. Peacemaking is more than a nonviolent movement. It steps out to help solve the root causes of sin and violence. It helps restore broken relationships.

The church must help bring justice into society. Jesus' kingdom mission focused largely on the poor, the oppressed, those in bondage, and those who needed liberation from unjust treatment. To bring justice in Myanmar society, churches must unite together and put it in action. To get unity, the three mission streams in Myanmar need to work from a common paradigm of mission toward unity, since theologians and missiologists have identified the kingdom of God as one common mission paradigm, saying, "Unity will prevail when individual believers understand that they comprise God's missionary body and see their mission mandate as the expansion of the Kingdom of God."[19]

Endnotes

[1] Chin Khua Khai, "Myanmar Mission Boards and Agencies," in *Evangelical Dictionary of World Missions* (eds. A. Scott Moreau, et al.; Grand Rapids, MI: Baker, 2000), 667.

2 See Wolfgang Huber, "Human Rights – A Concept and Its History," in Alois Müller and Norbert Greinacher (eds.), *The Church and the Rights of Man* (New York: Seabury, 1979), 1–10.

3 Article 18, Universal Declaration of Human Rights (1948), 2, 4; http://www.un.org/Overview/rights.html (viewed May 12, 2003).

4 David D. Barrett, *World Christian Encyclopedia* (Nairobi, Kenya: Oxford University Press, 1982), 203.

5 BBC Monitoring News file, London, December 24, 2000.

6 Suantak Vumon, *Zo History* (Aizawl, Mizorm, Idia: Vumson [1986]), 189.

7 Josef Silverstein, *Burmese Politics: The Dilemmas of National Unity* (New Jersey: Rutgers University Press, 1980), 104–10.

8 Wendy Murray Zoba, "Through Bombs and Bullets," *Christianity Today*, 41.10 (September 1, 1997), 50–52.

9 Seth Mydans, "Burmese Women Are Reporting Systematic Rapes by the Military," *The New York Times*, May 12, 2003, p. A 11.

10 *International Herald Tribune* (Paris), July 17, 2003, 8.

11 *Shan-EUgroup*, http://www.Shan-Eugroup (viewed May 12, 2003).

12 "Waiting for an Industrial Revolution," *Bangkok Post*, October 5, 2002.

13 "Burma" *Britannica: The Year Books* (Chicago: Britannica, 1988), 437.

14 Ibid.

15 Shan-EUgroup, http://www.Shan-Eugroup, 3 (viewed October 4, 2003).

16 Ibid.

17 Aung San Suu Kyi, *Freedom from Fear* (Middlesex: Penguin Books, 1991), 69.

18 *Radio Free Asia News*, RFA Reports, September 2003.

19 Paul E. Pierson, "Arthur F. Glasser: Citizen of the Kingdom," in Charles Van Engen, Dean E. Gilliland, and Paul Pierson (eds.), *The Good News of the Kingdom* (Maryknoll, NY: Orbis, 1993), 8.

13

Spiritual Foundations for Interreligious Dialogue and Reflection on Its Present-Day Practice

MONS. FELIX A. MACHADO

1. An Unexpected Encounter

The prime minister of India, who visited Rome in 1999, was accompanied, among others, by his personal secretary. Upon their arrival in Rome the secretary called me. He was told about my presence in Rome by a family friend of mine. The secretary came to take me to the hotel where the Prime Minister was staying. While I was finishing the celebration of the Holy Mass, the secretary waited for me in the church. Later, I had occasion to see the Prime Minister, and then the secretary expressed to me his desire to visit the Basilica of St. Peter's. I made an appointment with the secretary for the next day, after the Prime Minister and his delegation had met the Holy Father. Our visit to the Basilica lasted about an hour. The secretary had the intention of praying rather than go around the Basilica like a curious tourist. We were walking in silence in the Basilica, and in front of every statue the secretary made a deep bow with his hands folded in a prayerful gesture. When we approached the tomb of St. Peter in the crypt, the secretary fell flat on the ground and remained in that posture (*panchanga pranama*) for five minutes. When we walked through the crypt we came out in the porch of the Basilica as if to exit, and I said to the secretary, "Let us now go." He begged of me to return to the Basilica. Amidst the crowd he stood still at the back of the Basilica, with his eyes closed, hands folded and body inclined forward. After a few minutes of intense prayer he opened his eyes and said to me, "Now let us go."

Timidly I asked him whether he liked the Basilica. He said that his main intention was to pray in such a privileged place where for thousands of years millions of people had come to pray. Mind you, the Prime Minister we are talking about is a convinced and practising Hindu. He is even said to be an active member of Rastriya Swayamsevak Sangha (RSS), a fundamentalist organization which provides *hindutva* ideology to his political party, the Bharatiya Janata Party (BJP). The secretary as well is a convinced and practicing Hindu.

I was edified with the simple gestures of the secretary in St. Peter's Basilica. His sense of the "sacred," impressed me.[1] He was not the first Hindu in whom I encountered such personal and intense thirst and hunger for God. The personal secretary of the Indian Prime Minister was visiting Rome for the first time. In our conversations I had found out that he was well acquainted with the history, culture, art, architecture, museums, etc. of Rome. However, he had in mind the prayer in the Basilica of St. Peter's as priority. That was his long-time desire, and he seemed happy to have fulfilled it.

2. Moved to Reflection and Action by the Encounter

These are some of the questions which came to my mind: To whom was he really praying? Who must have heard his prayers? Who taught him this sensitivity to the "sacred"? What did he say or feel when he stood or fell flat in deep silence? I kept on remembering the words of Paul VI and those of John Paul II:

> Evangelization is to be achieved, not from without as though by adding some decoration or applying a coat of colour, but in depth, going to the very centre and roots of life. The gospel must impregnate the culture and the whole way of life of man. . . . This work must always take the human person as its starting point, coming back to the interrelationships between persons and their relation with God ... This proclamation is relevant also for immense sections of the human race who profess non-Christian religions in which the spiritual life of innumerable human communities finds valid expression. In these we hear re-echoed, as it were, the voices of those who for a thousand years have sought God in a manner which, while imperfect,

has always been sincere and upright. These religions, possessing as they do, a splendid patrimony of religious writings, have taught generations of men how to pray.[2]

Defending his action accomplished in Assisi in 1986 and inviting his closest collaborators to commit themselves to receive the conciliar teachings of the church, John Paul II said,

> Every authentic prayer is under the influence of the Spirit "who intercedes insistently for us … because we do not know how to pray as we ought," but he prays in us "with unutterable groanings" and "the one who searches hearts knows what are the desires of the Spirit" (Rom. 8:26–27). We can indeed maintain that every authentic prayer is called forth by the Holy Spirit, who is mysteriously present in the heart of every person … the unity that comes from the fact that every man and woman is capable of praying, that is, of submitting oneself totally to God and of recognizing oneself to be poor in front of him.[3]

A few months prior to his inviting the leaders of different religions to pray for peace in Assisi, the same pope had said to the representatives of various religions in India,

> As an inner attitude of the mind and heart, spirituality involves an emphasis on the inner man and it produces an inward transformation of the self. The emphasis on the spiritual nature of man is an emphasis on the sublime dignity of every human person. Spirituality teaches that at the core of all outward appearances there is that inner self which in so many ways is related to the Infinite. This spirituality of inwardness which is so predominant in the Indian religious tradition achieves its complement and fulfilment in the external life of man.[4]

3. Searching for Deeper Motivation for Engaging in Interreligious Dialogue

But my intention to narrate the episode of the visit of the private secretary of the Indian Prime Minister to Rome is to introduce my pondering on the topic entrusted to me, namely Spiritual Foundations for Interreligious Dialogue and Reflection on Its Present-Day Practice. I have been wondering if the term "interreligious dialogue" adequately and correctly communicates what the church intends by its teaching concerning relations with other religions. Does it not give an impression of engaging in a purely cerebral discussion? Is it not a term which seems to limit interreligious relationships to a few select experts? In the church's invitation to her faithful to commit to interreligious dialogue there is primarily an aspect of a religious person meeting another religious person, people of one religion encountering people of other religions. The "religious" dimension seems to me at the center of the church's call to interreligious dialogue. I am prompted to recall here another discourse of John Paul II:

> The fruit of dialogue is union between people and union of people with God, who is the source and revealer of all truth and whose Spirit guides men in freedom only when they meet one another in all honesty and love. By dialogue, we let God be present in our midst, for as we open ourselves in dialogue to one another, we also open ourselves to God. We should use the legitimate means of human friendliness, mutual understanding and interior persuasion.[5]

What makes my encounter with a Hindu an act of interreligious dialogue is his and also my openness to God[6] and therefore openness to others. Surely we are not talking here of the same belief in that God. But for both of us our meeting has a transforming value which is an essential element of spirituality. On my part, this encounter provokes in me a deeper realization of God (and who I am and who others are), whose source and modalities I, as a Christian, find in the Blessed Trinity. Thus my encounter with a Hindu (or a Buddhist or a Muslim or a Sikh) becomes for me an occasion for self-transformation.

4. Engagement in Interreligious Dialogue is Motivated by Christian Faith

The explicit practice of interreligious dialogue in the Catholic tradition dates back to the Second Vatican Ecumenical Council (1962–65). But even before *The Declaration on the Relationship of the Church to Non-Christian Religions (Nostra Aetate)* was promulgated (October 19, 1965), Paul VI had expressed the following challenge to the religious leaders (December 3, 1964) who represented different religions in Bombay (now Mumbai):

> We must therefore come closer together, not only through the modern means of communication, through press and radio, through steamships and jet planes – we must come together with our hearts, in mutual understanding, esteem and love. We must meet not merely as tourists, but as pilgrims who set out to find God – not in buildings of stone but in human hearts. We must meet man, nation must meet nation, as brothers and sisters, as children of God.[7]

In the course of these forty years the Catholic tradition has been evidently enriched by the challenge of interreligious dialogue. There have arisen also some important questions and concerns for the Catholic side as its faithful engage in dialogue with other religions and their respective adherents.[8] But the church keeps exhorting her sons and daughters to pursue the path of dialogue. At the dawn of this new millennium John Paul II said,

> A relationship of openness and dialogue must continue. In the climate of increased cultural and religious pluralism which is expected to mark the society of the new millennium, it is obvious that this dialogue will be especially important in establishing a sure basis for peace and warding off the dread spectre of those wars of religion which have so often bloodied human history. The name of the one God must become increasingly what it is: *a name of peace and a summons to peace.*[9]

Is the Catholic Church's commitment to interreligious dialogue purely for sociological reasons? Does this commitment on the part of the Catholic Church involve only anthropological concerns? Should we not at the same time seek and deepen theological and spiritual foundations for interreligious dialogue? In fact, the Catholic Church is motivated to dialogue with other religions mainly for theological and spiritual reasons:

> The Church ... feels itself called to dialogue principally because of its faith. In the Trinitarian mystery, Christian revelation allows us to glimpse in God a life of communion and interchange. In God, the Father, we contemplate a pervasive love unlimited by space and time. Every reality and every event are surrounded by his love ... the Church has the duty of discovering and bringing to light and fullness all the riches which the Father has hidden in

creation and history, not only to celebrate the glory of God in its liturgy but also to promote among mankind the movement of the gifts of the Father ... In God the Son we are given the word and wisdom in whom everything was already contained and subsisting even from the beginning of time. Christ is the Word who enlightens every person because in Him is manifested at the same time the mystery of God and the mystery of mankind (cf. *RH* 8, 10, 11, 13). He is the redeemer present with grace in every human encounter, to liberate us from our selfishness and to make us love one another as he has loved us. . . . In God the Holy Spirit, our faith allows us to perceive the force of life and movement and continuous regeneration (cf. *LG* 4) who acts in the depth of people's consciences and accompanies them on the secret path of hearts towards truth (cf. *GS* 22). The Spirit also works "outside the visible confines of the Mystical Body" (*RH* 6; cf. *LG* 16; *GS* 22; *AG* 15). The Spirit both anticipates and accompanies the path of the church which, nevertheless, feels itself impelled to discern the signs of Her presence, to follow Her wherever She leads and to serve Her as a humble and discreet collaborator. . . . The reign of God is the final end of all persons. The Church, which is to be "its seed and beginning" (*LG* 5,9), is called from the first to start out on this path towards the kingdom and, along with the rest of humanity, to advance towards that goal.[10]

5. Open to Encounter Others While Firmly Rooted in Faith

Every Christian who engages in the apostolate of interreligious dialogue must be aware of the deeper motivation for this engagement. This clarity with regard to the Christian believer's motivation is necessary in order to avoid facile irenicism, indifferentism, relativism, syncretism, or fundamentalism – all enemies, not only of the Christian faith, but also of interreligious dialogue.[11] Some Christians seem to think that their faith in the mystery of Jesus Christ, Lord and Savior, is the obstacle in their way to engage in friendly, open, respectful, and harmonious relationships with people of other religions. This faith is considered be an offence to others. But Christians must know that precisely it is their faith in the mystery of Jesus Christ that becomes the "launching pad," a starting point and a firm foundation for them to engage in interreligious relationships. This is what the Holy Father said to the participants in the "Study and Reflection Days" on the occasion of the tenth anniversary of the death of H. E. Mgr. Piero Rossano: "A serious and authentic interreligious dialogue must rest on solid foundations so that it will bear the hoped for fruit at the appropriate time. Being open to dialogue means being absolutely consistent with one's own religious tradition."[12] Openness to others can never be separated from fidelity to Christ's teaching. In the course of the last forty years, and even before that, we see such unconditional adherence to Christ, Savior and Lord of all, and openness to others in the lives of many Christians who committed their lives to the apostolate of interreligious dialogue. In fact, the absolute fidelity to Christ, as these examples would show, can become a solid starting point for meeting people and appreciating those riches which – as the Second Vatican Council says – God in his munificence has distributed to the peoples.[13]

A church document reminds us that "before all else, dialogue is a manner of acting, an attitude and a spirit which guides one's conduct."[14] It is important, therefore, to address the question of motivation in dialogue in order to shape the attitude and conduct of the Christian partner. A solid spiritual foundation becomes imperative for every Christian if our dialogue is to be fruitful and enriching.

6. Christian Theology and Anthropology Calls for Interreligious Encounters

While the church exhorts Christians to enter into dialogue and collaboration with the followers of other religions, she also admonishes them to bear witness to Christian faith and life.[15] The church proposes spiritual foundations for interreligious dialogue by appraising her theology – God is the Father of all[16] – and her anthropology – every human being is created in the image of God.[17] This God is revealed fully and completely in the salvific mystery of Jesus Christ, the Incarnate Son of God, who is "the way, the truth, and the life" (John 14:6),[18] and "his gospel in no way detracts from man's freedom, from the respect that is owed to every culture and to whatever is good in each religion."[19] The revelation of God in Jesus Christ is not opposed to the natural thirst every human person has for the absolute truth. In fact, the Church "knows quite well that the divine message entrusted to her is not hostile to the deepest human aspirations; indeed, it was revealed by God to satisfy, beyond every expectation, the hunger and thirst of the human heart. For this very reason the gospel must not be imposed but proposed, because it can only be effective if it is freely accepted and lovingly embraced."[20]

As baptized and active members of the church, Christians are animated by the Holy Spirit who is always present in the church in a particular manner. Christians are inhabited by the Holy Spirit and thus they become spiritual members. However, since the beginning of creation the Holy Spirit who hovered over the water (Gen. 1:2) has been active in the world, and will remain active until the end of time. Christians must recognize the variety of ways in which the presence of the Spirit is manifested, some of which may be quite surprising.[21] We cannot set bounds to the action of the Holy Spirit. The Spirit is free (2 Cor. 3:17). When Christians go to meet with people of other religions they should not think that the Holy Spirit is exclusively in contact with Christians alone. Rather, Christians should be ready to recognize the presence of the Holy Spirit in the others. The Holy Spirit in Christians must reach out to the Holy Spirit in the hearts of other people (e.g. the motto of Cardinal Newman, "Heart speaks to heart"). During his pilgrimage in India, John Paul II declared: "The Church's relationship with other religions is dictated by a twofold respect: Respect for man in his quest for answers to the deepest questions of his life, and respect for the action of the Spirit in man." Of course, Christians are called to continuously pray for the gifts of fortitude and discernment which are essential elements of spirituality. This is how Christians will learn to "discern" what is good and what is not good in their dialogue with people of other religions.

The possibility of the presence of the Holy Spirit is not only limited to individuals of other religions but can extend to religions themselves. This is affirmed in one of the documents from the International Theological Commission:

> Given this explicit recognition of the presence of the Spirit in the religions, one cannot exclude the possibility that they exercise as such a certain salvific function, that is, despite their ambiguity, they help men achieve their ultimate

end. In the religions is explicitly thematized the relationship of man with the Absolute, his transcendent dimension. It would be difficult to think that what the Holy Spirit works in the hearts of men taken as individuals would have salvific value and not think that what the Holy Spirit works in the religions and cultures would not have such value. The recent magisterium does not seem to authorize such a drastic distinction.[22]

Our faith teaches us that only in the church are to be found the means of salvation in all their fullness. This should in no way induce the Christian to assume a triumphalist attitude or to act out of a superiority complex.[23] The principle of *sentire cum ecclesia* needs to be recalled as the identity of every Christian is the church. In other words, it could be said that no Christian is a Christian when alone in an individualistic sense, separated or isolated from the church. Thus it is necessary "to think of our brothers and sisters in faith within the profound unity of the Mystical Body and therefore as 'those who are a part of me'."[24] Christians who engage in dialogue with people of other religions need to be anchored in the life of the church which, "by her relationship with Christ is a kind sacrament or sign of intimate union with God, and of the unity of all mankind. She is also an instrument for the achievement of such union and unity."[25] Only good citizens are worthy ambassadors of their countries. A commendable Christian partner in dialogue is one who represents the faith of the church in its integrity.

7. The Practice of Faith Shapes all Interreligious Encounters

Spirituality could be described as a mature fruit of a life of faith. Such a life is a fruit of a complete docility to the Spirit. As any other commitment, interreligious encounter is a consequence of faith. Christians need to sustain and strengthen this commitment, first of all by evangelical values: Christ's kenotic dimension (Phil. 2:5–8) takes on a special meaning for a spirituality of dialogue. "It is not a matter of losing one's own identity, but of taking the form and likeness of the other. It is a humble love that fosters dialogue."[26] Marcello Zago makes an interesting observation concerning the imitation of Christ, namely:

> not only does [Christ] reveal that God loves the world, but he gives himself
> entirely out of love. This love is expressed throughout his entire life, in his
> words and in his actions especially in favour of the poor (cf. *RM* 13–15). In his
> contacts with others, he engages in controversy only with the members of his
> own religion; he only turns against the Pharisees and the Scribes. He never
> engages in controversy about the religious traditions present in Palestine,
> which he knew and with which he came into contact: Romans, Canaanites
> and Samaritans. Not only did he arouse faith, but he was able to find it in
> pagans like the centurion or the Canaanite woman.[27]

The fundamental virtue of dialogue is charity[28] the qualities of which are universal, gradual, solicitous, fervent, and disinterested, without limits and calculations, understanding and adapted to everyone.[29] We need to bear in mind that engagement in interreligious encounters is not the result of our human strategies or calculations; rather, it is the work of the Spirit itself, the agent and main force of salvific work.[30] This is why attitude of discernment, that is, the discovery of how the Spirit works in people of other religions and calls them to become involved as cooperating agents in his salvific action, is necessary to practice interreligious dialogue.

Engagement in dialogue can help us deepen our own spiritual life which has its firm roots in God's unique revelation made fully manifest in Jesus Christ, Savior of all. We not only need to know the others; we need the others to know ourselves. Interreligious dialogue is a deeply religious activity. In our meeting with the people of traditional religion we can discover their emphasis on the search for harmony between living and the deceased, between people and the cosmos, and the social agreement accomplished through words, family, community, and life values. In our encounter with Hindus we may be struck by such spiritual values as that of their sense of the sacred and of the divine, the priority of experience and witness, the quest for the real inner self, the virtue of equanimity towards everyone and everything, and of *ahimsa* or universal love. In meeting Buddhists we may discover their efforts for the search for final liberation in an apophatic Absolute, called *sunyata* (void), and the development of inner life through the many forms of meditation. In the Buddhist perspective, inner attitudes are more important than external actions; the point of departure and arrival is inward perfection, which determines external behaviour. Ethics and asceticism, and especially altruism, may become grounds for cooperation and exchange. The basis for a dialogue with Confucianism may stem from the importance attributed to interpersonal relations and social cohesion. In the dialogue with Islam, Christians may be attracted by the faith in the one and only God, the creator and judge of all, by the very universalist claim to having received revelation and conveyed salvation, and by practical consistency. Muslims believe that belonging to the Islamic community (*Umma*) creates special bonds.

"The Christian who meets other believers is not involved in an activity which is marginal to his or her faith. Rather it is something which arises from the demands of that faith. It flows from faith and should be nourished by faith."[31] All practice of dialogue needs to be nourished, guided, oriented, and directed with the help of God. Dialogue is the result of the action of the Holy Spirit and "... the fruit of the Spirit is love, peace, patience, kindness, goodness, faithfulness, gentleness, self-control" (Gal. 5:22–23). The fruits of the Spirit are binders in interreligious relations. A Christian who engages in interreligious dialogue needs to be strongly anchored in prayer, which is a very effective means of obtaining God's grace. Both words and silence in dialogue must emerge from the Christian's union with God who is the Father of all. Proposing an eventual document on the Spirituality of Dialogue, the president of the Pontifical Council for Interreligious Dialogue wrote to the Episcopal Conferences throughout the world: "the more the partners in interreligious dialogue 'seek the face of God' (cf. Ps. 27:8), the nearer they will come to each other and the better chance they will have of understanding each other."[32]

8. Conclusion

The term "interreligious dialogue," which is normally used to indicate the new attitude of the church since the promulgation of *Nostra Aetate,* fails to communicate accurately the intention of the church in this matter; it does not fully correspond to the practice carried out by the church, particularly in the last forty years. Every interreligious encounter begins with openness to God or in the recognition of transcendental values of life. For Christians, interreligious encounter is rooted in their faith in God who is triune.

What is emphasized by the church in interreligious encounters today is the meeting of people of different religions on a deeper level, namely, on the level of spirituality. Spirituality involves an emphasis on the sublime dignity of every human person. Spirituality is an attitude, a motivation of the mind and heart which produces an inward transformation of the self. Awareness of a deeper motivation to meet people of other religions helps Christians to avoid facile irenicism, indifferentism, relativism, syncretism, or fundamentalism.

Christians are invited to be open to people of other religions while at the same time remain faithful to their own religious tradition. Openness to other religions at the exclusion of fidelity to one's own religious tradition generally results in relativism; fidelity to one's own religious tradition in today's pluralistic world, at the exclusion of openness to people of other religions, often ends in fundamentalism. Rooted in their faith, Christians are urged to engage in meeting people of all religions. God is revealed as the Father of all, he is manifested in Jesus Christ as the enlightening Word, and he accompanies the church through the Holy Spirit. The kingdom of God is the final end of all persons, and the church, "its seed and beginning," is called from the first to start out on this path towards the kingdom of God and, along with the rest of humanity, to advance towards that goal. Just as only good citizens are worthy ambassadors of their countries, so also commendable Christian partners in dialogue are those who represent the faith of the church in its integrity.

Questions such as the following are often raised in conversations among Christians: Why should a Christian engage in interreligious encounters? What is the aim of dialogue with other religions? If one understands the spiritual, anthropological, and theological motivation the Christian should have in order to engage in dialogue with people of other religions, one will be able to comprehend that answers to these questions cannot be sought outside the context of the Christians faith and teaching which is the foundation for Christian anthropology, spirituality, and theology of interreligious dialogue. It needs to be emphasized that the Christian partners' participation in interreligious engagement is not prompted by human options or carried out for any tactical or ulterior motives, but it is undertaken primarily because it is demanded, above all, by the exigencies of their faith. For Christians, engagement in interreligious encounters is a way of "being" in pluralistic society. It is important to recognize two points: (1) Our world today is a "map of religions." (2) Faith must be lived in its integrity amidst this world. What is the goal of interreligious dialogue? The answer to this question also must be sought in the Christian faith and teaching because for Christians interreligious encounters are intrinsically linked to their faith. Separating the two will harm both: neither will it be a genuine Christian interreligious encounter, nor will the Christian practice of faith be credible.

It is necessary to nourish our practice of interreligious encounters with solid spiritual food: God can never become a negotiable item or a marginal thought in our interreligious encounters. He is the center or foundation of all interreligious encounters. The compassion of God the Father, the forgiving love of God the Son, and the filial warmth of God the Holy Spirit, in other words, the guidance, direction, and orientation of the Trinitarian God brings all interreligious dialogue to fruition. The more the partners in interreligious encounters "seek the face of God," the nearer they will come to each other and the better chance they will have of understanding each other.

Endnotes

[1] John Paul II, To the Representatives of the Various Religions of India, *Insegnamenti* IX/1 (1986), 319–24, n. 7: "It is my humble prayer that the remarkable sense of the 'sacred' which characterizes your culture may penetrate the minds and hearts of all men and women everywhere. In this way, God will be honoured and the human family will experience ever more fully its oneness and its common destiny."

[2] Paul VI, Post-Synodal Exhortation Letter, *Evangelii Nuntiandi* (December 8, 1975), 53.

[3] John Paul II, Address to the Roman Curia, *l'Osservatore Romano* (English edn.; January 5, 1987), 11.

[4] John Paul II, To the Representatives of the Various Religions of India, *Insegnamenti* IX/1 (1986), 319–24, n. 2.

[5] Ibid., 5.

[6] Cf. Frére Roger of Taizé, *Les Sources de Taizé* (France: Les Presses de Taizé, 2001): "A simple desire of God is already a beginning of faith (*Lk* 17:5–6)" (59).

[7] Paul VI, Address to the Representatives of the Various Religions of India (December 3, 1964); *Insegnament,* II (1964), 693–95, n. 2.

[8] John Paul II, Apostolic Letter *Novo Millennio Ineunte* (January 6, 2001), 56: "Dialogue, however, cannot be based on religious indifferentism, and we Christians are in duty bound, while engaging in dialogue, to bear clear witness to the hope that is within us (cf. 1 Pet. 3:15). We should not fear that it will be considered an offence to the identity of others what is rather *the joyful proclamation of a gift* meant for all, and to be offered to all with the greatest respect for the freedom of each one: the gift of the revelation of the God who is Love, the God who 'so loved the world that he gave his only Son' (Jn. 3:16). As the recent declaration *Dominus Jesus* stressed, this cannot be the subject of a dialogue understood as negotiation, as if we considered it a matter of mere opinion: rather it is a grace which fills us with joy, a message which we have a duty to proclaim."

[9] Ibid., n. 55.

[10] Secretariatus pro Non Cristianis (now Pontifical Council for Interreligious Dialogue) *The Attitude of the Church Towards the Followers of Other Religions, Reflections and Orientations on Dialogue and Mission* (Pentecost 1984), nn. 22, 23, 24.

[11] Denis Isizoh, "Religions in Sub-Saharan Africa: Working and Walking Together; A Christian Reflection," *Pro Dialogo* 114.3 (2003): "The spirit that must animate interreligious dialogue includes: consistency with one's religious traditions and convictions; openness to understand people of other religious traditions without pretence, prejudice, and closed-mindedness; honesty; humility and frankness; renunciation of rigid principles; avoidance of false irenicism, intolerance and misunderstandings; realization that dialogue leads to inner purification and ongoing conversion."

[12] John Paul II, Discourse, June 16, 2001, *Pro Dialogo* 108.3 (2001), 291–93.

[13] *Ad Gentes*, 11; cf. also *Nostra Aetate*, 2.

[14] Secretariatus pro Non Christianis (now Pontifical Council for Interreligious Dialogue), *The Attitude of the Church Towards the Followers of Other Religions, Reflections and Orientations on Dialogue and Mission* (Pentecost 1984), 29.

[15] *Nostra Aetate* 2; cf. also John Paul II, Post-Synodal Apostolic Exhortation Vita Consecrata, n. 102.

[16] John Paul II, Address to the Roman Curia, December 22, 1986, *l'Osservatore Romano,* English Edition (January 5, 1987), 3: "The one God in whom we

believe, Father, Son and Holy Spirit, the Most Holy Trinity, created man and woman with particular attention, according to the narrative in Genesis (cf. Gen. 1:26ff., 2:7,18–24). This affirmation contains and communicates a profound truth: the unity of the divine origin of the whole human family, of every man and woman, which is reflected in the unity of the divine image which each one bears in himself (Gen. 1:26) and *per se* gives the orientation to a common goal (cf. *NA* 1) … Accordingly, there is *only one* divine plan for every human being who comes into this world (cf. Jn. 1:9), one single origin and goal, whatever may be the colour of his skin, the historical and geographical framework within which he happens to live and act, or the culture in which he grows up and expresses himself. The differences are less important elements, when confronted with the unity which is radical, fundamental and decisive."

17   *Nostra Aetate* 4; cf. also John Paul II, Encyclical Letter *Redemptoris Missio*, 55: "God who desires to call all peoples to himself in Christ to communicate to them the fullness of his revelation and love, does not fail to make himself present in many ways, not only to individuals, but also to entire peoples through their spiritual riches, of which their religions are the main and essential expression even when they contain 'gaps, insufficiencies and errors'." Cf. also John Paul II, Encyclical Letter *Centesimus Annus*, 24: "At the heart of every culture lies the attitude man takes to the greatest mystery: the mystery of God." Cf. also *Dominus Jesus*, A Declaration on the Unicity and Salvific Universality of Jesus Christ and the Church, which is published by the Sacred Congregation for the Doctrine of the Faith (August 6, 2000): it upholds the equal dignity of all persons, no matter of what religion: "*Equality*, which is a presupposition of interreligious dialogue, refers to the equal personal dignity of the parties in dialogue, not to doctrinal content, nor even less to the position of Jesus Christ – who is God himself made man – in relation to the founders of the other religions" (n. 22).

18   Cf. also other biblical texts: Matt. 11:27; John 1:18; 3:34; 5:36; 17:4; 14:9; Col. 2:9–10; 1 Tim. 6:14; Tit. 2:13.

19   John Paul II, Encyclical Letter, *Redemptoris Missio*, 3.

20   John Paul II, Homily on Pentecost Day (June 11, 2002), 3.

21   In his Encyclical Letter *Dominum et Vivificantem* (May 18, 1986), John Paul II refers to the Holy Spirit as the "hidden God" who as love and gift "fills the universe." He invites all Christians to go out to meet the hidden God, a meeting with the Spirit "who gives life" (n. 54).

22   International Theological Commission, *Christianity and Religions* (September 30, 1996), 84.

23   Cf. John Paul II, Apostolic Letter *Novo Millennio Ineunte* (January 6, 2001): During the Great Jubilee of the Year 2000, John Paul II invited Christians to do "examination of conscience, aware that the Church, embracing sinners in her bosom, 'is at once holy and always in need of being purified' (*LG* 8)," 6.

[24] Ibid., 43.

[25] Second Vatican Council, *Lumen Gentium* (November 21, 1964), 1.

[26] Marcello Zago, "The Spirituality of Dialogue," *Pro Dialogo* 101.2 (1999), 243.

[27] Ibid., 242–43.

[28] Cf. John Paul II, To the Religious Leaders of India in New Delhi (November 7, 1999), 2: "[The Church] sees this dialogue [with the religions of the world] as an *act of love which has its roots in God himself*. 'God is love', proclaims the New Testament, 'and whoever remains in love remains in God and God in him … Let us love, then, because he has loved us first … no one who fails to love the brother whom he sees can love God whom he has not seen' (1 Jn. 4:16, 19–20)."

[29] Paul VI, Encyclical Letter *Ecclesiam Suam* (August 6, 1964), 40–48.

[30] A recent study by FABC theologians is an example of discernment. Cf. *The Spirit at Work in Asia Today,* in FABC papers, n. 81, 96.

[31] Cardinal Francis Arinze, "Letter to Presidents of Bishops' Conferences on the Spirituality of Dialogue," *Pro Dialogo* 101.2 (1999), 264.

[32] Ibid., 266.